# SAVING THE CHILDREN

# SAVING THE CHILDREN

History of the Organized Effort to Rescue
Jewish Children in the Netherlands
1942–1945

*Bert Jan Flim*

*Abridgement by Jozien J. Driessen–van het Reve*
*Translated by Jeannette K. Ringold*

CDL Press
Bethesda, Maryland

Library of Congress Cataloging-in-Publication

Flim, Bert-Jan, 1957–
    [Kinderreders. English]
    Saving the children : history of the organized effort to rescue Jewish children in the
Netherlands, 1942–1945 / Bert Jan Flim ; abridgement by Jozien J. Driessen-Van het
Reve ; translated by Jeanette K. Ringold.
    p.  cm. — (Occasional publications of the Department of Near Eastern Studies and
the Program of Jewish Studies, Cornell University ; no. 6)
Includes bibliographical references.
ISBN 1-883053-88-9
    1. Jews—Persecutions—Netherlands.  2. Holocaust, Jewish (1939–1945)—Neth-
erlands. 3. Jewish children in the Holocaust—Netherlands. 4. World War, 1939–
1945—Jews—Rescue—Netherlands. 5. Netherlands—Ethnic relations. I. Driessen-
Van het Reve, Jozien J. II. Title III. Occasional publications of the Department of
Near Eastern Studies and the Program of Jewish Studies, Cornell University ; no. 6.

DS135.N4F5413 2004
940.53'1835'08309492—dc22                                    2004057103

The cover design utilizes a photograph courtesy of Mr. Ate Wieberdink (1991, Waalre)
of the monument at Tienray (Limburg) in memory of Hanna van de Voort (1904–1956).
The sculpture is by Mrs. Elly van den Broek (1989, Malden).

ISBN: 1883053-889

OCCASIONAL PUBLICATIONS OF THE
DEPARTMENT OF NEAR EASTERN STUDIES
AND THE
PROGRAM OF JEWISH STUDIES
CORNELL UNIVERSITY

NUMBER 6

Editorial Committee

Ross Brann,
David I. Owen,
Gary A. Rendsburg

# SERIES EDITOR'S PREFACE

It is perhaps appropriate here to explain how the publication of this book came about. This is the third volume in the Occasional Publication series of the Department of Near Eastern Studies and the Program of Jewish Studies that deals with the Shoah (Holocaust) and the second volume that concerns the Netherlands. *Yours Always: A Holocaust Love Story* by Kitty Zilversmit appeared in 1995 as volume 2 in the series. The memoir, printed in 1200 copies, quickly sold out and was particularly popular in high school classrooms thanks to the frequent lectures provided by the author. It was included in our series in part because of the author's association with the Cornell community through her husband, Don, a professor emeritus of nutritional science at the university. Both had survived the Nazi occupation of the Netherlands, he having escaped to the United States with his parents and she surviving in hiding throughout the war but losing her parents, two brothers, and a sister to the Nazi killing machine.

Subsequently, in 2000, thanks to the good offices of Mr. Leo Ulman, another survivor from the Netherlands and one of the "saved children," I was put in touch with Mr. Cornelus ("Kees") Willems (now deceased) of Amsterdam. Shortly thereafter Mr. Willems established the Paul and Berthe Hendrix Memorial Chair in Jewish Studies at Cornell University to memorialize the parents of his wife, Marianne Willems Hendrix (now deceased), who herself was among the "saved children." Both Marianne's parents had perished in the Shoah along with her two older brothers, Robert Alexander and Hans Leonard. Her brothers have been memorialized with a doctoral research fellowship at Cornell University. The first incumbent of the professorship was Gary A. Rendsburg (now at Rutgers University), who shepherded this book through the press and who also happens to be a child of Shoah survivors from Germany. All these circumstances combined to make the Shoah in the Netherlands a focus of interest at Cornell. It was through further contacts initiated by the late Marianne Willems Hendrix that I was approached by the Lest We Forget Foundation to consider the publication of this important study. These unusual coincidences together influenced the decision to include *Saving the Children* in this series.

On a more personal level, my son, Ethan, was a high school, International Rotary Club exchange student in Monnickendam, where he lived for part of his year with the family of Mario and Lucie Rodriguez Pereira, a local Dutch-Jewish family that had managed to survive the Nazi occupation in exile. Furthermore, my daughter-in-law is also Dutch. All these associations, coupled with my not infrequent professional and personal visits to the Netherlands, no doubt conspired to develop my interest in Dutch-Jewish history.

The immense loss of 73 percent of the Netherlands' Jewish community has been made known primarily through the *Anne Frank Diary*. But the wider story, particularly of the rescue of Jewish children, has been less available, especially in English. This book, focusing on the children and their rescuers, is intended to serve also as a textbook for teachers in high schools and colleges, as well as to inform a wider public of the heroism and suffering of those Jews and non-Jews who rescued about 1,000 children from the hands of the Nazi murderers—nearly a quarter of all the Dutch Jewish children who managed to survive the Shoah. While not enough children were saved, it is comforting to know of the successful efforts expended by so few during those terrible times. That their stories—by those who survived and by those who tragically did not—indeed their names, are recorded below is but very small compensation for what they achieved. We can be grateful that these stories now can be told, while, at the same time, we lament those that never will.

David I. Owen
Bernard and Jane Schapiro Professor of
Ancient Near Eastern and Judaic Studies
Director, Program of Jewish Studies
Cornell University

Ithaca, New York
August 25, 2004

# TABLE OF CONTENTS

# PREFACE

*To the Jewish children in the Netherlands*
*who were hidden during the Second World War*

The relatively high percentage of Jewish victims in the Netherlands during World War II often gives rise to the assumption that the Dutch people behaved badly under the German occupation by giving insufficient help to the Jews who were threatened.

The percentage of the Jewish populace who were murdered by the Nazis was higher in the Netherlands (73 percent) than in Belgium (40 percent) and in France (25 percent). Only 5,500 of the 107,000 Jews deported to concentration camps from the Netherlands returned.

One must necessarily ask whether less help was given to Jews in the Netherlands than elsewhere. That most certainly does not seem to have been the case. A relatively large number of Dutch people (more than 4,000) have been honored with medals by Yad Vashem, the Holocaust memorial center in Israel, for saving Jewish compatriots by arranging for them to hide in their own or neighbors' houses.[1] Despite such efforts, very many Dutch Jews were murdered. The reasons for this are complex. One factor in the explanation is the reign of terror imposed by the Nazi regime during the five-year occupation of the Netherlands. All the more reason to remember those who had the courage to help.

The organized effort to save Jewish children was the subject of systematic research over a period of several years. The results of this research should not remain unknown simply because they were first published in Dutch and are therefore accessible to only a relatively small number of readers.

---

1. *Lexicon of the Righteous Among the Nations* (Yad Vashem: International Institute for Holocaust Research, 2004).

The Lest We Forget Foundation (Stichting Vertaalfonds) was established with the purpose of publicizing *Omdat hun hart sprak. Geschiedenis van de georganiseerde hulp aan joodse kinderen in Nederland 1942–1945* (Ph.D. diss., Groningen, 1995; published by Kok, Kampen, in 1996), the research of Dr. Bert Jan Flim.

The Stichting Vertaalfonds asked Jozien J. Driessen–van het Reve to prepare an abridged adaptation of Bert Jan Flim's dissertation for a larger public. Her manuscript of May 5, 2000, entitled *Kinderredders* ("Children's Rescuers"), is a clear and informative account of the underground networks that came into being in the Netherlands in the years 1942–45 to help the country's Jews, who were being persecuted by the Nazi occupation regime and its collaborators solely because they were Jewish.[2]

This account is intended for high school and college students and their teachers, people involved in Holocaust education, and everyone who wants to further the cause of tolerance. It will be indispensable for in-service training and continuing education courses for teachers who need accurate and interesting resources to help teach their students about racism.

Readers interested in the Second World War and the Holocaust will find facts (not fiction) in this work. Through its use of lively quotations taken from interviews with the very people who so courageously worked to save Jewish children, the book conveys an accurate picture of the situation the rescue activists faced, the dangers they endured, their goals and hopes, and their postwar feelings about what they did and, sometimes, what they were unable to do. The book also shows how resistance groups managed to organize and operate under the very noses of a brutal enemy.

At the request of the Lest We Forget Foundation, Jeannette K. Ringold has translated the Dutch text into English. Dr. Ringold is a translator of books by such well-known Dutch authors as Marga Minco, Carl Friedman, and Anna Enquist. As a member of the speakers bureau of the Holocaust Center of Northern California, she has for many years appeared before audiences of middle school and high school students to tell them about her personal experiences as a hidden child in occupied Holland. She is uniquely qualified to place this account in its proper framework and atmosphere.

---

2. See also Bob Moore, *Victims and Survivors: The Nazi Persecution of the Jews in the Netherlands, 1940–1945* (London: Arnold, 1997); and the chapter on the Netherlands, based on Yad Vashem records, in Mordecai Paldiel, *The Path of the Righteous: Gentile Rescuers of Jews during the Holocaust* (Hoboken, N.J.: Ktav, and New York: Jewish Foundation for Christian Rescuers, 1993), pp. 92–146.

We have gratefully accepted many large and small donations and sub-sidies. Without the support of the principal sponsor, who survived in hiding as a toddler and wishes to remain anonymous (see page 193), it would not have been possible to produce the English translation this soon.

This book is an abridged version of the thesis "Omdat hun hart sprak" ("They Listened to Their Hearts") by Dr. B. J. Flim, University of Groningen, 1995. ISBN 9024260-264; published in 1996 by Kok, Kampen, the Netherlands.

The abridged version "Kinderredders" ("Children's Rescuers") was compiled in 2000 by the historian, Mrs. J. Driessen–van het Reve, Amsterdam (the Netherlands). ISBN 9080572-713.

The translation of "Kinderredders" was done in 2001 by Dr. J. K. Ringold, Menlo Park, California. ISBN 9080572-721.

Oss, The Netherlands
June 2004

Mr. L. Breemer, Amsterdam
Dr. B.J. Flim, Leeuwarden
Dr. G. Hes, Oss (deceased May 5, 2002)
Mrs. E. Heijnen-Hes, Oss
Mr. R. Matthijsen, Oss
Prof. E. van Thijn, Amsterdam

# INTRODUCTION

This book tells the story of those Dutch people who during the Second World War were involved in saving and hiding Jewish children. It describes in detail the work of two resistance groups:

- *The Utrecht Children's Committee*—students from Utrecht led by Jan Meulenbelt.
- *The Amsterdam Student Group*—students from Amsterdam led by Piet Meerburg and Wouter van Zeytveld.

Two other groups are discussed more briefly:

- *The Naamloze Vennootschap* ("Anonymous Association"), generally known as the NV—primarily young people from Amsterdam, South Limburg, and Twente who were members of the Dutch Reformed Church.
- *The Trouw Group*—members of the editorial staff and distribution system of the illegal resistance paper *Trouw*.

A very important fifth group consisted of the Jewish staff of the Hollandsche Schouwburg and the child-care center across from it on Plantage Midden-laan in Amsterdam.

Approximately one thousand children escaped death with the help of these resistance groups. This constitutes almost one-quarter of all the Dutch Jewish children who survived the war.

## WHAT WAS THE SUBJECT OF THE RESEARCH?

The research on which this book is based covered how the four groups came into being, how they were organized, and whether they differed from one another. It also considered how long the individual activists intended or were able to participate in rescue work, and looked into their backgrounds and motivations. Moving from the rescuers to the beneficiaries, it asked who the children were, who the host families were, how the children were treated, and how many of them survived the war.

## WHY THIS RESEARCH?

Many beneficiaries of the rescue efforts, hidden during the war as children but now adults, would like to know the full story of what they experienced. Some wonder whether their parents did the right thing in giving them to strangers. Many of the rescuers want to know about the other rescuers: who they were and what they did. Most of the activists in rescue work knew only their own tiny piece of the puzzle, because under the conditions of the German occupation, it was better for members of the resistance to know as little as possible. Now they can learn the whole story.

## HOW WAS THE RESEARCH CARRIED OUT?

The written sources that were available for research purposes could be stored in one file. For obvious reasons, the rescuers entrusted as little as possible to paper during the war. That is why the researcher sought out the surviving rescuers and children to interview them. For the success of an oral history interview, it is essential to create a bond of trust between the interviewer and the interviewee. The first, very careful, conversation is usually followed up with subsequent conversations and afterward by telephone inquiries. This took much time and energy.

The human memory is selective. In order to obtain reliable information about events that many individual interviewees remembered differently or selectively, most matters had to be examined more than once.

One-to-one conversations with rescuers and the rescued yielded the most information. The files on children whose parents were murdered by the Nazis were another important source. The history of the children in hiding was established by using the files of the National Commission for War Foster Children, the OPK. In addition, research done for a previous study of 310 hidden children yielded valuable information.[1]

---

1. Bloeme Evers-Emden and Bert Jan Flim, *Ondergedoken geweest – een afgesloten verleden?* (Kampen: Kok, 1995).

# PERSECUTION AND DEPORTATION
## May 1940–September 1944

### How It Came to Pass That Children Were Hidden

In the early morning of Friday, May 10, 1940, Holland was attacked by Germany. Rotterdam was bombed heavily. The Dutch army resisted for five days but had to surrender when the Germans threatened to bomb other cities as well. At the behest of Reichsführer Adolf Hitler, a German civil administration was set up in the conquered country. From then on, officials of the Dutch government had to do whatever the Germans said.

The Jews of the Netherlands suffered more than the country's other inhabitants during the German occupation. In accordance with Hitler's command, they, like most of the Jews in the other countries of Europe, were transported by train to extermination centers where they were killed.

### Persecution and Isolation
#### ISOLATION OF THE JEWS: MAY 1940–JUNE 1942

Jews had freedom of religion and the same civil rights as all other Dutch citizens.

In school, children had no idea whether their classmates were Jewish; it wasn't important. The great majority of the country's Jews were completely integrated in Dutch society. Some of them were observant, and others not at all.

The Jewish populace of Holland included new immigrants who had only recently fled Eastern Europe and Germany in the hope of leading a peaceful existence and others whose families had lived in the country for centuries. This hope was now crushed. Some of the country's Jews were so desperate that they committed suicide during the first days of the war. Oth-

ers, following the example of the queen and her ministers, tried to escape to
England via IJmuiden and other ports.

Everyone in Holland knew how Adolf Hitler's takeover in Germany in
1933 had been the start of slowly increasing misery for Jews. In the years
since, Germany had rearmed very quickly and had built up a formidable
army. In the fall of 1935 the National Socialist regime adopted the Nurem-
berg Laws. Henceforth, marriage and sexual relations between Jews and
non-Jews (called Aryans) were forbidden. Violators of the laws against
"racial mixing" were arrested. The laws defined anyone with at least three
Jewish grandparents as a "Jew." Two Jewish grandparents made one a "half-
Jew," and one grandparent a "quarter-Jew." Regardless of ancestry, anyone
registered as member of the Jewish community or married to a Jew was considered a "Jew."[1]

Once they were isolated in this way, the Jews could be persecuted at
will.

KRISTALLNACHT

Kristallnacht in 1938 was one of the most important steps in the escalating
persecution of the Jews in Germany. The German government decided on
a pogrom after a seventeen-year-old boy, Herschel Grynspan, shot and
killed a member of the German embassy in Paris in order to draw attention
to the lot of his parents and 17,000 other Polish Jews who had been driven
out of Germany. During the night of November 10, Nazis hunted down
Jews throughout Germany; 35 Jews were killed. Overall, 191 synagogues
were burned and 76 completely destroyed, and hundreds of homes and Jewish stores and warehouses were seriously damaged. The vast amount of broken glass on the streets gave this event the name Kristallnacht. During the
weeks that followed, 20,000 Jewish men were arrested, 400 of whom were
killed. In the aftermath, many Jews left or tried to leave Germany. It is estimated that approximately half of Germany's Jews left the country between
1933 and 1939.

The Dutch government regarded Hitler as a friendly head of state and,
in order not to antagonize him, was not inclined to allow Jewish refugees to
enter the country, although there were, of course, some exceptions. Many
hundreds were turned back at the border. Dutch Jews tried to help escapees
from Germany to settle in Holland or obtain passage to the United States.
From 1938 onwards, Walter Süskind, a Jew who had fled from Germany,
and now worked in Amsterdam for an international business, was one of the
people involved in this effort. He helped a number of friends and acquain-

FIGURE I

*The Netherlands crammed between Nazi Germany and the North Sea* (1940)
(➤ P indicates the extermination camps in Poland)
*Courtesy of Mr. Willem M. Ysebaert (Oss)*

FIGURE 2

*Map of the Netherlands: provinces, important cities, and sites*

Courtesy of Mr. Willem M. Ysebaert (Oss)

1. Noord–Holland ( a Amsterdam )
2. Zuid–Holland ( a The Hague )
3. Zeeland ( a Middleburg )
4. Utrecht ( a Utrecht, b Camp Amersfoort )
5. Friesland ( a Leeuwarden, b Sneek )
6. Groningen ( a Groningen )
7. Drenthe ( a Assen, b Camp Westerbork )
8. Overijssel ( a Zwolle, b Nijverdal )
9. Gelderland ( a Arnhem )
10. Noord–Brabant ( a Den Bosch, b Camp Vught )
11. Limburg ( a Maastricht, b Tienray )

tances to flee Germany. David Cohen, a professor of ancient history and phi-losophy, was also active in helping refugees. He was the chairman of the Committee for Special Jewish Concerns (Comité for Bijzondere Joodsche Belangen), established in 1933, and secretary of the Committee for Jewish Refugees (Comité voor Joodsche Vluchtelingen), which came under its auspices.

ESTABLISHMENT OF THE JEWISH COUNCIL

After the German conquest, the segregation of Holland's Jews, which made it easier to persecute them, began with an insidious series of small steps. In October of 1940, all Dutch civil servants had to fill out forms with the names of their parents and grandparents. Everyone received two forms, one to be filled in by Jews, and the other by non-Jews. Non-Jews declared that they were "not a Jew or married to a Jew." Jews had to report how many Jewish grandparents they had. Then, in January 1941, all Jews had to register. Out of a total population of less than 9 million there were 140,552 "full-Jews," 14,549 "half-Jews," and 5,719 "quarter-Jews" in Holland. More than half of Dutch Jewry (79,410) lived in Amsterdam.

In February 1941 a Jewish Council was created on German orders. Its task was to explain the many anti-Jewish regulations to the country's Jews and to see that they were carried out.[2]

To this end the *Jewish Weekly* was created, a periodical in which all the regulations were announced. The chairmen of the Jewish Council were Abraham Asscher, a diamond merchant in Amsterdam, and the above-men-tioned David Cohen.

ISOLATION

During the first two years of the occupation, the Germans gradually isolated the Jews, step by step, from the rest of the Dutch people. They achieved this by issuing regulations that pertained only to Jews. As of October 1940, when almost all of the 240,000 civil servants signed the Aryan declaration—only twenty are known to have refused, on principle, to sign—there suddenly were Jews and non-Jews in Holland. All the anti-Jewish regulations that fol-lowed were unconstitutional in both letter and spirit. The Dutch constitu-tion states, among other things, that every Dutch citizen can be named to any service to the nation (i.e., any public office). Shortly after the declarations of Aryan origin were handed in, the Jewish civil servants were dismissed. That same month, all businesses owned by Jews had to be registered. After

December 1940, non-Jews were no longer allowed to work in Jewish households.

In April 1941, the first national identity cards were issued at the Apollohal in Amsterdam. Full-Jews received cards marked with a capital *J*. Before this, identity papers had been unknown in Holland, except whatever documents were needed for traveling abroad. Much care had been taken in producing the new Dutch identity card; it was much more difficult to counterfeit than the German Kennkarte or the Belgian Carte d'identité. A Dutch civil servant named Lentz had done his best to make the document tamper-proof. Everyone had to hand in two passport photos, two fingerprints, and two signatures. One of each was put on the individual's identity card, and the others were on cards kept in the Central Card File (Centrale Karthotheek) in The Hague. Every community was designated by a letter, and the cards were numbered consecutively.

At the beginning of 1941 a regulation was enacted that encroached deeply on the lives of Jews; Jewish businesses were taken over by *Verwalters*, non-Jewish administrators. Unilever, the firm where Walter Süskind worked, was Jewish and thus came under the supervision of a *Verwalter*. In October 1941 the *Verwalters* were ordered to fire all their Jewish employees. The last date for discharging Jewish personnel was January 31, 1942. In addition, a new regulation promulgated in January 1942 required unemployed Jews to report to a labor camp.

As of October 1941, Jews were no longer admitted to the universities. Starting on January 17, 1942, all Jews who lived near Amsterdam had to move there in phases. Jews in large cities like The Hague and Rotterdam did not come under this requirement. Starting in May 1942, every Jew over the age of six had to wear a star. Jews had to hand in all works of art, jewelry, cash, checks, securities, and bank accounts with more than 250 guilders before June 30. All this was administered by the "robber" bank Lippmann-Rosenthal (LiRo) in Amsterdam. Jews were not allowed to go swimming, shop in non-Jewish stores, or walk in parks; their telephones were cut off. They were not allowed to change their residences or travel; their bicycles were taken away. These and many other regulations against the Jews were announced between September 1941 and the end of July 1942.

A TEACHER

Jan Hemelrijk, a teacher at a high school in Amsterdam, recalls the following:

When the German troops entered Amsterdam in May of 1940, many people who had dreaded their entry were soon reassured. The general opinion was: "It's much better than I expected!"; "They're behaving so correctly"; "Quite different from what we anticipated."

"You don't know them yet," said an experienced observer. "They're worse than the plague."

But who fears the plague when its consequences are not near at hand? And who worries about horror stories taking place far away?

"This year I won't be there for final exams," I let slip at the end of September during a family gathering with three of my high school students.

"How can you say such a thing? Why would they do anything to you? It's impossible! No one believes that. You're too pessimistic." Parents and students vied with one another to offer comforting reassurances. I listened, smiling.

Two months later I was suspended in the first "purge" because I was "of Jewish blood." People tried to console me and themselves with the thought: "You'll be back"; "It's only for a little while."

People thought that the beginning of the misery was already the end. . . . The scheme was clever. The Jews had to be isolated to be easy prey for their executioners. After they were denied access practically everywhere, except to their own houses, the Jewish children were removed from the schools at the end of the 1940–1941 school year. Yet they did not admit defeat. A people does not survive centuries of persecution without being tough. Jewish schools were established. And at the Jewish lyceum [high school] in Amsterdam, where I taught Latin and Greek several hours a week, students and teachers worked for nine months with a doggedness that assumed deliverance was still possible. There was great dismay when the offensive order to wear the Jewish star was announced. It was as if you had to expose yourself naked to the foul stares of the persecutors. Still, there was little resistance. A staff member of the Jewish Council, Pam, resigned when the Council helped to distribute the stars. This was more than he could tolerate. But for the Jewish Council there was no "This is the end." The Council bent before the growing storm in order not to break. "As thanks I will devour you last," the cyclops Polyphemus said to Odysseus.

The shadow of death hung over the first (and last) public end-of-year ceremony at the Jewish lyceum. Fifteen-year-old girls had received written orders from the Zentralstelle für Jüdische Auswanderung (Bureau for Jewish Emigration) to be at Central Station at one o'clock in the morning for a transport. To where? No one knew. The parents understood that they had to send their daughters as defenseless victims into the street in the middle of the night and would never see them again. They were not allowed to accompany the girls to the station. The daughters went, often after harrowing domestic scenes, in order "not to endanger their parents." As if the parents would be spared!

I witnessed desperate discussions in the homes of several girls and then left crushed because I had no solution. "Don't go!" was my urgent advice. "And then what?" was the desperate reply from desperate parents. Most of them did go, only a few had sense enough to go into hiding.[3]

## A CHILD

Starting in September 1941, Jewish children in the public schools were forced to transfer to special Jewish schools. In an interview for this book, Elly van Leeuwen, the daughter of a shopkeeper who sold bicycles, lamps, and radios, remembers the segregation of the schools:

> Then I went to the Jewish school. That was in the second or third grade, I don't remember exactly. And you couldn't go on the tram. We weren't allowed to go on the tram. Then we had to wear the star; you had a star on and you had to walk from one end of the city to the other. And those from that side of the city had to come to our side to go to school. And I remember that we had all Jewish teachers and all Jewish children in that school. . . . It was scary. For when families were picked up, the Germans came to get the children from school. The last day I went to school, the teacher was taken from the class. After that I didn't go to school anymore. That was third grade.

## EARLY RESISTANCE

During the first two years of the war, organized Jewish resistance against the regulations was practically out of the question. The only way to avoid them was by going into hiding. Very few people dared to do this in this early stage. There was a constant expectation that this regulation would certainly be the last one. Jews were explicitly forbidden to change their residences, and soon they were also no longer allowed to travel.

Jews who joined the resistance, by and large, joined the general Dutch resistance. Illegal newspapers like *Vrij Nederland* and *Het Parool*, established during the first year of the war, were important expressions of resistance.

An expression of resistance that became well known was the famous protest at the end of November 1940 by Professor R. P. Cleveringa, a legal scholar, against the dismissal of his Jewish colleague M. E. Meyers. The text of his speech was copied by students in Leiden and circulated in the other Dutch universities. The students at Delft and Leiden decided to strike, whereupon these universities were closed. Professor Cleveringa was arrested and was not released until eight months later. The University of Delft reopened after a few months. The University of Leiden remained closed. There was no strike in Utrecht.

The climax of the resistance in the early years of the occupation was the February strike of 1941 in Amsterdam. Municipal officials kept the trams off the streets, large factories participated. The people of Amsterdam had found the strength to resist the impending disaster that until then no one had dared to face. The strike was a protest against the arbitrary and violent rounding up of 400 Jewish men on Saturday and Sunday, February 22 and 23, in the "Jewish quarter" of Amsterdam. This action was a retaliation for a surprise attack by Jewish youths on a group of Dutch National Socialists and German soldiers who had marched, singing, through the Jewish area of Amsterdam. Such provocations had taken place before, and Jewish young men had begun to take boxing lessons so that they would no longer have to suffer such humiliations. When the small group of agitators, singing anti-Jewish songs, approached the Jewish quarter, a gang of Jewish youths jumped out of doorways and beat them so severely that one of them landed in the hospital. He didn't survive. Then, in reprisal, 400 Jewish men were rounded up randomly. As a protest against the deportation of these 400, the inhabitants of Amsterdam and of other cities in the province of Noord-Holland went on strike on February 25 and 26, 1941. This protest against the occupying power has since been called the "February strike." It was the first anti-pogrom strike ever carried out. The strike was put down violently. Three of the strikers were executed by a firing squad on March 13, 1941. The resistance against the treatment of Jews had been broken.

DEPORTATION OF THE JEWS:
JULY 1942–SEPTEMBER 1944

During the period of July 1942 through September 1944 one of the greatest disasters in Dutch history took place: the deportation of 102,992 Jews.[4]

Most of them were gassed a few hours after their arrival at extermination camps in Poland, mainly Auschwitz or Sobibor. In Sobibor, 34,294 Dutch Jews, brought in nineteen trains, were gassed immediately on arrival; 19 men and women returned from that dreadful place. Of the 56,545 Dutch Jews who were transported to Auschwitz, a selected minority was allowed to

work in the camp before going to the gas chambers or succumbing to disease
or exhaustion. Some survived. Most of the approximately 5,200 survivors
had been sent to Bergen-Belsen and Theresienstadt, which were concentration camps, not extermination camps.

The deportation of the Dutch Jews was a part of the *Endlösung der Juden-
frage*, the "Final Solution of the Jewish Question." The Final Solution turned
out to be the murder of European Jewry. The decision was made in 1941,
and the plans were ready in early 1942. The method for carrying out the plan
was adopted on January 20, 1942, at Wannsee near Berlin. Jews living in the
occupied parts of Europe would be brought by train to extermination centers in Poland and gassed there. But the Germans did not announce this.
What they did announce was that Dutch Jews between the ages of sixteen
and forty would be transported to Germany as part of an employment program under police supervision.

START OF THE DEPORTATIONS

On June 26, 1942, the chairmen of the Jewish Council heard from F. H. Aus
der Fünten that Dutch Jews between the ages of sixteen and forty would be
sent to Germany to work. This was to go into effect immediately, starting in
the second week of July. Aus der Fünten was acting head of the Zentralstelle
für jüdische Auswanderung (Bureau for Jewish Emigration), located on
Adama van Scheltema Square.[5]

The Jewish Council was ordered to send out the call-up notices and to
help prepare the travel forms. On July 15 the first transport left for Westerbork, a transit camp in the province of Drenthe; its final destination,
unknown to everyone, was Auschwitz.

The prospect of a trip to a labor camp in a freight car was not enticing.
It was generally assumed that the work in the new location would be quite
heavy. As a result, tens of thousands of Jews tried to obtain a so-called *Sperre*,
a stamp on their identity card that would postpone deportation, always with
the phrase *bis auf weiteres* ("until further notice"). The *Sperre* played an enormous role in the lives of those who had not yet been deported, so enormous
that a Dutch verb was created from it: *sperren*, with its own conjugation.
There is no need here to describe the variety of stamps, or the dates on which
the different *Sperre* were no longer valid because the "further notice" had
arrived. Suffice it to say that all the employees of the Jewish Council were
spared until May, and some even through September 1943, when their
*Sperre*, too, were canceled. On September 29, 1943, the last regular transport
left Amsterdam; it included the two chairmen of the Jewish Council,

Asscher and Cohen. They survived Bergen-Belsen and Theresienstad respectively.

## THE LARGE RAZZIA OF JULY 14, 1942

Berlin ordered the German occupation forces to deport 40,000 Jews from France, 40,000 from Holland, and 10,000 from Belgium.[6]

Every week, starting in mid-July, the administration in Holland had to send a transport of 1,000 Jews to Auschwitz. Those who were called up first had to report to the Bureau for Jewish Emigration on July 15, 1942 "to go to a labor camp in Germany." The Germans decided to hold a large razzia (raid) on the day before, July 14. Streets were blocked off in a predominantly Jewish area and people were loaded into trucks. That same day the Germans decreed that the 700 Jews they had rounded up would go to Mauthausen unless the 4,000 who had stayed at home presented themselves. The Jewish Council immediately printed and distributed this threat. Its importance was clearly understood. The 400 Jewish young men who had been rounded up during the razzia of February 22 and 23, 1941 and sent to concentration camps in Germany had ended up in Mauthausen, and by the end of the summer of 1941, most of their parents had received notices that their sons had died. (One survived because he was used as a guinea pig in a medical experiment in Buchenwald.) Everyone knew that Mauthausen meant certain death, but the threat had the opposite effect: fewer and fewer Jews reported voluntarily. On September 2, the German chief of police, Obergruppen-führer Hanns A. Rauter, ordered Amsterdam's police force to pick up the Jews at their homes. Those who had already been rounded up but could not be deported immediately were held in the Hollandsche Schouwburg, a small theater on Plantage Middenlaan, near Artis (the zoo).[7] The organization of the Schouwburg passed into the hands of Expositur, a department of the Jewish Council.[8]

At least 19,400 Jews pretended they were not home; they went into hiding and often escaped death.[9] Some did not decide to go into hiding until the very last moment.

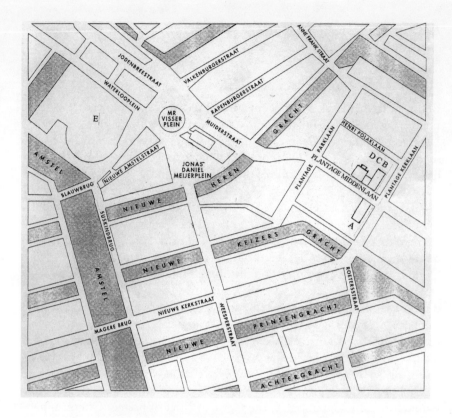

FIGURE 3
*Location of the Hollandsche Schouwburg and the child-care center
at Plantage Middenlaan, Amsterdam*
Courtesy of Mr. Willem M. Ysebaert (Oss)

A  Hollandsche Schouwburg
B  Crèche (child-care center)
C  Annex of the child-care center
D  Hervormde Kweekschool (Protestant Teachers College)
E  Town Hall and Concert Hall (built after 1945)

## THREE HIDDEN CHILDREN
JOSEEF VLEESCHHOUWER

During a razzia in 1943, the Vleeschhouwer family was caught and taken to the Muiderpoort station. A freight train stood ready to take them to Westerbork. Joseef Vleeschhouwer remembers the following bizarre scene:

> We went to Muiderpoort station. Cattle cars stood ready, and a lady was sitting in a corner with a couple of children. And my mother went to sit next to them. My brother and my two sisters were already sitting on the floor. And I was going to sit down when I heard my father call out "Lientje" to my mother. My mother got up and said: "Come on, kids, we're leaving." . . . And then we left and sat down behind a small building that stood in the middle of the platform, at the end of the platform. After I don't know how long, a Nazi came by, and he said: "*Einsteigen.*" And then my father said: "Let's pick up our stuff." After the German walked by, my father said: "Not too fast, take your time." We sat down again. A few minutes later another Nazi came over and said "*Einsteigen,*" and he kept watching us. Then my father said: "Walk around that little building, the other way around." We went to the other side. As soon as he saw that we had gotten up, the Nazi walked away. We sat down again. Eventually a German came who sent us to a line at a ticket window. . . . The line was cut off one person ahead of me. There was one person ahead of me. From there we were brought back to the Schouwburg. And from there we got away.[10]

In the end, the whole family managed to survive the war by going into hiding.

HENK VERMAAS

In November 1942 Henk Vermaas[11] and his parents were hauled out of their beds and taken to Westerbork. Here is Henk Vermaas's account of what happened:

> The terrible thing was being picked up from that house . . . because my father went with another group. This meant that we were in effect separated right there. Sitting in the house and then that terrible ringing of the doorbell at night. Those thugs who come in, and while you're packing some people are already robbing you. When you want to pack something, it's already gone! Dutch police! That, of course, was one of the great frustrations for the Jews—that they were taken by ordinary Dutch police! Accompanied by a bunch of anonymous thieves. . . . And I still remember this, I was sitting with a friend of mine from the

Jewish school, one of my friends on that train. And we were leaving our city,[12] you see. And there I was—sitting there talking as though nothing was happening. And then he said to me: "Shut up a minute. This may be the last time I see my hometown." And I remember that very well. Those stories about people not believing that things were getting serious—I don't believe them at all. That boy who was my age and hadn't studied up on anything and didn't know anything special, that boy already had the feeling of "This might be the last time."

Transports from Westerbork to the east often took place on Tuesdays. Henk Vermaas clearly remembers the mood of the evening before a transport:

The names were called out. . . . Alphabetically. And then, at a certain moment they were past your letter. You see, I was trained incredibly well during the war, I don't even say the letter. It was hammered in so incredibly well that even now I think: "Hey, don't say which letter it is." . . . But anyway, once they passed that letter, you had a week to see if it would be passed again. That really was awful. And I think that people were aware that really awful things were going to happen."

The Vermaas family was picked up and transported to Westerbork earlier than the German administration had planned because it needed houses in the city where they lived. This caused some official confusion, and in consequence the family, after a six-week stay in Westerbork, was allowed to leave for Amsterdam, where they remained legally for half a year before going into hiding.

CHELLA WINNIK

In 1988 Chella told me how difficult it had been for four people to go into hiding together. With her sister and her parents she had been hidden in three different places. For several days they did not have a roof over their heads. Chella Winnik describes the situation as follows:

We couldn't go anywhere. A man and his wife, a mother and a father with two girls, were walking the streets of Utrecht. Without a star. My father was dark. Not typically Jewish looking, but dark. And we had no money, not for food, nothing. We just walked, walked, walked. It got dark. Then my father took us to the market, where there were four empty handcarts covered with tarps. That night all four of us slept in those handcarts in the market. With tarps over them. When it got light again, we had to begin walking again. That's how we wandered around for several days. Practically without food. I don't know whether my father had stolen the food from someplace or other when he gave us something to eat. I'll never forget my father's face when he had to make us lie down in the handcarts on the market square.

## NOTES

1. L. de Jong, *Het Koninkrijk der Nederlanden in de Tweede Wereldoorlog*, pt. I (The Hague, 1969), p. 456.

2. J. Presser, *Ondergang. De vervolging en verdelging van het Nederlandse jodendom 1940–1945*, pt. I (The Hague, 1965), p. 64.

3. J. Hemelrijk, Sr. *Zeven maanden concentratiekamp* (Alkmaar, 1952).

4. During the Second World War, a total of about 107,000 Dutch Jews were deported. This figure includes the victims of the first razzia in 1941 and Dutch Jews who were living elsewhere in occupied Europe. Only 5,500 of the deported Jews survived the war. See Gerhard Hirschfield, "Niederlande," in *Dimension des Völkermords. Die Zahl der jüdische Opfer des Nazionalsozialismus*, ed. Wolfgang Benz (Munich, 1991), pp. 137–165, 162–165.

5. W.P.F. Lages was the official head of the Zentralstelle, but he left the daily affairs to Aus der Fünten.

6. J. Presser, *Ondergang,* pt. I, p. 246.

7. In December 1941, this theater was renamed the Joodsche Schouwburg (Jewish Theater) by order of the Germans, and only Jewish productions were permitted. In this book we keep the original name, often shortened to Schouwburg.

8. The Expositur was created in the spring of 1941, at the same time as the Zentralstelle für jüdische Auswanderung, to deal with emigration requests by Jews who had come to Holland from foreign countries. After the deportations began, the staff of "Expo" helped those who were leaving to fill in the forms correctly.

9. L. de Jong, *Koninkrijk*, pt. VII, p. 318, n. 1. This estimate is probably too low. According to Johannes Houwink ten Cate in the "Zündler Report," there were 39,000 Jews living legally in Amsterdam after May 1943, and somewhat more than 19,000 of them were deported. The rest must have gone into hiding. In addition, we should count the Jews from outside Amsterdam who went into hiding and those who disappeared from the scene before May 1943. See J. Th. M. Houwink ten Cate, *Alfons Zündler en de bewaking van het gevangenkamp aan de Plantage Middenlaan 24 te Amsterdam* (Amsterdam, August 1994/January 1995).

10. Most of the accounts of personal experiences come from interviews and telephone conversations with the person cited. The section entitled Sources (see below, page 167) lists the interviews and telephone conversations from which statements are taken. This one, for example, is from: Interview with Joseef Vleeschhouwer, November 12, 1988, Collection of the author (Groningen). Hereinafter the sources for quotations will no longer be indicated, but they can be found in the bibliography of Flim's book *Omdat hun hart sprak* (Kampen: Kok, 1996).

11. The interviewee did not want to be identified; this is the name he used while in hiding.

12. He mentioned a city in the eastern part of the Netherlands, but at his request the name has been omitted.

# THE FIRST RESCUERS
July 1942–April 1943

The raid on July 14, 1942 shocked everyone who witnessed it, and they in turn told others what had happened. Resistance groups began to form spontaneously, hoping at least to save the children. Jewish parents handed their children over to members of these groups who then took them to hiding places outside Amsterdam.

Over the next ten months, 58,023 Jews, in fifty-two trains, were deported from Westerbork to Poland. This meant that rescuers had to move quickly if they wanted to save a substantial number of Jews. Four rescue organizations will be described in this book, two started by students in Utrecht and Amsterdam, one by young Calvinists in Amsterdam, and the fourth by members of the resistance movement associated with *Trouw*, an illegal paper.

## COOPERATING STUDENT GROUPS: UTRECHT AND AMSTERDAM

News of the raid in Amsterdam on July 14, 1942 soon traveled outside the city.

In Utrecht, that same month, Jan Meulenbelt, a student, was called by his mother. She told him that she had four or five Jewish children in her apartment and asked him to help find a permanent place for them. She explained that she had unhesitatingly said yes when Ad Groenendijk, a social geography student who was one of Jan's friends, had asked her to take care of some Jewish children from Amsterdam. Ad had learned about the situation from his friend Cor Bastiaanse, who in turn had been told about the first summonses for Jews to report to the Zentralstelle (Bureau for Jewish Emigration) by Beppie de Hont, an eighteen-year-old Jewish girl from Amsterdam. Several of the parents who had received call-up notices decided to let their children go with Cor. Jan promised his mother that he would try to find a refuge for the children and then called some friends.[1]

Jan Meulenbelt was a research assistant at the Criminology Institute in Utrecht. He discussed the situation with his boss, Ger Kempe, and they concluded that the hiding of Jewish children had to be better organized. The Utrecht Children's Committee came into being as a direct result of their conversation. Meulenbelt and Kempe decided right off that it made no sense to hide children in Amsterdam where the raids were taking place. They realized, too, that the foster parents who took in children would have to be helped with food and clothing for them. They would also have to find someone who would take on the responsibility of getting the children out of Amsterdam.

Jan Meulenbelt contacted Jur Haak, a mathematics student at Amsterdam University. Haak was willing to arrange escorts for the children and asked Piet Meerburg to help. Haak's room on Lairessestraat became the regular meeting place, known as the "office," of the Amsterdam Student Group. Piet Meerburg, a law student, was already involved in the student protests in Amsterdam against German actions pertaining to higher education, and especially against professors who were members of the Dutch Nazi organization, the NSB (National Socialist Movement), and gave lectures favoring the Third Reich. Meerburg was a member of the Amsterdam Student Association, an organization for male students. As he later reminisced:

> I remember quite well how I actually took the step from student resistance to the next stage, that of the children. . . . I was studying with a friend of mine who was Jewish . . . and both of us were at the clubhouse. . . . And he was called to the telephone. He came back and said: "Well, I have to go home because—" I don't know exactly what was happening at his house. He went home and was picked up and never returned. That was the first group . . . of young Jews who were suddenly picked up and forced to work someplace in Noord-Holland. So it was not Westerbork. . . . That fellow never came back. And then I thought: "This is really too much. I'm sitting here like a clod, and meanwhile this is happening right under my nose. It can't be." Things like that make you really angry. It was then that I realized how serious it was; that these kinds of things really happened.

Piet Meerburg thought it was a good idea to limit their efforts to children.

> Look, we all sometimes helped adults. Of course. But we always knew that we couldn't do both. In point of fact, as we well knew, there were so many children. Besides, I think it appealed most to us. . . . Of course

we weren't cut out for armed resistance. . . . We weren't the right kind
of people for that, considering our background. We knew that all too
well.

In another interview he elaborates:

We were terribly aware of our responsibility. Very much so. Because
we were working with *children*. We were really quite aware of that. I
broke off contact twice with people who had what I call a "Lone
Ranger" attitude. And both of them were actually arrested and
executed by a firing squad. . . . We were very sensitive about that sort
of thing.

Jur Haak's younger sister, Tineke, had a friend, Wouter van Zeytveld,
who had just graduated from high school. Tineke was on vacation, after her
first year at the School for Social Work. The two of them decided to help Jur
and Piet. Wouter came from a left-leaning socialist family. He lived in the
Transvaal district of Amsterdam. He remembers how in his neighborhood,
where half the residents were Jewish, "people, whole families, were loaded
into trucks by the Schalkhaar police. It wasn't difficult to understand that
that's not right. You can't live next-door to that."

That same summer of 1942, Piet Meerburg dropped out of school.
Wouter tells about those early days:

There was absolutely no overall organization. These were simply
people who happened to know one another, or happened to run into
each other. . . . You spoke with Mr. X, Mr. Y, Mr. Z, or Mrs. X, Y,
and Z. And they, in turn, would say things like: "There's a child whose
parents are looking for a place to hide." Or you heard from someone
that somewhere there were people who were willing to take in a child.
It was a sequence of loose contacts and coincidences.

The first summonses went to people from sixteen to forty years old.
Most of the Jewish parents in this age group took their children with them
when they responded to their call-up notices. Some, though, wanted to
leave their children behind in Holland. Hetty Voûte, a biology student in
Utrecht who had been recruited for rescue work by Jan Meulenbelt, recalls:

During those early days, the adults did not yet have the feeling of "we
want to get out." They gave you the children. The first children we
took with us, we took from houses here in Amsterdam. And then you'd
say: "Don't you want to get away yourselves?" And they'd say: "Well,
we're young." It was as if they felt: "A work camp, we can handle that."

A time came when the students were able to place more children than were supplied from Amsterdam. In a roundabout way, a cooperative arrangement was established with a pediatrician, Dr. Philip Fiedeldij Dop, who had taken over the practices of two Jewish colleagues. One had committed suicide, and the other had gone into hiding. Just before Dr. Dop's Jewish colleague went underground, she told him that students in Amsterdam were helping to find places for Jewish children. He went to the hospital where she had said students were taking care of Jewish children. Dop recalls:

> When I arrived there I sat down in a friendly way and gave my name, and the students . . . blithely wrote everything down and told me whatever I wanted to know. Then I said: "Guys, you can't do things that way. You can't be so free and easy about telling a stranger what you're doing. I'm going to look somewhere else."

Through another doctor, Piet Meerburg heard what Fiedeldij Dop wanted. Using a false name, Meerburg phoned him but did no more than give him a telephone number. This cautious way of going about things inspired confidence, and Dop decided to work with Meerburg. Dop visited every Jewish family in his practice that had received a summons. He asked the parents if they wanted to let their children go into hiding in Holland. Then an appointment would be made for a student to come and take the child away. Wouter van Zeytveld remembers:

> You don't realize it fully until you have children yourself. The insanity of that sort of situation. But at the time it wasn't a problem for me. . . . The parents, by and large, they were fantastic, composed. They didn't know where the children were going. We didn't tell them; they weren't supposed to know. If they were picked up, they wouldn't be able to say anything. I remember one time, it was in the Transvaal district, I was with a family where the mother was very emotional. . . . And the fact that this actually irritated me a little . . . illustrates the relative matter-of-factness with which everything took place.

One of the students was Gisela Söhnlein, an acquaintance of Piet Meerburg. She recalled what it was like to go to a home to pick up a child:

> It wasn't dramatic. I mean, the children didn't cry, and the parents were very calm. . . . I think the parents must have told them that they were going to stay somewhere until they could take care of them again. The parents had done a lot of preparation at home. . . . I don't remember that any of the children were nervous. I think they were very calm. A bit scared.

Joseef Vleeschhouwer, who was hidden by the Trouw Group, was told what was going to happen by his father.

> I went into hiding when I was eight years old in September '43. . . .
> It must have been in the summer of '43 that one Friday evening, in accordance with tradition, my father had me stand before him to talk about the Bible passage for the week, and then he said: "But now we are going to discuss something else." I can repeat it almost verbatim. He said: "You know there's a war on, don't you?" Well, I did know that. "And the Germans are going to kill the Jews." And I knew that too. And then he said: "Of course it's important that we don't give them the chance. And that's what I want to discuss with you, because we have taught you not to fib and not to lie and cheat." And I should tell you that "lie" was a very nasty word at that time. That's why you had to say "fib." And my father said "lie and cheat." And he said: "But there is an important Jewish commandment, and that greatest commandment is to stay alive. You have to preserve life. And someone who wants to kill you, you are allowed to do things that are necessary to save your life, for example lying, or eating things that are not kosher, not ritually allowed." He gave me detailed instructions about this. And as fate would have it, around fourteen days later we went into hiding.[2]

At the outset there was sometimes written contact between parents and children. Parents occasionally were given a photo of their child so that they could see that the child was all right. But many parents reported for the labor program or went into hiding themselves, and in those cases contact was lost quickly.

## HOW DID PEOPLE BECOME INVOLVED?

Rut Matthijsen, a chemistry student in Utrecht, heard about the raids for the first time when a fellow student asked if he and some others could use his room for a meeting. Rut said it was fine. He had stayed in Utrecht during the summer of 1942 because he was doing lab work in mineralogy and crystallography. He was inspired by the people who met in his room (among others Jan Meulenbelt and Ger Kempe), and since he had failed an examination he decided to take on an assignment. And that is how an apolitical student became involved in hiding Jewish children. After the summer he dropped out of school temporarily and devoted himself full-time to saving children.

One by one, other students were asked to help. Students recruited in their own circle through organizations and student houses. In 1940, there were a total of about 15,000 students in all Dutch universities. Utrecht had the most students: 3,500. The Utrecht Student Association (for men) and the Utrecht Women Students Organization were both rich sources of volunteers in Utrecht. Anyone who was not a member of either of these groups was most likely a member of some other student organization. Jan Meulenbelt, for example, was a member of the Dutch Society for Student Teetotalers.

Meulenbelt described how he recruited his friend Frits Iordens:

> He was tall, blond, cheerful, and terrific. He was against the Nazis. He was, as it were, so tall, blond, cheerful, and outspoken, and so naturally anti-Nazi, that at first glance you would never have suspected that he was the excellent interpreter of Bach that he was. . . .
>
> In the early summer of 1942, Frits was still studying law, playing the piano and the violin, and drinking beer as if there were no war. After the summer vacation he returned from his parents' home in Arnhem to Utrecht because he really wanted to study quietly in his room on Maliebaan. During that summer vacation, when he had time, he had been a leader of the local branch of a resistance group in Arnhem, but he gave it up in order to devote himself to the last phase of his academic training.
>
> I remember that I didn't understand that at all. I didn't know at the time that death doesn't really exist for his type of spirited personality. The choice of his pursuit worked out so well because his happy nature was at that moment not yet open to the moral alternative: playing music and studying, or helping children and adults to escape certain death. . . .
>
> It is impossible to forget the atmosphere that reigned in that room on Maliebaan when I visited him a few weeks later. I had come to persuade him to join a group that was about to collapse because of the insoluble problems of hiding people. Iordens was sitting at the piano and said no. He said it cordially. He even said it politely. But he said no. Frits Iordens continued playing Bach. Until he turned around and said: "All right, I'll join you." It became a full-time job.[3]

In order to do this work, Frits Iordens, the law student, went back to his parents' home in Arnhem. There his visits to friends and acquaintances yielded a considerable number of possible placements. Students from Utrecht took the children to Arnhem.

Anne Maclaine Pont, Frits Iordens's girlfriend, was an art history student. She knew many people in Overijssel province. Anne became friendly with Baron Philip van Pallandt of Eerde, a country estate in Overijssel. Seven Jewish children were lodged in a small house on the estate. One of Anne's

cousins, twenty-five-year-old Annemieke de Wit, took care of children in
Het Onland, a house near Lochem.

It wasn't easy to find hiding places outside one's circle of friends and relations. In the summer of 1942, Hetty Voûte worked with Jews who belonged
to the Westerweel resistance group. Hetty recalls:

> We went crazy looking. The same thing over and over. And you'd
> ask the grocer you trusted: "Don't you have anything?" Here and
> there. In Noordwijk I went into houses at random. Around Noord-
> wijkerhout I visited farm after farm. To see if there wasn't someone
> who would finally say yes. Maybe the farmer with that beautiful farm-
> house. . . . And then he said: "If it is God's will that these children are
> taken away, then it's God's will." Then I said: 'If it's God's will that
> your farmhouse burns down tonight, then that's also God's will. And
> your neighbors won't come to help you either."

At the end of the summer, Jan Meulenbelt asked Hetty to join the Utrecht Children's Committee.

> At a certain moment Jan said: "Do you want to join us?" At that time
> "us" was Jan Meulenbelt, Rut Matthijsen, Anne Maclaine Pont, Frits
> Iordens, Ger Kempe. It didn't start running well until I began working
> with Jan, who had all his contacts in Amsterdam. Then I had to go to
> an address only once, and from then on I had my work cut out for me.
> For then they'd say: "My neighbor wants help also." And then you
> were at the neighbor's, and she would say: "My cousin wants to also."
> So then you'd go two or three times a day to another address. And
> then you'd go to Utrecht with these children.

Jan Meulenbelt was and is regarded by everyone as the organizer of the
group. He ran the show; he had an overview and tried to give structure to
this group of widely divergent and strong personalities. In Hetty's words:

> When people did things that were too crazy, Jan would blow the whis-
> tle, and they obeyed him. . . . I think that we all felt responsible in one
> way or the other because Jan wanted to know exactly what was
> happening.
>   From the start, Jan had the notion: "What you're doing with chil-
> dren, that's not so bad. . . . They won't hold it too much against you."
> . . . Jan was very strict about that. You had to restrict yourself to chil-
> dren.

Gisela Söhnlein was asked to join by Hansje van Loghem, Piet Meerburg's fiancée. Gisela, a law student in Amsterdam, lived in the EOOS soror-

ity house. She also knew Anne Maclaine Pont because they had once had the same piano teacher in Zwolle. Gisela's mother and stepfather lived in Utrecht. Gisela could travel free of charge because her stepfather worked for the Dutch railroad. Because of this she was able to serve as a link between the Amsterdam and Utrecht groups. She thought it was fantastic to be asked:

> Because we had a very unpleasant situation. We lived on Rubensstraat across from the building on Euterpestraat where the Gestapo was. They looked right through our house, so to speak. At night there were always those raids and Jews were picked up. And you'd hear those people crying, and car doors slamming, and dogs barking. My bedroom was in the front part of the house, and I simply couldn't sleep a wink. And yes, for me it was a relief when someone said: "Would you please help us?" Well, I did, immediately.

In Amsterdam Gisela would be told that the "supply" consisted of a certain number of children of a certain age, so many boys and so many girls, and whether they were "pr" or "not pr" ("pr" was the abbreviation for *gepronon-ceerd*, meaning that they looked Jewish). She would then report this at a group meeting in Utrecht, always held in a different place selected by Matthijsen. Then the Utrecht students would look for suitable hiding addresses. Sometimes Gisela took the children with her to Utrecht.

Other members of Gisela's sorority were also asked to join. Meerburg's fellow-workers selected themselves, as it were. Gisela recalls:

> I was never really afraid. I still don't understand why not, but that's how it was. . . . I was convinced that it had to be done, and I simply did it. I have to add that I did have a sense of adventure. . . . That was an aspect that shouldn't be neglected. . . .
>
> [In Utrecht] there was a student who had a certain expression. . . . She looked so terribly suspicious, like she was hiding something, that even from a distance you thought: "Something's up, she's doing something she shouldn't do." We stopped working with her.

On the way back to Amsterdam, Gisela often took along ration cards and money "organized" by the Utrecht group for their counterparts in Amsterdam.

Thanks to the cooperative arrangement with Fiedeldij Dop, there were more children available in Amsterdam than the Utrecht group could place. Piet Meerburg decided to himself go and find places where they could be hidden.

I know that I went to Friesland in July or August to see if I could find anything; it was in '42, right after the first raid. At that time I mainly approached ministers . . . and pastors. Because you had to start somewhere. That was generally a very safe approach. I checked whether the person to be approached could be trusted, but then just went to them. The strange thing is that people simply didn't believe what was happening in Amsterdam. If you told them about raids you had seen with your own eyes, they simply didn't believe it. . . . But they soon changed their minds.

"FOUNDLINGS"

A very small number of babies did not have to go into hiding but were able to lead a "legal" existence. Here is how it happened. A newborn baby would be "abandoned" on the doorstep of the hiding address. The baby was then "found" by the foster parents, who registered it at the civil registry office. The child was issued an identity card with the name of the foster family. In this way Jewish babies were "aryanized" (Piet Meerburg's word). But it didn't happen all that frequently. Meerburg and his group managed it five times; a total of ten cases are known among the 1,000 children saved by the rescuers. Piet Meerburg elaborates:

> We always did it with two of us. Either Wouter with one of the girls, or I with one of the girls. The girls never wanted to do it alone because it was an enormous psychological burden. I still remember that I once did it with Tineke in Laren [a village near Amsterdam]. So they knew that we had placed the child on the step and rung the bell. . . . We did it at night or during the evening. And then, well, then we left. . . . Afterwards we went to my mother's place in Bussum [near Amsterdam]. Tineke Haak was very upset. And the same thing happened every time. They couldn't do it alone. The act of handing over the baby, of abandoning it—for these girls it was terribly difficult.

After January 15, 1943, this approach was no longer possible. All foundlings were considered to be Jewish children and were sent to the orphanage. On April 6, 1943, a diligent regional police commander wrote a letter to the Bureau for Jewish Emigration (Zentralstelle für Jüdische Auswanderung) in which he urged that all adoptions registered after the German invasion in May 1940 should be investigated carefully.

One little boy was abandoned as a foundling and then was betrayed: Remi van Duinwijck. Named Remi after the main character in the popular novel *Sans famille* (by the French author Hector Malot), he was found on

Duinwijckweg in Bloemendaal and was picked up at his foster parents' home (his fate will be described in Chapter 3).

A better way to aryanize Jewish children was to register the baby as a child born out of wedlock. Marion van Binsbergen, a woman who sometimes worked with the Amsterdam student group, registered three children. Once she did it twice in five months. Another woman was a thirty-six-year-old lawyer named Lau Mazirel who had a practice in Amsterdam. She registered several children. Lau's life partner, Robert Hartog, relates:

> The last year she hit upon the idea of having twins. She was always sorry that she hadn't thought of it earlier. And all our children survived just fine. Except when after the war she asked the municipal registrar to correct things, it took them aback. They even refused to believe that the two children registered before the war were really hers.

An acquaintance who was intermarried once called Rut Matthijsen and asked if he could supply a Jewish baby. Their newborn had died. Rut consulted Piet Meerburg. Together with Wouter van Zeytveld he went looking in the Transvaal district of Amsterdam. The fifth set of parents was willing to give up their baby. A few days later the couple was picked up; they were murdered. The baby was placed in the cradle of the dead child. Matthijsen recalls:

> Meanwhile the woman had been making noises and such so it would seem as if there were a live child in the cradle. It was play-acting for the neighbors, but it was rather awful for her. . . . And I buried the dead child in Bilthoven, in a deep grave in my mother's garden. It's probably still there.

FINANCING

At the end of July 1942, the group in Utrecht was taking care of twenty children and was running out of money. Rut Matthijsen and Ger Kempe tackled the problem of finances and of obtaining the needed ration cards. As to money, some parents who were still living in Holland could give money, for example 50 guilders per month. This was only asked of parents who could afford it. For other children, other sources had to be tapped. Kempe found a lady, an unmarried lawyer, the secretary of the commission that supervised the Protestant elementary schools; "Aunt Nel" was able to provide large sums of money and sometimes even gave addresses where the children could go. Matthijsen tried to raise money from fellow students. He approached the president of the Student Association council, J. P. Bol.

Jan Bol contacted as many Student Association members as he could and told them: "This weekend you have to ask for money at home. We now have an activity, helping, and we're counting on your support." And I'll be darned, within a week we had four thousand guilders.

The money soon ran out. Matthijsen asked Carel Nengerman, a fellow fraternity member and housemate, for money. Nengerman's father, the director of an insurance company, had died. Carel contributed 6,000 guilders. Matthijsen concludes: "Those were true club friendships." Matthijsen himself sold his stamp collection, which brought in 300 guilders.

When these students decided to give up their studies and devote themselves full-time to children's rescue work, they assumed that the organization would help support them. This became possible when a huge prize was netted by Willem Pompe, Ger Kempe's boss and the director of the Criminology Institute. As a religious Catholic, Pompe was on friendly terms with the archbishop, Dr. J. de Jong. Pompe had a talk with him, and the students were then invited to write a letter to the archbishop.

From the letter it appears that by August the number of children in their charge had increased to between seventy and eighty. On August 31, 1942 the archbishop in turn wrote a letter to the Dutch bishops asking them to earmark collection money for the students. Each of the four bishops turned over 2,500 guilders from the "collection for special needs," giving a total of 10,000 guilders to the Utrecht Children's Committee. The request for financial support came at a good time. Only four weeks earlier, all Catholic Jews had been deported despite efforts by the church to save them.[4]

At the end of 1942, Geertjan Lubberhuizen, a chemistry student and a friend of Frits Iordens, joined the group. He was on the editorial staff of the fraternity paper, *Vox Studiosorum*. If it worked out, Lubberhuizen would take a child to a hiding address. His fiancée, Willy van Reenen, worked in Arnhem as a pharmacist's assistant, and from time to time she helped him take Jewish children to Arnhem. From the beginning, however, Lubberhuizen was busy raising money, and eventually he was the one who solved the financial problems of the groups in Utrecht and Amsterdam (see Chapter 4).

Early in 1943, Anne Maclaine Pont asked Anna de Waard, a former classmate at the Protestant High School in Zwolle, to go "on collection" in the vicinity of the small town in Groningen where she had been born. Anna was a student in Utrecht and a member of the Utrecht Women Students Organization.

I would visit a prospect and say: "There is a great need, for there are Jewish children and adults who have to be helped. I know people who help them. And they need money." That way you didn't need to name names. Only your own name. And I had the greatest success . . . with the Dutch Reformed farmers in the countryside in northern Gronin-gen. They gave the most. Sometimes even one hundred guilders. Well, that was quite a sum at the time. Bear in mind that my room was expen-sive—and it was thirty-five guilders. It wasn't easy to convince people that Jews were people too. Because they weren't very pro-Jewish in those parts.

RATION CARDS

Food was rationed in Holland throughout the war. Rationing began on June 15, 1940 with bread and flour; coffee and tea were added later. Dry goods were also rationed. Every Dutch citizen received a distribution card (*stam-kaart*) on which the monthly ration coupons were checked off. Hidden chil-dren took along their own distribution card with a supplementary insert, but of course they couldn't show their registration card or the insert when a new registration card was filled in. At that time a number would be checked off or torn off and a new ration card was issued. Therefore it was essential to find friendly distribution clerks who were willing to exchange the numbers for ration cards without anyone showing a distribution card.

Hetty Voûte was able to establish connections with thirteen cooperative distribution clerks in the towns of Schoorl, Berg en Dal, Loosdrecht, Amers-foort, Nijkerk, Woerden, Driebergen, Voorburg, and Borculo.[5]

> I know that I was responsible for picking up ration cards, which was nasty work. First I had to go everywhere to find out where there were decent people working in the distribution offices. We did this in a very official way. You took one of the children along with its current regis-tration card. In it was the insert you needed to get the ration card. But you had to find distribution offices that were willing to exchange it for you. And gradually I knew places throughout the country where it could be done.

By the end of 1942, getting ration cards was no longer limited to Utre-cht. Wouter van Zeytveld also worked in this area after handing over his function as liaison between the Amsterdam and Utrecht organizations to Gisela Söhnlein. Wouter contacted trusted distribution clerks on Kalver-straat and "somewhere in east Amsterdam." These people were willing to issue ration cards when the children's distribution cards were presented. Once such a contact had been established, one of the students was asked to pick up the ration cards on a monthly basis.

PROVISIONAL ADDRESSES

When there was a shortage of homes, the students resorted to temporary emergency addresses, so-called provisional shelters. Hetty Voûte, for example, often took children to her parents' home on Kromme Nieuwe Gracht in Utrecht and once in a while to her brother in Amsterdam. Piet Meerburg and Wouter van Zeytveld also had children stay at their parents' homes for several days. In addition, Wouter van Zeytveld had a safe house in one of the poor districts of eastern Amsterdam.[6]

In the fall of 1942, Jan Meulenbelt asked Truitje van Lier for help. Truitje, together with her friend Jet Berdenis van Berlekom, ran a day-care center on Prins-Hendriklaan in Utrecht. In response to Meulenbelt's request, a kind of provisional shelter was created in an official child-care center, Kindjeshaven ("Children's Haven"). The child-care center had been operating since October 1940 and had been set up by Truitje, a law student in Utrecht and a former member of the board of the Utrecht Women Students Association. She had decided to do something for children "because they are always the ones to suffer." Because Truitje wasn't officially qualified, she worked with Jet, who had a diploma in child care.

Truitje took in children from the Utrecht student group as well as from a Communist group and a Dutch Reformed resistance group. Truitje herself also obtained addresses in the neighborhood, and people who were afraid to take a child themselves could become "foster parents" for fifty guilders per month. The children were in the child-care center under fictitious names. Through the Jewish Council cards had been obtained that stated that they were half-Jewish. To explain the Jewish appearance of a child with a non-Jewish father, Truitje invented a sick Jewish mother. She pretended that the non-Jewish father could not take care of his child because he had gone to work in Germany.

For emergency cases, Truitje and Jet could always fall back on Jet's parents, who lived in Bilthoven. That's where they took "Coal Flipje," the three-year-old son of a Jewish family from Amsterdam. During a razzia the little boy had been hidden in a coal bin by a friendly civil service worker, and he remained there for two nights. Truitje recalls:

> He came to us after he had been there for several nights. He was nothing but coal. He peed coal, his snot was coal. . . . Of course it was chaos. A couple of children together, that means screaming and crying and turmoil. And he wasn't exactly able to cope with it. I took him to Mrs. Van Berlekom, and he stayed there for quite a while. To calm down.

Good medical care was essential. Truitje found Dr. Sjamsoeding, a Utrecht pediatrician, who was willing to come by for free:

> He was worth his weight in gold. He was a pediatrician who lived near Kindjeshaven on Frans Halsstraat. And the children had to be vaccinated, of course. And it had to be done safely, which Dr. Sjamsoeding always did.

## CARD SYSTEMS

In November 1942, the number of Jewish children sheltered by the Utrecht group had grown so large that a card system had to be set up to keep the distribution of ration cards and everything else up to date. Hetty Voûte kept the data in a loose-leaf leather folder that stood in the bookcase under the title *The Collected Stories of John Galsworthy*. In it every Jewish child had a page with its name, a code number, a registration card number, and the "office" that was in charge of the child. The region was indicated by the abbreviation *Afd.* ("Department"). Every month the receipt of a ration card was checked off for each child. If you leaf through the folder, you see that in November 1942 ration cards were issued for forty-eight children. Later the number increased sharply, and it rose explosively in May of 1943, when sixty children were added to the card system.

The number of forty-eight children in November 1942 is much lower than the number (between seventy and eighty) mentioned in the letter of August 1942 to the archbishop. The discrepancy came about because the committee was only able to obtain ration cards for the forty-eight children for which it had registration cards. These children were included in the card system. There was no need to obtain coupons for some of the other children because the foster families had sufficient means or were able to deal with the ration cards on their own. Ration coupons for the remaining children were bought on the black market. This explains why the money ran out so quickly. The receipts for the second half of 1942 show a minimum total outlay of 21,600 guilders.

In addition, there was the cost of room and board for some of the Jewish children, support for the "permanent" workers, Jan Meulenbelt, Frits Iordens, and Rut Matthijsen, and tickets for the many train trips.

In November 1942, a system for managing money was set up. Cash was kept in a tin index-card box in the room of Bert Sedee, a medical student who had no other involvement with rescuing children. For that reason it was considered a safe address. Sedee doesn't remember ever opening the box. In early December a poster campaign was organized against the regulations proposed by Secretary-General Van Dam regarding forced labor by students. Since Bert Sedee was involved in the campaign, Rut Matthijsen began to worry about the safety of his room. He went there late one evening. Sedee wasn't in, but Rut took the card box to Jan Meulenbelt's room. The next day the Gestapo arrested Sedee in his room. He was released at Christmas, and later was able to escape, via Paris, to London.

Because many of the Jewish children were put up in and around the city of Utrecht, the city was divided into districts, and district heads were appointed, similar to the "managers" in Arnhem.

According to Hetty Voûte's card system, in February 1943 the Utrecht group was taking care of ninety-eight children in hiding. In April 1943 the number increased to 171 children.


JANUARY–APRIL 1943
THE THREESOME IN SNEEK

Piet Meerburg had not yet eliminated the province of Friesland as a refuge for Jewish children. With the help of Fiedeldij Dop, he was still able to supply more children than the group in Utrecht could accommodate. At the sickbed of an uncle, Meerburg encountered his cousin Mia Coelingh, who taught religion in public schools in and around Sneek, a town in Friesland. Mia Coelingh was also assistant minister in the Liberal Reformed church in Sneek. When her father had recovered somewhat, she decided to help Piet. She informed her parents of this decision, and they immediately gave one hundred guilders for the children's rescue work. She asked Gérard Jansen, a curate whom she had known since before the war, for help. Together they approached Willem Mesdag, a Baptist minister. Mesdag's children had been in Mia Coelingh's class. At the end of 1942 Mesdag had briefly hidden a colleague, the rabbi of the Sneek Jewish community and his wife.

The three decided to limit themselves to children. Piet Meerburg says: "I remember Jansen. . . . He would arrive at the station with packets of butter hidden in the panels of his robe. That's the kind of guy he was. Terrific. Really a terrific man."

Mia Coelingh adds:

His alias was Jan Zwart. He had a good sense of humor, was very compassionate and open to others. The first time he helped out, he had to bring a Jewish adult to a hiding address. And he had borrowed a baker's cart for the purpose. So this curate had gone to a baker and asked:

"Please let me have your cart." And so this Jew went into the baker's cart. The carts used to have lids, and the lid was closed. . . . And that's how he took that Jew to his hiding place. He was incredibly resourceful; he was never at a loss. He was always able to enlist people to help.

Mesdag's house became the center of activities in Sneek. It was there that the threesome met. It was also there that most of the Jewish children that Meerburg's group brought in by train were initially received. Mesdag's oldest daughter, Nina (her name is Nine in Dutch; to prevent confusion with the number nine we have changed her name to Nina in this translation), still remembers:

Mia Coelingh lived in a rooming house. It was, of course, inconceivable for young women with babies to keep going there and then leave without them. It just wasn't possible. And that is how Mia came to us. We were a family with five children, and we always had friends and confirmation candidates in the house. We still had a door with a latch that you could open from the outside. And then you came in and called out: "Hello! Anybody home?" All sorts of people were coming and going. And that's the way my parents did it.

Iet van Dijk, a medical student in Amsterdam, took the trip to Sneek dozens of times with one or more Jewish children. She was blonde, short, and exceptionally driven. In 1943 she was the most important person escorting children in the group around Meerburg and Van Zeytveld.

But Meerburg and Wouter van Zeytveld also traveled to Sneek. Mia vividly remembers the first young child:

She was a ravishingly beautiful girl with beautiful curls, about eight or nine years old. And she was placed in a very small worker's cottage that was right behind my house. She was such a sweet child, such a beautiful girl, that the whole neighborhood turned out. That very evening and the next day, several people from the neighborhood were on my doorstep: "Miss, can I have a girl like that too?" . . . They were literally pushing. Piet and I had agreed that I would contact him one way or another if I could place another child. So that's what I did. And the second one was a very skinny child who had just had chicken pox. It looked so pathetic. And I had to take the child to the second mother. At which point the second mother had quite a shock: "I ordered a beautiful child like the other one." I said: "You don't order anything here! You're supposed to save a human being. And this one just had chicken pox." But I went on: "And if you don't want it, that's OK. I have plenty of addresses. I'll come and get the child in a day." But the child stayed, and it all went fine.

KRIJN VAN DEN HELM

Willem Mesdag also instructed Piet Meerburg to Krijn van den Helm, a tax
clerk.[7]

This was Meerburg's second "golden" contact in Friesland. Krijn was a
Baptist. In May 1940 he had been a sergeant on the Grebbelinie front, trying
to hold back the Germans. He hadn't aimed very carefully because his religion forbade killing. But when a soldier next to him was fatally hit, Krijn
fired back. He regarded the bombing of Rotterdam and its defenseless civil-
ians as a crime.

Krijn had taken the fifteen-year-old daughter of a business acquaintance
into his house when her family had been ordered to report for "work in Germany" in August of 1942. In September 1941, Krijn van den Helm was
transferred to the tax office in Leeuwarden. His boss was Jan Evenhuis, who
didn't care much for the German administration. Wouter van Zeytveld
remembers this well:

> I felt that the whole office was working exclusively for the resistance.
> They no longer did any real work. It must have been a huge mess.
> Frisians are strange people. Once they say yes to something—and it
> does take them a while to decide—but once they say yes they're so
> fanatical you can practically build a house on it.

Krijn van den Helm and his friend Harm Kingma helped to hide Jews.
Van den Helm's initial contacts were trusted colleagues in the tax department. Early in 1942, 665 Jews lived in Leeuwarden; at least 100 of them had
gone into hiding by May of 1943. It is uncertain how many Van den Helm
helped. After May of 1943, there were—officially—no more Jews in Leeuwarden.

After February 1943, Iet van Dijk, Hans van Loghem, and Tineke Haak
(sometimes in the company of Meerburg or Van Zeytveld) regularly made
the trip to Leeuwarden. Meerburg and Van den Helm became good friends.
Each time they took along Jewish children who were met "under the clock"
of the station in Leeuwarden by Van den Helm, his wife Joop, or Harm
Kingma. The children were then taken to hiding addresses in the Leeuwarden vicinity. Meerburg was not the only "supplier" of Jews to the organization in Friesland. Van den Helm continued to hide adult Jews independently.

## AMSTERDAM–WEST FRIESLAND

In addition to the Amsterdam-Friesland route, the rescuers established an Amsterdam–West Friesland (the northeastern region of the province of Noord-Holland) route. At its center were Cees Kracht and his wife, Lien Kracht-Van Dok, who lived with their two young daughters in a small laborers' cottage in Wijdenes. Cees designed central heating systems, and Lien worked from time to time as a maternity nurse. Both came from very leftist families. Cees had refused military service and served ten months in solitary confinement at the Special Convicts Prison (Bijzondere Strafgevangenis) in Scheveningen. Cees and Lien were friends of the Jewish psychiatrist Van Emde Boas in Amsterdam. At the end of 1942, Van Emde Boas referred Wouter van Zeytveld to Wijdenes.

A small network of friendly, like-minded families soon was formed in West Friesland. Cees and Lien Kracht brought in Jan de Ruiter and his wife. They lived in a large house in Hoorn, and they sometimes hid as many as fourteen Jews at once in their attic. Jan de Ruiter worked in the textile trade, and in consequence knew many Jews from Twente (Overijssel). In addition he looked actively for places for Jewish children and tried in every way possible to get hold of ration cards. During the winter of 1942–43, the children were brought by Wouter van Zeytveld and Tineke Haak. Lien Kracht still remembers them materializing in the snow with four-year-old Bob, whom they themselves took in: "Wouter and Tineke were pulling a sled with the child and some suitcases on it. Someone had given them the sled."

It is no longer possible to track down how many children were taken to West Friesland. We do know, however, that the network took care of itself financially.

## THE CARD SYSTEM IN AMSTERDAM

The group in Amsterdam also kept a card system. Three separate lists were maintained because of safety considerations. The first list had the names of the hidden Jewish children, the second, street names and house numbers, and the third, the communities where the children were hidden.[8]

None of these lists was found after the war, and only 166 names have surfaced in other ways. All told, the Amsterdam group took care of an estimated 350 Jewish children.

DECLARATION OF LOYALTY

In the early years of the occupation, students were not sent to Germany as workers. But in the spring of 1943, the declaration of loyalty brought a change in their relatively safe position.

On February 5, 1943 an attempt was made on the life of General H. A. Seyffardt, a Dutch Nazi who was recruiting volunteers for the eastern front. The attempt was carried out by the CS-6 resistance group (see Chapter 5). Before he died, the general attributed the attack to students. The next day (a Saturday) razzias took place in universities and colleges; 602 students were arrested and sent to Camp Vught. They were told that in order to resume their studies they would have to sign a "declaration of loyalty" that stated that the signer would not engage in anti-German activities. Those who refused to sign would be sent to Germany.

The students urged one another not to sign the declaration under any circumstances; those who were undecided were worked on by "brainwashing" squads. Their professors as well as the Dutch government in exile in London condemned the required signing in strong terms. Sixteen percent signed. Many students went into hiding.

The risk of not signing the declaration of loyalty was diminished for the students in Utrecht because of a successful raid on the student administration of the university in December 1942. The raid was carried out by Anne Maclaine Pont, Frits Iordens, Rut Matthijsen, Geert Lubberhuizen, and Gijs den Besten—all of them, except Gijs den Besten, members of the Utrecht Children's Committee—who entered the university building and burned the student files. Jan Meulenbelt and Ger Kempe were not informed about the raid beforehand because the others knew that Jan wanted them to stick to rescue work and avoid any other form of resistance that might jeopardize the goal of rescuing Jewish children. They did not learn the details until the end of the war.

Hetty Voûte was completely available for children's rescue work after January 1943 when she joined the nucleus of the Utrecht Children's Committee. Now she also took children to their foster homes. Very often she did this together with Jan Meulenbelt, and the two of them took children all the way to South Limburg.[9]

Hetty remembered what it was like to call for the children. Unlike Gisela, she found it very difficult.

> I have the worst memories of that. Actually, I think it's only now that I realize how horrible it was. You went inside. Just an address, and everything was standing ready. Packed. A bundle, and a child or two.

And then you left with them. You took their papers and went down-stairs. And no one knew your name, they didn't know where you were going, they knew you wouldn't keep in touch with them. . . . And sometimes, because you still had to go to another address, you felt that it was taking them too long! . . . And then you arrived at Amstel station and the conductor would say: "Do you know how much you usually pay?" With a baby carriage. Meaning: Watch out, it looks suspicious.

One time Hetty was escorting some very Jewish-looking twins. They had to change trains at Woerden. Hetty recalls:

We're standing on the platform in Woerden and suddenly one of the two little boys calls out, with his small, shrill voice: "Solly, your cap!" . . . I thought, he'd better get that cap back fast, otherwise we're in for it. And right then you could see that the Dutch were not Nazi sympa-thizers. Everyone was watching, and it was obvious that they knew what's what, but no one says a thing, nothing happens, and you just go about your business.

Once on the train, it was easier:

You just sit down in the train with them. If they're babies, then it's no problem at all. If they're a little older, then you tell them: "Better not talk. It's better not to talk too much on the train." And the children are so docile. There was no crying as far as I can remember. They do exactly as you say. As if they feel instinctively that whatever is happen-ing here no longer has anything in common with a normal child's life. They don't whine.

WHO WAS RESPONSIBLE?

The children's committee entrusted the ultimate responsibility for the chil-dren to the foster parents. Meerburg and his group, however, saw themselves as responsible from the moment they called for a child at the home of the bio-logical parents until he or she had been delivered to the permanent foster par-ents. Meerburg explains:

Once we had a letter from parents who had been caught and sent to Westerbork: would we please bring the child to Westerbork. We discussed this for a very long time: do we have the right to refuse? Aside from the fact that it would have been a little difficult for us to go and stand at the entrance of Westerbork with a child in our arms, we also felt that we had taken over the responsibility from the parents: we didn't do it.

There were no regular checks on the well-being of the children. Hetty didn't think it was necessary:

> If people dare to take on the responsibility for a child, then they have the freedom to do it their way. . . . You saw how the children were received. I don't think I ever felt uncomfortable. These people were quite aware of what they were doing.

Not long before this, Hetty was almost caught and had to go into hiding. One of the people she sent to distribute ration cards to sheltering families was picked up with a thick stack of ration cards. Under interrogation, using Hetty's pseudonym, she said that she had been given them by Jet Juttink, who lived on Kromme Nieuwe Gracht in Utrecht. Hetty recalls:

> One afternoon when we were all together, my mother came upstairs and said: "They were just at the door for Jet Juttink. I told them I wasn't renting out any rooms." We gathered everything together as fast as we could. Everything. We had a lot of stuff lying around.[10]
> We hid it all. Fifteen minutes later they came back because they realized that they wanted me. And they told my mother: "If she's not here tomorrow morning, then we'll take you." I thought that was so terrible. And my mother said: "For goodness sake, it doesn't bother me at all." So the next morning she was sitting ready with some needlework, a sponge, and a good book. . . . That was February '43.

Mrs. Voûte was not taken. Hetty went into hiding in Ommen with Adri Knappert, a reliable member of the Utrecht group who lodged a good many Jewish children in her house. But she felt that she couldn't do enough there, so she left for Utrecht as soon as the coast was somewhat clear.

Hetty was able to take the room of another hidden student who had been living with a grocer, the Das family. She stayed there until her arrest in June 1943. She was able to continue her work, which included keeping the card system up to date. Hetty recalls that Mr. Das, whose children were quite young, set only one condition:

> One evening he asked me to come in and then he said: "I think everything is all right, but you're not Jewish, are you? . . . Because I think that's too great a risk." I said: "No, I'm not." He'd figured it out well before that.

Around the beginning of 1943, Gisela Söhnlein also began doing more and more. She no longer limited herself to escorting children to Utrecht, she also took them to the final foster family. The declaration of loyalty in March 1943 meant that Gisela had to drop out of school, just like all the other students who were active in rescuing children. A side effect was the closing of the EOOS sorority house. Gisela decided to live with her parents in Utrecht. She stayed there until June, when she and Hetty were arrested. Her original task of traveling as courier between the Amsterdam and Utrecht groups was no longer so essential because both groups were now operating more independently. When the EOOS house was closed in March, Piet Meerburg and Wouter van Zeytveld had to find another hiding address. In September 1942 there had been a raid on the house on Keizersgracht where Piet roomed, and he had barely been able to escape over the roof. After the raid he hid in the EOOS house together with Wouter. In September 1942, when Wouter received a summons to do forced labor in Germany, he was no longer able to continue living with his parents in Amsterdam's Transvaal neighborhood. Piet and Wouter found shelter with Jetty van den Berg, one of Tineke Haak's cousins. They were able to stay at this address for almost half a year because it was kept very secret.[11]

## GROWING INDEPENDENCE OF THE BRANCHES

The growing independence of the Amsterdam group was the subject of discussion at many meetings in Utrecht as well as in Amsterdam, motivated by the fact that the Amsterdam students had opened their own "line" to Friesland. Once the die was cast and the Amsterdam group began functioning independently in March of 1943, Jan Meulenbelt and Frits Iordens started thinking about the status of the other "branches." Hetty and Jan Meulenbelt had discussed this too.

Paul Terwindt, alias "Uncle Piet," was one of Iordens's first co-workers in Arnhem,[12] and he became responsible for the Arnhem branch in October 1942. He was indefatigable in tracking down families willing to take in children. Soon Terwindt extended his activities to the provinces of Limburg and Noord-Brabant. He traveled countless times to south Limburg, where he searched for and found new addresses.

Some children were moved several times. In January 1943, Terwindt moved eight-year-old Lottie Broekman from one address in south Limburg to another; she was a difficult child. Another child difficult to place was Jaap Grootkerk, who was mentally handicapped. After a long search, Paul Terwindt and his co-worker Tini van de Bilt found a family willing to take him. They were already caring for a large number of children. Although this branch became more independent, the children's committee regularly sent them new supplies of ration cards, and Jan Meulenbelt made sure that he was informed of happenings in all parts of the organization. A report about the

activities of the branch in Arnhem, written by Paul Terwindt around the end
of 1944 or early in 1945 for the Military Authorities (Militair Gezag) in the
liberated southern part of the Netherlands, gives us some insight into its
methods:

> If at all possible a child had to experience normal family life as a cousin.
> In communities where school principals cooperated, the child could
> be placed unnoticed in a school among non-Jewish children. But going
> to school was a goal that usually turned out to be unrealistic either
> because there was no cooperation or the risks were too great. The chil-
> dren were regularly provided with food ration cards and were checked.
> Often it was necessary to move the child to reduce risk because people
> began to be suspicious about the child's long stay. And so children were
> first placed in Arnhem, Oosterbeek, Bennekom, Wageningen, and
> Velp by the Utrecht Children's Committee until the students them-
> selves had to go into hiding. After that, the children were picked up
> directly from the Jewish parents in Amsterdam-Oost, where the razzias
> were taking place day in day out, night in night out, in ever increasing
> intensity. Taken by non-Jews to "the clock" in Central Station, they
> were then transported by train to the south or the north, depending
> on where foster homes were available.

Terwindt recalls:

> In Arnhem a secret file was started. It contained 150 addresses with
> names and family relationships. The addresses of foster parents did not
> appear on the cards. They were noted in code in a penmanship work-
> book.

It is, alas, no longer possible to track down this file. Most likely it is in the attic
of one of Terwindt's descendants.

### NEW WORKERS

As a result of the declaration of loyalty, four new part-time workers joined
the Utrecht Children's Committee. The first was a medical student, Jelle de
Jong, a tall heavy fellow who was originally from Friesland and had a strict
Calvinist outlook on life. He was in the same year at the university as Rut
Matthijsen. Little is known about his role on the children's committee. The
same is true for his girlfriend, Jaco Stamperius,[13] a medical student who took
many children to hiding addresses during the spring of 1943. Jelle de Jong
was probably asked to become contact person for the city of Utrecht. He
acted very firmly; some of the students with whom he worked even found
him dictatorial.

To coordinate matters, a central contact address was established for the city of Utrecht, at Boothstraat 17, where messages could be left for the members of the committee. This large student rooming house was not very far from the Begijnekade, where Jelle de Jong rented a room.

The third newcomer was James van Beusekom, a medical student in the Utrecht Student Association (Studenten Corps). He lived in the same house as Jelle de Jong. The similarity between his name and Jan Meulenbelt's alias (Van Beusecom) caused much confusion but was pure coincidence. James van Beusekom took many children to their hiding addresses, and he often did this with Gisela Söhnlein. At the foster homes they would introduce themselves as "Liesje de Koning" and "Karel van Nieveld."

The fourth newcomer, Alice Brunner, was an English student at Amsterdam University. She too had refused to sign the loyalty declaration and therefore had to leave the university. She became active in the rescue operation while living in her mother's house in Utrecht but can no longer remember who asked her to join; perhaps it was her younger sister Gabriëlle, who as a biology student in Utrecht knew Hetty Voûte. At any rate, Alice Brunner began to distribute ration cards and clothing in a neighborhood of Utrecht. This made her district chief, which, according to her, was hardly a full-time occupation. It meant, among other things, that she had to pick up instructions and supplies from Jelle de Jong.

Meanwhile Geert Lubberhuizen was involved in obtaining and counterfeiting identity cards, permits (*Ausweise*), and registration cards. When the students were asked to sign the loyalty declaration and the committee members went into hiding, Geert counterfeited new identity cards for them. He set up a workshop in the attic of a surgical resident who was training with a surgeon well-disposed toward the Germans and therefore not under suspicion. For safety reasons Geert called himself Bas Ruys. Counterfeiting was a rather expensive activity because Geert always needed paper. He couldn't stand begging for money. He thought of a plan to offer future backers something in exchange for their money. He was looking for something that he could "sell" for a decent sum. The profit would flow into the coffers of the children's committee.

At the end of March 1943, Lubberhuizen received help from Rut Matthijsen, who had been "unemployed" since February, when he had been caught by accident. Rut had been taking ration cards, registration cards, and a considerable amount of food to an address in a southern district of Amsterdam where Jewish children were hidden. On the way he was stopped by an officer of the Crisis Control Service (Crisis Controle Dienst), known as the

CCD, looking for black marketeers. The man was curious about the contents of Rut's suitcase. When sizable quantities of cheese and sausage were found, Rut had to go along to the police station. There they also found the ration and registration cards as well as several addresses. Fearfully awaiting interrogation, Rut decided to jump out of the window.

As a result of the fall, he ended up in the hospital with a concussion and a policeman standing guard at the door of his room. Somehow Ger Kempe managed to visit the hospital to give Rut a convincing cover story. Rut was to say that the food and ration cards came from the parents of students who were sending their children a little extra because of the bad food situation in the western part of the country. When stopped by the CCD officer, he had remembered the February 6 razzia of students and panicked. That is why he had jumped out of the window—he was afraid he would be sent on a one-way trip to Vught, like the unlucky victims of the razzia. Rut dished up this story when questioned and, to his surprise, was released, even though he still had to spend four weeks in the hospital to recuperate from his concussion. The food and the ration and registration cards were returned to him without comment.

After his stay in the hospital, Rut was out of circulation. Kempe, who had meanwhile become active in the Packard spy group, advised him to start collecting military information in and around Utrecht. Rut did not feel like doing that. He went to see Geert:

> The security there, especially after February 6, was perfect for Geert Lubberhuizen. . . . That's where he made the first counterfeits, on his own; I don't know how he started: scratch out and then erase and so on. He did it very well. He could also draw fairly well. So when I went there at the end of March, I saw that he was quite busy. Very calm, no dangerous hiding work. . . . And then we sat down and philosophized: "What do I do now?" . . . And he said: "Well, how about it? We need counterfeits."

Rut accepted the offer. For the rest of the war he worked as a counterfeiter.

## THE NAAMLOZE VENNOOTSCHAP (NV)

Nineteen-year-old Marianne Braun and her almost sixteen-year-old brother Leo lived on fashionable Minervalaan in Amsterdam in July 1942, when they received a summons to report for transport to Westerbork and employment in Germany. Together with their parents, they had come to Holland from Austria in 1938. Two years later they had adopted the Calvinist faith. Their parents went to their minister, Constant J. Sikkel, at the church on Raphaelplein, to ask what they should do. In his next sermon, Sikkel posed the question, in guarded terms. Among the congregants were the brothers Jaap and Gerard Musch, in their late and early twenties. After the service they offered to help find a refuge for the children. This would not be very easy, because the children did not want to go into hiding unless their parents could also do so. Jaap and Gerard Musch, together with their friend Dick Groenewegen van Wijk, decided to start looking for hiding places not just for this family but, more systematically, for Jews in general. Gerard and Dick looked unsuccessfully for two and a half months in the province of Groningen. Jaap Musch was more successful. Pastor Sikkel introduced him to the Dutch Reformed minister Gerard Pontier in Heerlen (in the mostly Catholic province of Limburg). With his aid Jaap moved in with the Bockmas, a miner's family from Friesland who were living in Heerlen. Jaap continued his work while boarding there.

Meanwhile the Brauns and their children were in different temporary refuges. Dick went to visit the parents and ran into them at the station. They were on their way back to Amsterdam because they could no longer stand it in their chicken coop. With great difficulty Dick got them to turn back. He promised to find them another place. This adventure made the trio decide to specialize in children: children were easier, because they usually did what they were told. The three found willing households around their base in the southern part of the country, and then arranged for the children to come. The flow of children was organized by the Kinsbergen family in Amsterdam, who had many Jewish acquaintances. In October 1942, the Woortman family was recruited; the husband, Joop, was a waiter who formerly had owned a taxi business and had many Jewish acquaintances. Joop Woortman went into Jewish areas of Amsterdam and talked parents into giving up their children. Meanwhile Dick Groenewegen van Wijk looked for places in and around Heerlen, and Gerard Musch worked the area near Kerkrade. They continued to make regular visits to the children who were already hidden in order to bring ration cards and other necessities. Sometimes they picked up children in Amsterdam. To attract less attention on the train, they pretended to be couples, using Rebecca van Delft and Jooske de Neve, former classmates of Marianne Braun; later, when Rebecca was no longer available, Annemarie van Verschuer stepped in.

They paid room and board for the children to poor miners and their families. Looking for addresses was no simple task, but sometimes foster parents knew families that were willing to help. In this way the pool grew larger and eventually also included Catholic foster families. Annemarie van Verschuer thoroughly detested looking for foster families.

> I always found it frightening. . . . I found it more frightening than taking the children from Amsterdam to Heerlen, for you never knew how people would react. And like a door-to-door salesman you had to persuade people to take in a child.

The Bockma house, where Jaap Musch had a room, became the group's meeting place. It was a large fourteenth-century Limburg farm with a sizable courtyard. Upstairs there were enormous attics. Mr. Bockma worked in a mine and also had a milk route. There was never enough money or food. The almost-adult Bockma children sometimes helped by escorting children to hiding addresses.

By the end of April 1943, eighty children had been placed in the Heerlen-Kerkrade area. Money and ration cards came primarily from Amsterdam via Joop Woortman. In this way a professional group of children's rescuers had been created: the Naamloze Vennootschap (NV), or Anonymous Association.

## THE TROUW GROUP
### HESTER VAN LENNEP AND GESINA VAN DER MOLEN

The illegal underground newspaper *Trouw* began publishing in January 1943. Its founders were all from Protestant circles. The members who were involved in children's rescue work are called the Trouw Group.[14]

Hester van Lennep had an institute for skin care on Keizersgracht. Women with children could regularly be seen leaving the building. She took the first child she helped to her mother's house in Hilversum. He was the son of the colleague of an acquaintance, a notary. Hester's acquaintance asked her advice on how his Jewish colleague should go about finding a hiding address for his children. That was in the second half of 1942. By May of 1943 Hester had found places for ten to twenty children. Her nephews, Gideon and Jan Karel Boissevain, were in the armed resistance. They named their group CS-6 after their parents' address, Corellistraat 6. It was this group that killed General Seyffardt on February 5, 1943.

Hester was helped by her friend Paulien van Waasdijk, her partner at the institute for skin care. Her nephew Gideon had hidden an adult, Sándor Baracs, at Keizersgracht 488. Gideon once had to go away for several days, so he asked Hester to take care of Sándor. Hetty and Sándor fell in love. Half a year later they were both members of the Trouw Group. Once Sándor had good counterfeit papers, he began to actively search for hiding addresses. Sándor took *Mein Kampf* seriously: "I said to everyone: 'Go into hiding! This is not labor (*Arbeitsdienst*) but deportation! This is deportation and death!' "

Through April 1943 the Jewish children hidden by Hester van Lennep often had a parent who had been treated at the institute of skin care or knew someone who had been there. As the number of requests for help grew, Hester van Lennep started looking systematically for places among her non-Jewish acquaintances. Slowly but surely the residents of Jewish neighborhoods learned that there was a woman living at Keizersgracht 484 who was able to help Jewish children disappear. Hester describes how word got around the Jewish neighborhoods:

> Through the grapevine. Through Jewish acquaintances who had other Jewish acquaintances and would say: "Gee, I know someone who can do something." It grew by itself. Before you knew it you were in the middle, and then you think: "Well, do you really want this?" But you simply couldn't go back. Once you were in it, you had to go on.

She used the "snowball" method when looking for addresses: "When I placed a child at my mother's, I'd say: 'If you know anyone else who would be willing to do something like this or would be willing to help a child, then please give me that person's name.' I always got some addresses."

The Boissevain boys helped by escorting children and looking for new addresses. When Hester didn't accompany a child herself, she arranged to meet the escort on a street corner. When contact was made, she and the escort would walk part of the way together, with the child in between the adults and holding one or the other's hand. The adults were supposedly involved in a lively conversation. At the next corner Hester would leave the child and the other adult. Another child gone.

Hester obtained ration cards from CS-6 but also by other means. Her older sister introduced her to Gesina van der Molen, who put her Trouw contacts at Hester's disposal. Gesina was one generation older. Born into a Calvinist family in Groningen, she had studied law, remained unmarried, and lived with her Catholic friend Mies Nolte in Aerdenhout. Gesina was one of the very few people who in 1940 refused to sign the Aryan declaration. Later, as a member of the editorial staff of the illegal magazine *Vrij Nederland*, she was imprisoned for several weeks. She acted the innocent old lady and was released. Together with Mies Nolte she went into hiding in Amsterdam. When she began working at Trouw, she developed a large network. Trouw kept contact with the National Organization to Assist Those in Hiding (Landelijke Organisatie voor Hulp aan Onderduikers), known as the LO. That is

FIGURE 4
*Farm of the Bockma family at Heerlerbaan (Limburg)*
Book of photographs NV group

why there were always enough ration cards, clothes, and money for those who went into hiding with the help of the Trouw Group. Hester van Lennep and Sándor Baracs had many more options when they linked up with the Trouw Group.

## NOTES

1. Richter Roegholt, *De geschiedenis van de Bezige Bij 1942–1972* (Amsterdam, 1972), pp. 9–51.
2. See note 10, Chapter 1.
3. Jan Meulenbelt, "Portret van Frits," *Nieuw Utrechts Dagblad,* March 17, 1955.
4. Dfl. 10,000 from the bishops; Dfl. 4,000 from members of the Utrecht Student Association; Dfl. 6,000 from Carel Nengerman and Dfl. 1,600 from "tante Nel." In total Dfl. 21,600.
5. Hetty Voûte, Letter to Yad Vashem; see "Sources." The total of thirteen offices is taken from J.J. van Bolhuis, ed. *Onderdrukking en Verzet: Nederland in Oorlogstijd,* vol. 3 (Amsterdam, n.d.), p. 695.
6. At Gerrit den Os, a metalworker and amateur opera performer. One unlucky day he was picked up while there was a Jewish baby in the house. The assailants took the baby and gave it to their cousin. Thereupon Wouter van Zeytvelt and Iet van Dijk went to the cousin's house, tied the cousin to a chair, and rescued the child. Since they were unable to return home before curfew, Wouter, Iet, and the child slept on the floor of the Colonial Institute, where Iet could get in. Source: Interview with Piet Meerburg and Wouter van Zeytveld, January 28, 1988.
7. Ype Schaaf, *Dodelijke dilemma's in het Friesche verzet. Het veemgericht en Esmée van Eeghen* (Franeker, 1995), pp. 67–70.
8. Piet Meerburg, Letter to the author; see Sources.
9. Sometimes the trip took too long. On one occasion Hetty and Jan Meulenbelt could not get back to Utrecht until long after curfew. They hid in a freight train.
10. The children's committee stored clothing and shoes in the attic of Hetty's parents' house.
11. Piet Meerburg, Letter to the author; see Sources. See also Data about G.H. Salomé, born October 12, 1918, for which the questionnaire of Mr. P. Dolfsma served as a model, Collection Stichting Onderlinge Studenten Steun (Amsterdam).
12. D.D. Vollgraff, Report of conversation with Jan Meulenbelt; see Sources.
13. She had to give up her activities after a few months because she was pregnant. In her case we can say, therefore, that she was a temporary part-time worker.
14. The name "Trouw Groep" is used throughout his book. Actually, this is incorrect, since it refers to a (separate) part of the Trouw organization.

# JEWISH RESCUERS OF CHILDREN
January–November 1943

Jews who were rounded up on the street during razzias or seized in their homes were temporarily locked up in the Hollandsche Schouwburg on Plantage Middenlaan if the train for the transit camp at Westerbork was not ready. In October 1942, the Jewish Council was authorized to place Jewish children under the age of thirteen in a child-care center located across the street from the Schouwburg. When a transport was scheduled to leave for Westerbork, they were reunited with their parents and together driven in trucks to the train station.

The Jews who rescued children were members of the Jewish staff of the Hollandsche Schouwburg and the child-care center. Without the guards noticing, they handed the children over to people on the outside who could help them go into hiding.

Several hundred Jewish children were smuggled out of the child-care center by the Jewish children's rescuers and by members of the four resistance groups (and by many others as well).[1]

## THE DEPORTATIONS FROM PLANTAGE MIDDENLAAN

Out of the total of 61,744 Jews who were deported from Amsterdam, 15,000 to 18,000 passed through the Schouwburg or the child-care center.[2] Those who were not immediately deported were held in the Schouwburg until it was possible to deport them. In the summer of 1943, many Jews, including special-punishment cases, were sometimes stuck for months on end in the Schouwburg and the child-care center.

The population of the Schouwburg consisted primarily of young adults with children. At first most of them were Jews who had been working in industry on projects needed by the German army, but whose deferments

(*Wehrmachtsperre*) had expired. After May 1943, the only Jews still in Amsterdam were those who had deferments (*Sperre*) because they worked for the Jewish Council. But this type of *Sperre* became increasingly unsafe through the spring and summer of 1943, and they were now being arrested together with their families. Both groups of Jews, the *Wehrmachtsperre* and the Jewish Council *Sperre*, must have been in the prime of their lives and often had young children. We may assume that one-third of the 15,000 to 18,000 Jews taken to the Schouwburg were children who ended up in the child-care center: 5,000 or 6,000 children. An estimated 500 to 700 children were rescued from the child-care center.

## THE CHILD-CARE CENTER

Before 1941, the child-care center was an ordinary day-care center where children went during the day if both parents were working. The child-care center was meant for poor Jewish mothers who took their children there so that they could work. In the thirties, the cost was 25 cents a day per child.[3]

Non-Jewish children could go there as well. The staff was made up of Jews and non-Jews. The child-care center was housed in the large building of a former Talmud Torah school on Plantage Middenlaan where until that time poor Jewish boys had received a free religious and secular education. The synagogue on the second floor remained in use, except for a small cubicle where the staff could change their clothes before and after work. The new child-care center was the most modern in Amsterdam; it had spacious rooms, big windows, and a large, partially paved playground. And, very unusual for the time, it also had small toilets for the girls and small urinals for the boys.

In 1926 Miss (she insisted on being addressed as "Miss") Henriette Henriquez Pimentel became director of the child-care center. Born on April 17, 1876, Miss Pimentel was a small, stocky woman with short gray hair. She was firm but had a heart of gold and was quite attached to her dog, Brunie. Her work became increasingly demanding because more Jewish mothers were forced to supplement the family income as a result of the 1929 economic crisis. The child-care center, which was able to handle one hundred children under the age of six, was used to full capacity every day. The staff of the center combed the children's hair daily to check for lice. If twenty or more lice were found on a child, the mother was not permitted to leave the child. The babies were completely undressed in the reception area and then dressed in clothes belonging to the child-care center.

The child-care center was the only institution of its kind in Holland that offered an accredited two-year training program for child-care workers.

FIGURE 5
*The Hollandsche Schouwburg at Plantage Middenlaan, Amsterdam*
From the collection of the Netherlands Institute for War Documentation, Amsterdam

Even after the deportations began, the students had classes three evenings a week and were taught by the director, doctors, and other experts. Because most of the children in the child-care center were Jewish, the kitchen was kosher.

The transformation from child-care center to annex of the Hollandsche Schouwburg took place in one single night in October 1942. Babies, toddlers, preschoolers, and even older children up to age thirteen had to await the moment of deportation in the child-care center. Henriette Pimentel asked three young child-care workers, Betty Oudkerk, Fanny Philips, and Sieny Kattenburg, to stay overnight and sleep in the child-care center with the children. Each of the three had a small room in the attic and was put in charge of a section for the night. Sieny Kattenburg (eighteen years old) was assigned to the children up to four years old. She and her parents discussed whether she should live in the child-care center:

> My parents agreed with me completely. . . . The only bad thing was that
> I saw them very little because I had to be in by eight. After eight we

FIGURE 6
*Nursery section of the day-care center, opposite the Hollandsche Schouwburg*
Courtesy Mrs. Cohen-Kattenburg (Amstelveen)

weren't allowed on the street. So we worked from early morning till late at night. We had to help with each transport. We had to take the children to their parents. No one else was allowed to do that. Transports left at ten in the evening, so we hardly came home anymore.

The job of child-care worker in the child-care center offered protection "until further notice" against deportation. But this protection did not include Sieny's family. She saw her whole family taken away. Her parents and her brother were deported on May 26, 1943 and did not return.

The babies in the child-care center were often fed by their mothers. Betty Oudkerk, Fanny Philips, and Sieny Kattenburg accompanied the mothers to the child-care center and back to the Schouwburg. They wore special armbands allowing them to visit the Schouwburg. It was their task to maintain contact between the children in the child-care center and their parents in the Schouwburg. Sieny was in the Schouwburg dozens of times. The staff of the Schouwburg was allowed to visit the child-care center. Maurice Hirschel worked in the Schouwburg and came almost daily to the child-care center together with Drs. De Vries Robles and Roos, who were in charge of the children's medical care. Harry Cohen, a worker in the Expositur, was often there to bring messages. He even remembers hiding Jewish orphans on the mezzanine to prevent them from being assigned to fill up shortages on transports. In the child-care center he became friends with Sieny Kattenburg. Another visitor was Lex van Weren, a trumpet player in the Jewish orchestra that was disbanded in 1942. After his dismissal he got a job with the Jewish Council. In his free hours, he and other musicians provided some entertainment in the child-care center. All in all, many people were able to enter and leave the child-care center. This included Germans, of course. Contacts between child-care staff and visiting Germans were maintained exclusively by Pimentel and Süskind. No one else was permitted to speak with them. One evening the Germans burst into the dormitory of the youngest children, stomping their boots on the stairs and in the hall. They encountered Sieny:

> Twenty Germans entered the room wearing those helmets and boots. So I went to face them. Like this. And then I said: "Out! Clear out! How dare you wake these little children!" And they left like quiet little lambs. And from then on they called me *das freche Weib* [impudent bitch].

The separated parents and children were awaiting deportation or, in some cases, freedom. But most of the parents understood the separation. Sometimes, for whatever reason, the parents might be held in the Schouwburg for a relatively long time. When this happened, the children were occasionally taken across the street to visit them for a few hours. On the day of the transport the families were reunited. Sieny kept the paperwork on arrivals and departures for her section.

In addition to the simple paperwork in the child-care center, there was the card index in the Schouwburg and the registration at the Bureau for Jewish Emigration (Zentralstelle). All Jews were registered on entering the Schouwburg. The lists were checked when families had to be reunited before departing on a transport. In December 1942 there was a considerable decrease in the number of people deported. This gave some breathing space in which to use the opportunities for escape via the child-care center.

## RUCKSACKS, LAUNDRY BASKETS, AND BABY CARRIAGES
JANUARY–APRIL 1943

Walter Süskind was in charge of the Schouwburg. In January of 1943, he was introduced to Joop Woortman, head of the Amsterdam branch of the NV, by Hans Kinsbergen or his mother Lea, both of whom knew Walter Süskind and his brother from the thirties, when they had all lived in the German city of Giessen. Walter Süskind found the non-Jewish helper he was looking for in Joop Woortman. Contacts with the other groups were established in the months that followed.

The escape methods used in this early period were elaborate and very dangerous. One by one, babies were hidden in something portable and carried out unnoticed. Child-care workers took them all the way to Central Station and handed them over to members of the NV.[4] Older children were sometimes able to escape when a tram passed along Plantage Middenlaan, blocking the view of the guard outside the Schouwburg. Semmy Woortman-Glasoog, twenty-seven years old at the time, used the tram method several times; once she and a colleague at the day-care center did it together:

> When we heard the tram coming . . . we slipped out, each carrying a heavy child. And we ran along beside the tram so that the guard couldn't see us. At the next corner there was a stop, and we got in. Everyone on the tram started laughing, they'd all seen where we came from, but no one betrayed us.

Jooske de Neve, also a member of the NV, picked up children the same way.

> Nine out of ten of the tram conductors were terrific guys. They knew exactly what was going on. . . . Those anonymous people in such a tram—the feeling of solidarity is incredible.

We know that one of the Schouwburg guards looked the other way on purpose. Alfons Zündler, a member of the SS, knowingly allowed people to escape from the Schouwburg and the child-care center.

THE UTRECHT ESCAPE AND SOME OTHER CASES

The Utrecht Children's Committee helped three children to escape in a one-time operation. In January 1943, three children who had been placed in the Rivieren quarter of Utrecht by the Utrecht Children's Committee were caught on the same day and taken to the child-care center in Amsterdam. Anne Maclaine Pont and Frits Iordens set out for Amsterdam. Frits, dressed in an SS uniform, "requisitioned" the children. The frightened staff of the child-care center quickly complied. The children were taken to new addresses and survived the war. Sieny Kattenburg recalls a similar operation carried out by a Jewish resistance member:

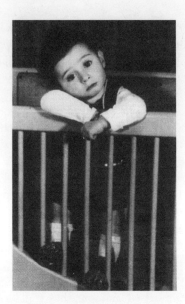

FIGURE 7
*"Remi van Duinwijck" in the child-care center*
Vrij Nederland, January 18, 1986

There was a certain Karel. He was called Karel in the resistance. . . .
His real name was Louis Busnak. He managed to come to the child-
care center in a German uniform with some other people, and they
"requisitioned" children. As Germans. He drove away with the children in a car, and they were taken by his group and hidden. . . . It was
a one-time operation.

That same month, two brothers and their sister were in danger. They
had been hidden by the Utrecht Children's Committee since early in the fall
of 1942. The older brother, "Johan," was in hiding with the W. family in
Utrecht. His brother and sister were in other homes nearby. Johan's foster
father was a sadist. He often made Johan recite the multiplication tables from
one through twenty while jammed between a table and a wall. If he made
a mistake, he had to "come upstairs." The W. family apparently began to fear
that this might become known in the neighborhood, for in January 1943
Johan and his younger brother, who was staying with a brother of Mr. W.,
were both handed over to the police by their foster mothers. Johan recalls:

That woman was sitting at the table, and she told me that I would be sent to a concentration camp. . . . Of course I was scared stiff. In the afternoon she and the wife of that other bastard where my brother was staying took my brother and me to the police headquarters in Utrecht. Believe me, I remember that. We went by bus. We were given some peppermints and left at the police station.

Their sister had a lucky escape and was quickly placed with a family in The Hague. Unfortunately, she was caught a few months later, deported, and gassed. Johan and his brother were taken to a prison and then to the child-care center. After a while an aunt came to visit them and got them out. Johan no longer remembers how this happened. However, it is certain that both boys again came under the protection of the Utrecht Children's Committee and were hidden in the province of Utrecht.

In early 1943 the students in Amsterdam were the ones who "supplied" Jewish children. Hester van Lennep also received children from the day-care center. Babies were transported in rucksacks or laundry baskets. In the spring of 1943, baby Ronald Rozenbroek was delivered in a rucksack to Hester van Lennep's home:

When I opened it there was a baby: he hadn't been changed and his skin was raw, covered with boils, terrible. I took him to my doctor, Dr. De Groot on Leidsegracht. . . . He gave me an orange cream and I covered that little boy with it. . . . A real supporter of the House of Orange.

After a week the baby had recovered sufficiently so that he could be placed in hiding in a children's home.

The Jewish Council had a clothing storeroom on Plantage Kerklaan (near Plantage Middenlaan). Miriam Cohen, who was in charge of the "baby section" of the child-care center, remembers that children were hidden here too:

We had a dressing room around the corner where people's clothes were brought. Because they brought so much luggage, we had a room around the corner, on Kerklaan. There was a woman called Nel. . . . And sometimes children were hidden there. A baby in a rucksack would be taken to the dressing room. It looked like a bundle of clothes. But there was a baby inside. . . . It went out the front door. When there was a tram stopped right there so that no one from across the street could see it. . . . And then you'd say: "Here's another package." That way Nel knew there was a baby inside it.

At first Süskind and Pimentel only saved children if their parents in the
Schouwburg consented. They could not make the decision on their own,
because if the parents weren't notified, they would protest if they had to
leave for Poland without their children. And that, of course, would have
killed the entire organization.

The ensuing discussions were handled by Sieny Kattenburg, Fanny Philips, and Betty Oudkerk. They had to ask the parents if they were willing to
give up their children. These hellish missions, carried out the evening before
a transport, remain etched in Sieny Kattenburg's memory:

> You'd go there and you had to try to speak to these people—in a
> corner, away from everyone else—quickly and very carefully: . . .
> "Wouldn't you like to leave your child with us? . . . We'll make
> sure that he or she goes to people who will provide good care until
> you return." . . .
> Most of them refused.

Sometimes, however, the parents themselves would ask the Jewish staff
of the Schouwburg about finding a refuge for their children. This information would be passed on to the child-care center. Margot Herz remembers
a baby that was going to be placed in hiding:

> She was a very beautiful little girl. The father was from Rotterdam.
> His name was Laufer. I don't know the child's name The father was
> in the Schouwburg and the baby was going to be picked up that night.
> All night long the father sat next to the child's crib.

There were exceptions to the rule that parents had to give permission in
advance: children who were caught while in hiding and brought to the
child-care center as punishment cases. Their parents had agreed earlier that
these children could go into hiding. In addition, many of the parents were
in hiding themselves. Süskind and Pimentel were concerned about the pos-
sibility of the parents, but not the children, surviving the war. Children who
were caught were classified as orphans because the whereabouts of their parents were unknown. The number of orphans in the child-care center grew
explosively. If the required number of Jews for a transport could not be
reached for some reason, the orphans were used to make good the shortfall.
Thus they were at even more risk than the others, so it was important to
smuggle them out as soon as possible.

One toddler caught while in hiding became so well-known that he
could not be spirited away without people noticing. As mentioned before
(see Chapter 2), the unknown foundling, "Remi van Duinwijck," was

caught in October 1942 and taken to the child-care center. There he became Pimentel's favorite, but unfortunately also the favorite of one of the German guards, who even bought a big teddy bear for him. Remi was the best-known child in the child-care center, and as a result no one was able to sneak him out of there. He was deported with a group of orphans in April 1943.[5]

The card index in the Schouwburg had to match the number of Jews who were (officially) present in the Schouwburg and in the child-care center. Süskind's colleague Raphaël (Felix) Halverstad doctored the records so that Jewish parents could leave with fewer children than they had on arrival. Sometimes he would get Aus der Fünten, the German supervisor, drunk while the bookkeeper removed or altered the cards of the children who were going into hiding. Afterwards the same changes had to be made in the Zentralstelle. Another trick was to give the parents "surrogate" babies. The parents were prepared for this. As Sieny Kattenburg remembers:

> In such cases we took a doll or a piece of cloth or a blanket . . . or a dressed-up pillow in our arms across the street. And the parents couldn't show it to anyone, because it couldn't be talked about at all; no one except for those involved was to know.

The parents had to play their role to the end. They had to show happiness at being reunited with their "baby." They were deported with the dressed-up pillow in their arms.

Of course this wasn't possible with older children. But there could be a miscount while they were walking from the Schouwburg to the child-care center. If the German guard was tipsy with alcohol, it was possible to miscount on purpose. Süskind would then, for example, count as follows: "85, 86, 87, 78, 79, 80." The children who were counted extra were hidden in the child-care center, on the mezzanine. These were older children who were then illegal. It meant that ten fewer were deported. Sometimes it didn't work. Sieny Kattenburg recounts:

> Sometimes we got a signal from the Schouwburg that we had to bring back a child we had hidden upstairs in the child-care center to be picked up to go into hiding. This meant that something had gone wrong. Sometimes the Germans asked for a child. And then I had to rush back to the Schouwburg with the child.

Sieny Kattenburg describes the pain she felt on the eve of a transport:

> You had to wake the children. There were other children who were not going on the transport and you didn't want them to start crying. They were all really young, from newborn to four or five years old. . . . And

then the children were dressed very quickly and were given a bottle
or something to eat and drink, and then I went downstairs with the
small children. The fear of these children. They felt it. They were
always very quiet; they said nothing and didn't cry and they were so
pale, and they went downstairs. It was awful. And then the tension
across the street, the assault vans. Those people who were being
brought outside, often screaming. The children who then had to go
to their parents. The fear of the parents. That fear. It was terrible. It
was the very, very worst.

## THE SMUGGLING SYSTEM:
### MAY–SEPTEMBER 1943

In May 1943, there were still 39,000 Jews living legally in Amsterdam.
Between May and November, 19,300 were deported, but 4,200 were
allowed to stay because they were married to Christians. This means that
approximately 15,500 Jews were able to avoid deportation, and thus that 38
percent of the Jews who were legal residents of Amsterdam in May of 1943
went into hiding.[6]

Starting in May 1943, it was possible to remove more children from the
child-care center. Smuggling with rucksacks and bundles of clothing continued, but two new methods were devised: taking walks and the Protestant
Teachers College.

### THE PROTESTANT TEACHERS COLLEGE

The Protestant Teachers College (Hervormde Kweekschool) was located at
27 Plantage Middenlaan, separated by only one building from the child-care
center. In April 1943, the occupants of the house in between (no. 29) were
deported and it became an annex of the child-care center. That same month,
Henriette Pimentel, the director of the child-care center, asked Johan van
Hulst, the principal of the Protestant Teachers College and now her neighbor, if she could use the back of the college's yard as a playground for the
children.

Van Hulst granted permission. A short time later, in May, Pimentel
asked if the Protestant Teachers College could accommodate some toddlers
for their afternoon nap. Van Hulst responded that it would be possible in a
large classroom that was not being used at the time. Since the child-care center was becoming very crowded because so few transports were leaving from
the Schouwburg, this made it convenient for children from the center to
take their afternoon nap in the Teachers College. Small beds were brought

in. Then the final, logical step was taken: the empty classroom became an
avenue of escape. Director Pimentel had carefully and step by step created a
secure way to get children away from the center. From then on, Joop
Woortman of the NV group could simply ring the bell at the Teachers College and escape with the children on Plantage Middenlaan. This had to be
done during school hours because the children only stayed in the Teachers
College during the day. Van Hulst recounted:

> There was almost no partition. Care-givers from the child-care center
> brought them through the garden to the Teachers College, and then
> I heard there or on the telephone: "Someone will be coming soon to
> speak with you." I understood right away that this person was going
> to take a child.

Van Hulst recalls that the elderly concierge, Mr. Van Wijngaarden, a
former sailor who lived in a room on the second floor of the Teachers College, usually opened the door. "I myself didn't open the door when the bell
rang, but he let people in. He knew what was going on. The fact that he was
completely trustworthy played an important role. And he couldn't stand the
Germans."

Johan van Hulst had worked at the Protestant Teachers College since
1938. He was married and had two children. In the summer of 1942, five
Protestant teachers colleges were notified by Secretary-General of Education
Van Dam that state subsidies would be stopped because their hiring policies
were too independent. As a result, the evangelical teacher-training colleges
in Haarlem, Leiden, and Rotterdam closed. In Amsterdam, after consultation with the board of the teachers colleges, it was decided to try to keep the
school open with private support (including the Reformed Church). The
principal cast one of the few opposing votes and decided, with two colleagues, to resign. They received reduced pay. Van Hulst was appointed
principal as of September 1, 1942. He traveled to The Hague to inform Van
Dam personally of the decision to carry on:

> Then I said: "Well, Mr. Van Dam, there is still a Dutch constitution.
> And it says that "teaching is independent, subject to oversight by the
> authorities." For the time being, you are the government. Teaching is
> independent, therefore we intend to go on. If you wish to exercise your
> right to oversight by sending Mr. Mussert as an inspector, I'll be happy
> to let him come. That is oversight by the authorities." I knew that he
> was no friend of Mussert. It turned out to be a very long conversation
> because he said: "You can't go on, you don't have any money." I said:
> "I'm not here to ask for a subsidy, I come only to tell you that we are

going to continue. . . . And we won't stop unless you send the police."
. . . We managed to carry on without the subsidy for the duration of
the war.

Students from Haarlem went to Amsterdam, so the new school year
began with twice as many students as had been enrolled at the end of the pre-
ceding year. Van Hulst saw the appalling scenes in the Schouwburg across
the street. He had no illusions about the fate of the deported Jews: "In *Mein
Kampf* there is a chapter with the heading 'I become anti-Semitic.' . . . The
chapter is perfectly clear. Hitler had only one goal: the destruction of world
Jewry."

Starting in May of 1943, Van Hulst had the opportunity to do something
about it. He was willing to take risks. Early on, he personally took a child in
a rucksack, and it immediately began crying in the tram. To his delight, this
was the first and last time that happened. The greatest uncertainty in Van
Hulst's plans was the attitude of his eighty-four students.[7]

As one might expect, they soon became aware of what was going on.
Their reactions to the deportations reassured him.[8]

At the outset they stood and watched curiously when there were razzias.
Van Hulst had to bellow to get them back in school, to the great hilarity of
the Germans across the street. More emotional reactions followed:

> I saw that some of the girls got very upset. They were close to fainting.
> And one young man wanted, no matter what, to go in there and beat
> up those Germans: "We don't have to take that. . . . I don't care what
> happens to me. At least I'll have done something." And then I had to
> say: "Hey, take it easy. You can't help anyone that way. Not yourself
> and not the Jews."

The first final examinations during Van Hulst's principalship were
scheduled for May 1943. The instructors wondered whether Van Dam
would get even by not sending any official external examiners. But that's not
what happened. Three examiners showed up on the day of the examinations, among them J. J. Feringa, education inspector in Hilversum. Van
Hulst remembers:

> At that time I had already arranged a separate classroom for the Jewish
> children. All our students knew about it. Without exception, because
> they passed the room every day. And they regularly saw the interaction
> between the child-care center next to the school and the classroom,
> with Virrie Cohen as intermediary. Mr. Feringa was an examiner. He
> was with me in the room, and at one point one of these babies began
> to cry. . . . Then he said: "Sir, are those Jewish children?" I said: "Yes,

Mr. Feringa, those are Jewish children. They belong in the child-care center, and they are here, and they will return there tonight." Then he shook my hand and said: "I wish you the best of luck."

Gesina van der Molen, the outside examiner in history, also heard the babies. Her reaction is etched in Van Hulst's memory:

> I was meeting her for the first time. And she too said: "Who are those children?" I replied: "Mrs. Van der Molen, they're Jewish. And they are here temporarily." Then she thought for a moment and said something that I'll never forget: "Now I know why God has brought me here." Before the final examinations of all the candidates were over, she had taken twelve of the children with her.

This was the first of the many visits to the college by members of the Trouw Group. Later Gesina van der Molen asked Hester van Lennep and Sándor Baracs to help her smuggle children from the child-care center.[9]

Hester, known as "Aunt Julia" in the child-care center, recalls her first visit:

> On July 7 I got Barendje from the child-care center. It was the day before my birthday. I remember it so well because my mother came to visit me, and she saw Barendje sitting on a little chair with a jam sandwich on the tin ashtray. . . . That was the first time I was in the child-care center.

In many cases children were brought to Hester van Lennep's skin care institute to convalesce before being taken to a permanent refuge. The house of Gideon Boissevain on Prinsengracht was also used as a temporary shelter. It was decided beforehand which children would go with her. Hester van Lennep never had a say in the matter, and didn't want to.

> Sometimes it was like an assembly line. It happened that I'd get two or three children out of there on one day. . . . I'd arrive and would get a child, and then I'd look to see if it was a boy or a girl.

The NV group and the Trouw Group made the most of the opportunities for escape presented by the Protestant Teachers College. When children were being picked up, Van Hulst was on the look-out. After he gave a signal, the rescuers disappeared quickly through the front door. Twice Van Hulst entrusted children to his students. When a student asked to take along a child, he would hesitate: "I'd stall because naturally I didn't want to involve the students too much. But it was easier if they didn't live in Amsterdam."

Van Hulst had to cultivate supposedly friendly relations with the Germans across the street, he had to make sure there was enough money to keep the school open, and he couldn't tell his wife about his resistance activities.

> Our first child was born in 1937, and the second in 1939. I thought: "If anything happens to me, how will the children judge this later? Will they say: 'We wish father had been more careful. We wish he hadn't put his life in the balance, he should have considered us more.'" Those are very difficult issues.

## THE AMSTERDAM UNIVERSITY STUDENTS AND THE CHILD-CARE CENTER

The Teachers College was used carefully and not too often by the Amsterdam university students. Piet Meerburg remembers being handed a child in the garden behind the Teachers College at least once. Meerburg recalls that the students also used the office of the Jewish Communal Organization, the home of the Lewin family on Plantage Parklaan, and the clothing depot on Plantage Kerklaan:

> We had two fixed addresses, on Plantage Kerklaan and Plantage Parklaan, where the kidnapped children were stripped of their Jewish stars and given other clothing, a new name, and a certificate showing that they were refugees from Rotterdam. The certificates had been pinched from the Evacuation Bureau on Westersingel in Rotterdam.

Each student left with two children. Meerburg always went to the Plantage district with Iet van Dijk or Hansje van Loghem. Not much is known about Iet, who also belonged to the Amsterdam Student Group. She picked up many children in the Plantage district. She and Mieke Mees, a medical student, took away more children than anyone else. Iet van Dijk traveled primarily to Friesland (in the north), and Mieke Mees went primarily to Limburg (in the south). Both women died before they could be interviewed for this book.

## TAKING WALKS

Older children couldn't be hidden in a rucksack or a bundle of clothes. Henriette Pimentel, the director of the child-care center, dreamed up the idea of going for walks in order to smuggle the older children out of the child-care center without anyone noticing. The Jewish child-care workers, probably helped by Walter Süskind, who maintained good relations with Aus der

Fünten, managed to convince the German guards in the Schouwburg that it was necessary to let the children in the child-care center out for fresh air at fixed times. Groups of children, supervised by the staff of the child-care center, were allowed to take short walks in the neighborhood. This expedient saved the lives of a few hundred Jewish children. Walter Süskind and his colleague Felix Halverstad, Virrie Cohen as representative of the child-care center, and one person representing all four child rescue groups would meet beforehand, in the annex of the child-care center, to plan things. Several rescuers, among them Joop Woortman, Piet Meerburg, and Sándor Baracs, participated in such discussions, but of course it was always one after the other, never all of them at the same time. Meerburg remembers:

> Then they said: "We have such-and-such children who would like to get out. What are the possibilities? Do you have a place for them? How long will it take?" And then we'd check with our contacts in Friesland and Limburg to see if we could place the children, and we'd agree to take the children there the following week.
>
> They would contact one another by phone, ostensibly talking about ersatz tea and ersatz coffee. When Meerburg received the message that a "package of ersatz tea" was ready for him, he knew there was a blond Jewish child to be picked up. Blond meant that the child had to be taken to Friesland. "Ersatz coffee" indicated dark children, who mostly went to Limburg.

There were two ways to handle the count when the children returned from their walks. The first was to get more children out of the center than were counted. Mirjam Cohen managed this several times by handing an extra child through the window to the accompanying child-care worker after the count was taken. Sometimes a child would be hidden under someone's clothing. Dick Groenewegen van Wijk, a member of the NV group, recalled:

> I've picked up children who went out for a walk from the child-care center. Once in a while they were allowed to get fresh air under supervision. Fifteen children would be accompanied by three caretakers who were also Jewish. And it had been decided in advance: "The three who are walking in the back, they're coming with us now." To say it simply: we were walking along a street and then we'd get to a corner, and then the group would turn left and the two of us would walk side by side, pick up the last three children, and continue straight ahead. That way you'd save three more children. It was a prearranged and well-organized enterprise.

Only very few people were let in on the second method, which was to bring the group of children back to the original number just before they returned to the child-care center. When trumpet player Lex van Weren was appointed a child-care worker by the Jewish Council. He was not told about the disappearances:

At one point I, as child-care worker, was allowed to go for a walk with the children with the help of several nurses from the child-care center. Taking a walk, I don't know another word for it. Twenty to thirty children were chosen, older children I thought, of course no babies. And our route was from the Schouwburg/child-care center, Roeters-straat, Sarphatistraat to Wibautstraat. But at that time it wasn't Wibaut-straat yet, it was a large sand lot. . . . We got to that sand flat and rested there. The children dug holes and I'd count. I'd go crazy counting because I was more or less responsible. Once, as we were leaving the sand lot, I started counting again. Twenty children? No, eighteen children! Well, I was scared stiff. Where were the missing children? It was inexplicable. . . . The children had been counted when we left, so I was a nervous wreck on the way back. But the strange thing was that when we walked into the child-care center, there were twenty children again.

Barely recovered from the scare, Van Weren went to his boss, who told him to pretend not to notice anything. The same thing happened on the next walk. Van Weren again feared for his life, and because he had been made responsible for the children he was partially let in on the secret. The line of children was augmented in two different ways: at the hiding place in the Teachers College, where the right number of children had been taken in advance from around the back, and at the child-care annex.

The tram method continued to be used as well. During the summer of 1943, Lau Mazirel, who had close relations with Meerburg's group and with Joop Woortman, went to the day-care center several times to get children and then was guided outside using the tram method. Some of the children she saved were taken to hiding addresses arranged by the Amsterdam students.

Between May and September 1943, hundreds of Jewish children disappeared via the Protestant Teachers College and during the walks.

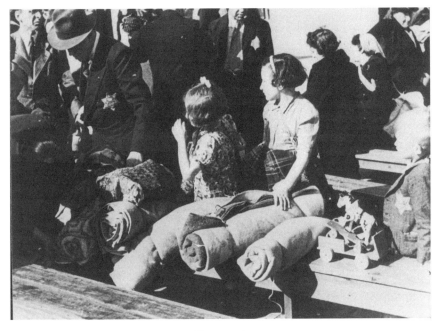

FIGURE 8

*Jewish children with their toys waiting at the Polderweg collection point (Amsterdam)
for deportation, May 26, 1943.*

From the collection of the Netherlands Institute for War Documentation, Amsterdam

## THE FINAL DAYS OF THE CHILD-CARE CENTER

On June 28, Harry Cohen heard from the Registrar's Office that he and
Sieny Kattenburg would be able to get married at noon. Sieny recalls the
events:

> At ten in the morning I had no idea that I'd be married at noon. Harry
> came running into the child-care center. He had a *Sperre* [permit post-
> poning his deportation], so he could stay! "We're getting married!" We
> got married on the double. We weren't allowed to go to the city hall,
> city hall came to Plantage Parklaan. . . . We were planning to go into
> hiding, and it was better to do it as a married couple (the Dutch were
> very moralistic). Our parents had already been deported.

Henriette Pimentel was a witness. Less than a month later, Henriette
Pimentel and Rebecca Boas, the assistant director of the child-care center,

were deported together with thirty-six others named on the same list—mostly child-care trainees. Margot Herz was also on the list.

> Two men in leather jackets, civilian clothes, showed up. With lists.
> They called out our names. I was upstairs and had to come downstairs.
> I came down, and there we were told . . . to go upstairs to get our identity
> cards and our rucksacks and get dressed. I went halfway down the stair-
> case, I saw it all, and I turned around. Behind me was Jetty Frankenhuis.
> . . . We went into the attic. The attic was above one of the rooms. We
> could see everything. There were holes in the ceiling, so we were able
> to watch. We heard our names called. Well, we didn't respond, and
> after a while it became quiet and all we saw was the little dog walking
> around. Then we knew that they had taken Mrs. Pimentel. That night
> we stayed up there and very early the next morning we got out.

Margot Herz obtained a fake identity card from a Jewish resistance worker, Gideon Drach. She went into hiding and survived the war. Other staff members—among them Virrie Cohen and Sieny Cohen-Katten-burg—were added to the list so that it would come to thirty-eight. Sieny remembers:

> Together we ended up at Polderweg. Three thousand people who had
> been rounded up were brought there.[10] Also children and staff from
> the child-care center. Then, in the middle of the night, they called out:
> "*Frau Cohen aus das Kinderhaus*" [Miss Cohen of the child-care center].
> Virrie Cohen . . . stepped forward. No, they didn't want her, they
> wanted the impudent bitch. Then I had to step forward. . . . They left
> me off in front of the Schouwburg. The only thing they said was: "*Und
> jetz sind Sie Directrice von das Kinderhaus*" [You are now the director of
> the child-care center]. Well, the child-care center was closed. I went
> to the Schouwburg, and everyone was there, including Süskind and
> my husband. They looked at me as if I were a ghost. I went back to
> the child-care center. We opened it, and the next day Virrie came back.
> Virrie was a certified nurse—about seven years older than I. She
> became the new director, taking the place of Henriette Pimentel.

Thanks to her father, the co-chairman of the Jewish Council, Virrie Cohen had been removed from the list at the last moment. New razzias soon filled the child-care center to overflowing. Under her direction the smug-gling out of children continued unabated. However, everyone knew that all this would soon come to an end because almost all the Jews had been deported or were in hiding. Virrie Cohen recalls the unspoken feeling of doom that hung over the child-care center:

One of the weird things I remember is, for example, that when we had eaten, we'd lift the tablecloth at the four corners and take it to the kitchen, where we'd throw away anything that was broken. We'd continue using the rest. Because the next day anything could happen.

Among the Jewish children to whom we have talked, very few have vivid memories of the child-care center. Chella Winnik was one of the oldest children who stayed there. The guards couldn't decide whether she belonged in the child-care center or with the adults in the Schouwburg:

> I'd be in the child-care center and there'd be an inspection and a German would come . . . and take me with him. "What are you doing here?" Back to the adults. Then I'd be with the adults for a night or two days and I'd have to go back to the child-care center. . . . It was terrible having to go back to the child-care center every time because I'd have to say good-bye to my parents every time because I didn't know whether I'd ever see them again.

Together with their parents, Chella and her younger sister, Lea, had been hidden in several different places since the end of the summer of 1942. After a year they were betrayed and taken to the Schouwburg. On August 5, Chella was with her parents when they found out that they would have to go on a transport the next day. Her father told her that a hiding address was being arranged for her and her sister.

> My father gave me the keys to the house. He still had them with him. Of our last house on Kromme Mijdrechtstraat. "Look, here are the keys for you, and we'll see each other there again." My mother had only a very small billfold with her. With a photo of her inside it. "Take that as a memento, we'll see each other again." I still have that billfold. I think that Lea has the keys. . . . Sure enough, there was a transport the next morning. With my own eyes I watched through the windows of the child-care center as my parents got into the car. That's the last image I have. Both of them getting in and my father looking up quickly. That's the last.

Her parents were murdered in Auschwitz at the end of August. Chella and Lea remained "illegally" in the child-care center for a few more weeks. They were hidden in the storage space on the mezzanine of the center during nights before transports. They escaped from the building three times (unseen behind a passing tram) and returned when the danger was over. Lea Winnik still remembers these escape attempts:

The whole neighborhood had been blocked off. And Virrie Cohen rushed up to us and said: "Go out of here. Get out any way you can!" . . .

We ran away fast. I don't remember how. The bridge was blocked off, so that no one could get out. We walked around. But two children—where can you go? And then we remembered that our former maid lived somewhere on Jodenbreestraat. Well, it was getting late and we went to see if she still lived there, and yes, she lived there. We rang the bell and went upstairs. It wasn't so nice for her because she was scared: "What can I do with two children? I've got enough worries myself." . . .

Then she went to the window and said: "Look, there's a man on the corner. I don't know who he is, but I've heard that he places Jewish children in hiding. What can happen to you children? Go downstairs and ask if he can help you, because I can't help you, and the end of the story is that you have to go back to the child-care center." Well, we did go downstairs. We went over to the man and I pulled like this at his shoulder. Don't forget, I was a ten-year-old child. At his sleeve. And then he said: "Who are you?" And Chella said: "Listen, we've heard that you help to hide Jewish children. We ran away from the child-care center. Can you help us?" And looking at us he said: "What's your name?" Chella didn't want to say her real name, but there was nothing to lose, so she said: "We're Chella and Lea Winnik." And he wrote it down. Then he looked at us and he said: "You know what? When the razzia is over, just go back to the child-care center. And I'll get you out." Chella was angry. She said: "You see, that's a Nazi sympathizer. Who would send us back to that child-care center?" But we went back.

The man in the long coat was Joop Woortman. Around the middle of September 1943, Chella and Lea Winnik were told that they'd be going for a walk. This time it was two groups at the same time, the last four of which would be pulled out by NV members. In this way as many as eight children, including the two sisters, could be saved at the same time. This shows how adept the NV was at finding hiding places during the last phases of deportation. The eight children were put up in different homes in Venlo and in neighboring Blerick in the province of Limburg.

The Germans emptied the child-care center on September 29, 1943, one day before Rosh Hashanah, the Jewish New Year. The Jewish Council was dissolved, and after a few months in Westerbork, most of its personnel were sent to Theresienstadt or Bergen-Belsen. Mirjam Cohen was also sent to Theresienstadt and survived.

The days before the clearing of the child-care center were hectic. The NV had been tipped off by Süskind and Woortman, and they made a final attempt to get as many children as possible away. Jaap and Gerard Musch and Dick Groenewegen van Dijk went in person to Plantage Middenlaan and took fourteen children with them. Never before had such a large number been saved at one time. Later, Dick Groenewegen characterized this operation as "actually rather irresponsible." An understatement, because fourteen children accompanied by three young men must have been conspicuous in the train. Nevertheless, the caravan reached its destination in south Limburg without problems.

That same week, Virrie Cohen secretly accompanied fifteen children to the office of the Jewish Community on Plantage Parklaan. An article in the newspaper *Het Parool* of May 2, 1981 mentions a certain Michael who was one of these children.[11] Michael was thirteen years old when he arrived in the Schouwburg with his caregivers (his parents had already been deported). He stayed in the child-care center for two and a half months and regularly had to hide to avoid being deported. In the article he recounts:

> Right before the Germans put an end to the whole organization, I was taken to the building of the Jewish Community together with fourteen other children ranging from infants to thirteen years old. We had been hidden there before during a sudden inspection by the Germans. Our greatest worry was keeping the little ones quiet and feeding the youngest ones. We chewed biscuits for them. While we were sitting there, some people came to look at us, students we recognized because we'd seen them before in the child-care center. They took us with them one by one. I was the last to go. Because of my age, it was difficult to place me. I was put up in Amsterdam for three days, and then I had to buy a ticket to Limburg at Central Station. At Venray, a lady with a blue dress and a yellow purse walked by. That was my signal to get off the train.[12]

The lady in blue was one of Meerburg's couriers. Michael was taken via a roundabout route to foster parents in Oirlo, where he survived the war.

Van Hulst also tried his best to save as many children as he could:

> Aus der Fünten visited the child-care center. . . . Then he ordered a razzia to be held a few days later; everyone was to be taken away, and the child-care center and the Schouwburg were to be liquidated. It all happened in a horrible way. The houses were searched one by one, and all the Jews who were found were kicked into trucks in a most criminal manner. . . . And then Virrie Cohen came to me: "The child-care center is jam-packed. Come with me and take a few that you can put up temporarily in the Teachers College; maybe they can be picked

up today." You have to imagine that you're standing there—eighty, ninety, perhaps seventy, perhaps a hundred children—and then you have to decide which ones. . . . That was the most difficult day of my life. You know that you can't take all of them. You also know that the ones you don't take are sentenced to death. So I took twelve. Later you ask yourself: "Why not thirteen?"

Twelve children ranging in age from nine to twelve. Van Hulst had no place to take them. He asked them if they had anywhere to go, and the answer was affirmative. After that he let them out the door one by one. One boy returned that evening. The people to whom he had gone weren't home. This was reported to Virrie, and a hiding address was hastily arranged for the boy. The next day Van Hulst was visited by an unknown woman with a typically Jewish appearance but no star on her clothes:

"She said to me: "My two children were lost, and you saved them." I said: "Madam, you have the wrong party. I don't know you. I have never saved any children." "Yes, but my children say that the principal of the Teachers College, he let us go and he got us out of the child-care center." I said: "Madam, please think carefully. Your children are lying, Make sure you tell them that." She said: "Yes, I understand completely. But I do thank you very much."

Van Hulst's role in saving children was now ended, but he took care of people in hiding until the end of the war. On April 14, 1945, a woman he had never seen before came to the school and warned him that the SD was on its way to arrest him. Van Hulst disappeared immediately. Soon afterward the SD arrived at the school, but of course Van Wijngaarden, the elderly concierge, knew nothing. Van Hulst remained in hiding during the last three weeks of the occupation.

At the end of September 1943, Betty Oudkerk was at Amstel Station about to be deported when she was placed in a group of mixed-marrieds by one of Süskind's coworkers. In this way she escaped deportation and together with a sister went into hiding with a farmer near Nieuw-Vennep.[13]

Maurice Hirschel went into hiding the day the care center was closed. All he knew was that he had been told to go to an address on one of the canals of Amsterdam. It turned out to be the home of Auke Smit, a young economist whom he knew from his college years. Smit told Hirschel to take the train to Vught station, where he arrived safely and finally ended up at a monastery in Stein in south Limburg, a refuge arranged for him by the NV.

In Virrie Cohen's memory, the days after September 29, 1943 seem like a chain of confusion. She still remembers that the remaining children from the child-care center were housed across the street. They were probably deported on Friday, October 8, 1943. That day, starting at 2:30 p.m. and for the next four hours, two buses went back and forth between Middenlaan and Panamakade, where the trains were waiting.[14]

Virrie was busy every moment in the Schouwburg and the child-care center, arranging things for the impending departure. She was pulled in two directions. On the one hand, she wanted to follow the dictates of her heart and leave with her family for Westerbork and whatever unknown fate awaited them. On the other, Piet Meerburg and Walter Süskind tried to persuade her to go into hiding. Virrie still remembers how Meerburg finally convinced her:

> He told me he would make sure I made it because I would have to help find the children again after the war. . . . So I walked back and forth between the Schouwburg and the child-care center. I may even have slept for a while in the Schouwburg. Someplace. And then Piet Meerburg said to me: "When the time seems right, just walk away. You're always going back and forth; they won't notice. Just go to Weteringschans." Dr. Roos lived there.[15] And I seem to have done just that.

Maurice Hirschel gave her some money because she no longer had anything. With the help of Dr. Roos and several other people, Virrie finally ended up in Tienray in north Limburg.

Meanwhile, on September 29, arguing that she would be able to help her parents when they returned, Harry Cohen persuaded Sieny to leave the child-care center. Sieny recalls the way she and Harry Cohen disappeared from the scene:

> We walked out of the child-care center. It was early in the morning. . . . Harry had obtained fake identity cards. Without a J. . . . Then we were walking in the street and we were stopped. Well, talk about tension. . . . You're stopped by a German, a damned Nazi, who screams at you: "ID card!" So my husband gets his ID out of his pocket. We still had our stars on. And I thought that he had pulled the wrong ID cards out of his pocket. I died of fright. I just died of fright. And then he asked what business we had walking there. "Well," my husband says, "we're taking a walk around the block and then we're going back to work." And walk we did. We had to go to Stadionkade. That's quite a distance to walk. And we walked that whole distance without saying a word. Both of us were petrified. Only our legs moved. Stadionkade has a bend, and that's where we stopped. Moved closer together and

then carefully took off the stars, which we had already loosened a little. Then our time in hiding began.

Felix Halverstad also went into hiding.[16] There were no longer any Jews residing legally in Amsterdam except for a few employees of the Jewish Council, among them Walter Süskind and Lex van Weren. After October 8, 1943 Amsterdam was officially *Judenrein* (cleansed of Jews).

## THE LAST CHILD-CARE CENTER

In reality Amsterdam was, of course, far from *Judenrein*, because a relatively large number of Jews were in hiding in the city, and from time to time some of them were caught. Many others were hiding in the Amsterdam vicinity. Hidden Jews who were arrested were still held in Amsterdam. The Schouwburg continued to serve as a holding center for Jews until November 19, 1943. The building of the child-care center was closed on September 29. In its place, the former annex next-door served as a shelter for Jewish children who were caught. From November 9 to November 19, arrested Jewish children were probably imprisoned in the Schouwburg. After that date, arrested Jews, children as well as adults, were locked up in the Huis van Bewaring (municipal jail) on Amstelveenseweg. On September 13, 1944 the last transport left Westerbork because the railroad strike made further transports impossible. In the summer of 1944, Excelsior Dry Cleaning moved into the building of the child-care center. In 1950 a new child-care center was established on Sarphatistraat, "Henriëtte House," run by Virrie Cohen and named for director Pimentel.[17] Walter Süskind remained in Amsterdam until September 1944, at which time he and his family were deported.[18] They did not return.

## NUMBERS

Approximately 35 percent of the total number of Jews placed by the four groups discussed in this chapter came from the child-care center (11.5 percent of the 1,100 people rescued were adults)

| Group | Children from the child-care center | Total number rescued | Percentage rescued from the child-care center |
|---|---|---|---|
| Utrecht Children's Committee | 10 | 400 | 2.5 |

| Amsterdam Student Group | 140 | 350 | 40.0 |
|---|---|---|---|
| NV | 160 | 250 | 64.0 |
| Trouw | 75 | 100 | 75.0 |
| Total | 385 | 1100 | 35.0 |

The total of 385 constitutes almost two-thirds of the 600 children smuggled out of the child-care center. The other third were smuggled out by private parties and by other resistance organizations.

One out of ten children in the child-care center were saved. Virrie Cohen never fails to point out that these 600 children were rescued thanks to the children who *did* go on transport. The children who were not rescued, numbering between 4,400 and 5,400, formed a smoke screen behind which the children's rescuers did their work. Virrie expressed it as follows:

> In my memory I can still see children walking in a line across the street, out of the child-care center—into the Schouwburg. Wearing rucksacks. They had to go when there weren't enough adults for a transport. Aus der Fünten himself came over to select the children. I could do nothing to stop it. . . . I let the children walk across the street. I didn't hold them back. What do you think keeps me awake at night? Not the children I found again in Limburg after the war, but those lines of children that I let go across the street.

NOTES

1.  For example, members of the Boogaard family (active in the resistance) from Nieuw Vennep, some members of the Westerweel Group, and many private individuals like Truus Jetten from Roermond, the antique dealer H. van Schlichte-Bergen from Amsterdam, and Greta Borzykowski-Stroz, the "Polish mother" who was herself deported.

2.  The others were taken to assembly points at Adama van Scheltemaplein (Zentralstelle; especially in 1942) or Borneokade (from 1943 on). The trains at Borneokade mainly took the sick and the aged. Transports also left from Muiderpoortstation (Polderweg assembly point) and, later in 1943, from the Huis van Bewaring (jail) on Amstelveenseweg. See J. Th. M. Houwink ten Cate, *Alfons Zündler en de bewaking van het gevangenenkamp aan de Plantage Middenlaan 24 te Amsterdam – volgens de geschreven bronnen* (Amsterdam, August 1994/January 1995), pp. 85–86.

3.  Interview with Virrie Oudkerk-Cohen; see Sources.

4.  Interview with Margot Herz; see Sources. See also Ines Fellner-Cohen, Testimony for Yad Vashem, February 28, 1987, Yad Vashem Archives (Jerusalem).
5.  Interview with Margot Schwartz-Herz; see Sources. It was learned only recently that his real name was Koentje Gezang.
6.  J. Th. M. Houwink ten Cate, *Alfons Zündler*.
7.  W. van der Horst, *De grond waarop wij stonden. Geschiedenis van de Hervormde Kweekschool/Hervormde Pedagogische Academie Amsterdam 1907–1984* (Amsterdam, 1993), p. 87.
8.  One student came from a National Socialist family. She was well disposed toward the occupiers but out of respect for Van Hulst said nothing.
9.  W. van der Horst and R. Kingma, ed., *De crèche en de kweekschool* (Kweekschool cahier no. 8), Amsterdam, 1987, p. 26.
10.  The actual number was 619 people.
11.  He did not want his real name to appear in the newspaper. We will conceal it too.
12.  Roy Buijze, "Micheal, de laatste geredde," *Het Parool*, May 2, 1981.
13.  Elisabeth Goudsmit-Oudkerk, Letter to Yad Vashem; see Sources.
14.  J. Th. M. Houwink ten Cate, *Alfons Zündler*, p. 93.
15.  Karel Roos was exempted from deportation because his wife was not Jewish
16.  Halverstad went into hiding in Amsterdam. Source: J. Michman, Undated interview with Mrs. Dwinger, Collection E. Verhey (Amsterdam).
17.  A. Scherphuis and A. van Ommeren, "De crèche 1942–1943," Supplement to *Vrij Nederland*, January 18, 1986, p. 19, 20.
18.  H. Wielek, *De oorlog die Hitler won* (Amsterdam, 1947), p. 262.

# EXPERIENCED CHILDREN'S RESCUERS
## May–September 1943

After ten months the organizations began to function smoothly. Between May and September 1943 they were able to remove a good many children from the child-care center. During this period, some of the rescuers themselves were arrested as the German and Dutch man-hunters perfected their methods. Harsh German actions increased anti-German feelings, and this made many more people willing to take in Jewish children. The rescuers would have been unable to do anything without reliable people willing to give the children a home.

### THE STRIKES IN APRIL AND MAY 1943

The April-May strikes broke out when it was announced that the 300,000 Dutch soldiers who had fought the Wehrmacht in May 1940 would be considered prisoners-of-war and, as such, would be sent to work in Germany to improve its war economy.[1]

On February 7, 1943, the day after the attempt on General H. A. Seyffardt, the Dutch Nazi who recruited men to serve on the eastern front, it had already been decided that all career officers were to be sent to Germany as prisoners. Six days later, Himmler asked Hitler's consent to make prisoners of all the soldiers who had fought against Germany in May of 1940. On Thursday, April 29, 1943, Hitler gave permission. Since Holland had compulsory military service, there were veterans of the 1940 fighting everywhere in the country. Inhabitants of even the smallest hamlets resisted. The fiercest reactions took place in the provinces of Overijssel, Limburg, and Friesland, precisely the area where the rescuers has found so many homes willing to hide children. Businesses, stores, and offices closed in all the cities, beginning with Hengelo. People flatly refused to work for the Germans any longer.

Farmers in Friesland, Twente, and Limburg preferred to dump their milk into ditches rather than give it to milk collectors. The miners shut down the mines.

On April 29, Obergruppenführer Hanns Rauter, the German police chief of the Netherlands, proclaimed summary police jurisdiction, thereby giving his men authority to fire on people engaged in any kind of civil disturbance. Ninety-five strikers were shot dead. Posters threatening the death penalty were hung everywhere. Many strikers were arrested. Eighty were summarily executed. Hundreds were sent to prisons or prison camps. Most were freed after a week.

Radio London gave no clear guidelines, and the trains kept running. Nevertheless, on Monday, May 3, there were still strikes not only in many places in Friesland, but also at the Bata shoe factory in Best (Noord-Brabant), at Philips in Eindhoven, and at some textile factories in Twente. On Saturday, May 8, the last trouble spot was controlled. The strike was finished.

On May 5, it was announced that the students who had not signed the declaration of loyalty would have to report the next day for work in Germany. On May 7 it was announced that all men between the ages of eighteen and thirty-five had to report for work in Germany; this would take place by age groups. On May 13 all radios had to be turned in. The anti–German feeling in the country grew more intense. Those who did not want to go to Germany had to go into hiding. The children's rescuers profited from the fact that hiding was now becoming the normal way of life.

## THE UTRECHT CHILDREN'S COMMITTEE

The Utrecht Children's Committee received "new" children from the Amsterdam students or from their parents. May 1943 was one of the busiest months. In that one month, the number of names in the card system rose from 171 to 231. Several people who had been active as rescuers from the very beginning were now doing other things. Geert Lubberhuizen and Rut Matthijsen were forging documents, no longer just for rescuers and older Jewish children, but also for students who had gone into hiding and for artists. At the same time, though, Rut continued to be responsible for the "office" where the Children's Committee held its daily meetings. It was at the meetings that information was exchanged, and money and papers were distributed.

As a safety measure, Jan Meulenbelt, Frits Iordens, and Rut Matthijsen went to Driebergen, where they stayed at the home of one of Hetty Voûte's cousins for a while. Ger Kempe and his boss, Professor Willem Pompe, could not remain at the Criminology Institute after the conflict regarding the declaration of loyalty. They had to go into hiding. Kempe worked for an espionage group but continued to attend the meetings of the children's rescuers. Kempe did what he could to support Jan Meulenbelt. Anne Maclaine Pont and Frits Iordens arranged an escape route for Allied pilots who had been shot down; they took them to Belgium, and from there they were taken farther by the Belgian and French resistance. In a really urgent situation, Frits was always willing to help out. Rut Matthijsen remembers:

> Contact was somehow established with the Boutelje family, a shop-keeper in Utrecht. . . . Anne and Frits visited there with some regularity because a "good" policeman, Smorenburg, was a close friend of the family. . . . He was important because his brother was a policeman who collaborated with the enemy. Once, when foster parents in the Rivieren district learned that the police were coming the next day to pick up the children they were sheltering, Frits Iordens put on the "good" Smorenburg's uniform and took the children away the evening before.

The only "old hands" in Utrecht who continued to work full-time at rescuing children were Hetty Voûte, Gisela Söhnlein, and Jan Meulenbelt. They were the ones who picked up sixty children in Amsterdam in May 1943 and delivered them to safe refuges. They also searched out new places for children who were already in hiding. In addition (but working separately) Truitje van Lier kept the Kindjeshaven available as an important first shelter for babies. In May 1943 Hetty Voûte took four-month-old Amalia Roe there. Another newborn baby, Herbert Ehrlich, and his three-year-old brother, had to be picked up in a great rush at their parents' home. After ten months, Herbert got very sick. Truitje and Jet made a supreme effort to get the baby through the critical stage. They managed to get him into a hospital, but the doctors were unable to save him, and he died.

Truitje has vivid memories of the spring of 1943:

> You can't imagine what it was like. They came every half hour. And I borrowed sleds and portable cribs everywhere, and then I'd put a basket on a sled and I'd have another cradle. No one was traveling anymore, so you could get cradles. There was no end to it. It was really awful. And I took in too many, but there was no way to refuse. If not, they'd be gone. . . . That was when the big razzias broke out in Amsterdam.

After some time most of the children were picked up again and lodged elsewhere throughout the country. Truitje and Jet received extra ration cards for the authorized children through official channels. They obtained ration cards and sometimes extra money from the Children's Committee. In addition Truitje had her own contacts, Truuke and André de Wolf, who regularly gave her ration cards. A Calvinist resistance group in Amsterdam provided them as well. Truitje remembers:

> Once there was a man from the Calvinist group. He was terribly nause-ated because he had just eaten all the ration cards. We tried to bring him to. He had eaten them when the police picked him up. So he came to tell us that he didn't have them. He was so sick, that poor man. I kept him with us for a while until he recovered.

Reliable new workers joined the organization to satisfy the need for res-cuers: Jelle de Jong, An de Waard, James van Beusekom, Manfred Lewin-sohn, Alice Brunner, the sisters Olga and To Hudig, and Ankie Stork. All of them except Ankie Stork, who was a newcomer, had already done some work for the committee. They took care of the already hidden children by bringing them ration cards and checking to see whether everything was going all right in the household. If there were any complaints or requests, they reported them to the office. Foster parents could also send messages to the contact address at Boothstraat 17.

Jelle de Jong, a fellow student of Rut Matthijsen, coordinated the district heads, who were each in charge of ten to twenty children. All told, the dis-trict heads were in charge of about one hundred children. In addition to their meetings in the office, the committee members also got together at the weekly rehearsals of a Bach choir. An de Waard recalls:

> For a while we were together in a Bach choir. . . . Anne, Frits, Jan Meulenbelt, and Hetty Voûte were probably members, but I don't recall them being there. It was in the beginning. When was the choir discontinued? I'm not sure; I guess when the men could no longer show up. . . . Someone would say: "Hey, do you think you can find a hiding address for me? Because I've got a really Jewish-looking child who has to be placed in a home that's really secure. This kid can't go out on the street at all. And I have another one who doesn't look so Jewish. Do you have anything else?" That's how we exchanged infor-mation that could lead to placements.

The district heads tried on their own to solve small problems like bed-wetting with the foster parents. More difficult problems were passed on to the office. An de Waard remembers:

> Of course, there were times when a child didn't feel at home for some reason and didn't fit in with the family, and then became a behavior problem. . . . If the foster family then said: "This is impossible, we can't control the child," we fell back on the people who arranged placements and looked for someplace else.

Sometimes An de Waard took a child with her on the train. She would turn her ring around to give the impression that she was a married woman traveling with her child. Gisela Söhnlein often traveled together with James van Beusekom:

> . . . sometimes you put on a kind of boy-traveling-with-girl act. I traveled with others, but most of the time with James. Once I took a really tiny baby to Rozendaal with James. It was really ridiculous, because I looked so very young, and so did he. And you wondered what exactly people thought of a couple like us, with suitcases and a child. If anyone asked, we said "Rotterdam" or something like that. . . . I must say that he had a heart of gold.

Ankie Stork traveled a lot with Manfred Lewinsohn. He was also involved in obtaining money and supplies. He used the alias Manfred Boutelje, but was called Manfred for short. Ankie Stork describes him as follows:

> He was a very likeable guy. Afterwards it turned out that he was Jewish. And he spoke with a slight accent. I always wondered where he came from. But he was very trustworthy, I would say, not a swashbuckler. He was dependable; he was a dependable worker.

Manfred Lewinsohn became involved as a part-time rescuer at the beginning of 1943, through Frits Iordens. A Jewish mother with two children who was in hiding, Sara Blok-Roozeboom, delivered ration cards to addresses given her by Lewinsohn.

## EARNING MONEY

A lot of money was needed both for train tickets and to support the rescuers. Geert Lubberhuizen needed money to buy paper for his forged documents. While visiting her uncle, Anne Maclaine Pont was given a scrap of paper with a poem entitled "De Achttien Dooden" (The Eighteen Dead). When

### The Eighteen Dead by Jan Campert

A cell is just two meters long.
And just two meters wide,
But smaller is the little space
In which I shall be laid.
Though I have not yet seen it.
There, nameless I shall lie,
And eighteen more beside me.
Tomorrow all will die.

Oh, fair and fertile meadows,
No more be bound in chains,
My lovely, lowland country,
Find peace, repose again.
What other can a plain man do,
But kiss his wife and son,
And leave to fight a battle
That is lost, but will be won?

A bitter task I undertook,
But had no other choice.
The heart will dare, and will succeed,
Freedom will raise her voice.
Then honor will the spirit know,
And triumph be the crown,
For at the feet of conquerors
This land will not bow down.

By force and by deception
A country is enslaved,
Imposed on by a brigand law,
The nation torn, dissolved.
But German aspirations to

The land it overran
Are fruitless. We, defiant still,
Will fight till all is won.

The vermin-catcher of Berlin
Piping his evil tune,
Hunts down a generation free,
Till all of us are gone.
No more I'll see my loved one,
Or break with her my bread,
Why then the race for glory.
And who deceives the dead?

O you who read, remember them,
My comrades, how they stood,
Faced death without dishonor,
As every proud heart should,
How, for their land and nation,
Their lives they paid in fee.
And remember, after darkness
Comes the light. We shall be free.

I watch the early morning light
Creep through the window high.
Dear Lord, now let thy will be done,
May death come easily.
And if it be that I have sinned,
Forgive me, as I pray
To face, nor flinch, the firing-squad
Which ends my life this day.

Written by Jan Campert, after the execution, on March 13, 1941, of fifteen members of the Dutch resistance group, De Geuzen (named after the resistance groups that fought against Spanish oppression in the sixteenth century) and three activists who had participated in the February strike. These executions shocked the Dutch population. The poem became the anthem of the Dutch resistance, and the money collected from the sale of copies of the poem was transferred to the resistance.

The poet Jan Campert, who was also involved in the rescue of Jews, perished in Neuengamme concentration camp on January 12, 1943.

### FIGURE 9

*De Achttien Dooden ("The Eighteen Dead"),*
*a Dutch resistance poem by Mr. Jan Campert*

English translation by Mrs. Rena Minkoff

she showed it to the others, someone, perhaps Geert, suggested making it into an illustrated broadsheet that could be given as a gift to people who contributed money. The poem was written by Jan Campert (1902–1943). Anne Maclaine Pont asked her cousin Ankie Stork to sell the broadsheets in Nijverdal (Overijssel), where her parents lived.

For many years Ankie Stork had been taking piano lessons from Alice Heksch, a Jewish woman who came to Almelo for the lessons. Once Alice was no longer allowed to travel, Ankie began traveling to Amsterdam from Utrecht, where she was a student at the university. After the deportations started, these trips were very grim; Ankie never knew ahead of time whether Alice would still be there. She decided to do "something." In the end, Alice Heksch was able to go into hiding with her husband and children.

Ankie had great success selling copies of the poem in Nijverdal and its environs. "The Eighteen Dead" was Geert's first product. Every committee member usually had several copies available. The pamphlets were sold for five guilders apiece. Most of the proceeds went to children's rescue. On September 1, there were envelopes containing more than 75,000 guilders in change for Geert. The Utrecht Children's Committee no longer had money problems, and the Amsterdam Student Group benefited too. The committee decided to support people in hiding as well as artists who had been unwilling to become members of the *kultuurkamer.*

LIQUIDATION

In early June of 1943, James van Beusekom sent a message stating that his contacts in Amsterdam had received a letter from Jews in Westerbork who said they had been betrayed by Dirk de Ruiter and Mies van Ginkel.

Dirk de Ruiter and Mies van Ginkel had been recruited by James van Beusekom and had been appointed by the Utrecht Children's Committee to take care of Jewish children until final refuges were found for them. Thanks to a Protestant clergyman in Vught, the Utrecht Committee had been given the use of a hostel in the nearby village of Esch. A young Jewish woman in hiding, Clara Hes, helped the couple with household chores. Dirk de Ruiter and Mies van Ginkel lived as husband and wife but were not married. At the time of their appointment, they themselves had pointed out the issue of the resistance paper *Vrij Nederland* for March 21, 1943 in which they were designated as not trustworthy. The article in question read as follows:

*Warning*

We have been asked to warn against the following persons: . . . Maria Euphemia van Ginkel, Dintelstraat, Amsterdam, living with Dirk de Ruiter, calling herself Mrs. De Ruiter. She is a fortuneteller and has connections with the Sicherheitsdienst [SD; Nazi security service]. De Ruiter socializes primarily with spouses of prisoners.

The couple insisted that none of this was true. And because they had made such a good impression by telling everyone about this article, the Utrecht group decided to give them a chance. But James van Beusekom had new information. The two were capable of betraying everyone. Not only the children they now had in their care, but the rescuers who had called for and escorted the children. They also knew about the contact address at Boothstraat 17 in Utrecht.

The committee met in Utrecht and devised a plan. The situation was serious. Once the children were out of harm's way, Jan and Rut would take two armed members of an action group to the house to kill the couple. The events that followed this emergency consultation were a turning point in the history of the Utrecht Children's Committee, so it is important to relate them in detail.

In all probability, the brutal way the German regime had dealt with the strikers in April played a role in the decision to liquidate the couple. There was much discussion in the group about risks, moral dilemmas, and the consequences of what they were doing. Rut Matthijsen recalls:

We were . . . uncompromising people who thought things through. Consider Anne and Ger Kempe and some others. They simply said: "If the Germans threaten: 'We're going to shoot a few hostages if you don't stop hiding Jews,' then you have to say: 'Well, that's how it will be. They have the power to do it, but you can't let yourself be coerced by such things.'" There were several fundamental ideas that we had drummed into one other.

Contact was made with the Oranje-Vrijbuiters action group.[2] Rut knew its leader, because he had helped to place two Jewish boys in Woerden.

The first part of the plan worked fine: Hetty and Gisela made several trips to Esch and each time came up with a plausible excuse to take some of the children with them when they left. The fear that the couple were traitors was confirmed by Clara Hes, their domestic servant, who had overheard the couple arguing. She said that Van Ginkel had been very upset because Jewish children were no longer being brought to the hostel. She threatened: "I'll report the whole mess unless more start to come." The day before the assault, Hetty and Gisela took Clara Hes to safety.[3]

On June 11, 1943, the agreed date, there were still two children in the hostel. When they arrived, Gisela and Hetty found to their horror not only Dirk de Ruiter and Mies van Ginkel but their foster son. Hetty and Gisela lunched with the family and then proposed taking the children for a little walk. They got out of there as quickly as possible, and then Rut Matthijsen, Jan Meulenbelt, and the two men from the action group swung into action.

However, the two action group members had only one pistol, and, to make matters worse, its caliber was too small. Dirk de Ruiter was killed, but Mies van Ginkel survived the assault. No one had counted on the foster son, who was only wounded and managed to escape. From a nearby farm he alerted the Boxtel police and also gave them the name Van Beusekom and the contact address, Boothstraat 17, in Utrecht. By that time Jan, Rut, and the two action group members were on their way back to Utrecht.

The chief of police in Boxtel, Samuel Kerkhove, was eager to join the SD, and saw the information from the foster son as a chance to show how alert he was. He immediately phoned Utrecht and reported the whole thing. James van Beusekom was lucky; since he had gone on to Amsterdam, he got away. But the police raided the contact address in Utrecht and arrested everyone. Several people, including some Jews, had been hiding there. They were deported to Germany and never returned. The police also began arresting people named Van Beusekom, among them James's parents, who lived in Middelburg (Zeeland).[4]

The foster son told the Boxtel chief of police that everyone involved in the attack, including Hetty and Gisela, had come to the house by bicycle. Kerkhove checked at the train station to see whether any bicycles had been shipped from Boxtel to Utrecht that day. And indeed Hetty and Gisela had sent their bikes by train. Jan and Rut, however, anticipating a police check, had left a false trail by sending their bicycles to Eindhoven, intending never to pick them up.

That evening, in the office, the raiders gave their report. Kempe, who hadn't known anything about the attack, was not amused.[5] Frits Iordens, who apparently felt much the same, said: "It was not handled very elegantly." The dark look they received spoke for itself.

The next day Hetty Voûte celebrated her birthday in Noordwijk with her mother and her friend Olga Hudig, to whom she told the whole story. Back in Utrecht, she ran into Jan Meulenbelt and Rut Matthijsen, who were getting ready to take the train to their overnight address in Driebergen. After saying good-bye to them, she went to the station to get her bicycle, which had arrived from Boxtel, and was promptly picked up by the SD.

> I returned to Utrecht by train and thought: "I'll just quickly get my bike." The bicycle was standing right in front. I thought: "Gee, what luck." Well, the SD were standing right there too. They had followed the bicycle. So then I had to go with them to the police station. And on the way I had my beach permit in my pocket, so I had to eat it."

The SD officers delivered Hetty to the police station and left immediately to keep watch over Gisela's bicycle. Hetty assumed that Jan Meulenbelt and Rut Matthijsen's bicycles were also at the railroad station in Utrecht. She foresaw a disaster:

> I thought: "I can't let it happen. Any minute those boys and Gisela will come to get their bicycles and they'll all be run in." So I said to the policeman: 'It's my birthday. I have no idea why I'm here. I have to call home. They're waiting for me.' Well, that wasn't allowed at all. So I said: "Just step out into the hall, you don't have to see what I'm doing." That's what he did, and I called home. I got my brother on the phone, and I said: "Tell Olga that I'm here." They did, and Olga warned the guys.

Meanwhile, Gisela had gone to her parents. After they got Olga's message, Jan Meulenbelt and Ger Kempe tried to warn her. But because the telephone might have been bugged, they had to express themselves in very guarded terms. Gisela explains:

> The next day Jan called me, I think; he said: "You have to come here right away." He didn't say why. I said: "Listen, I was just going to have dinner in the city with my parents." It was Whit Sunday. He said: "Well, go ahead, but then come here right afterwards." But he didn't tell me not to go to the railroad station.

Gisela decided to pick up her bicycle on the way, and she was arrested in the bicycle shed at the station:

> It was as if I'd been hit on the head. A dull blow. Not more than that. Yes, and "What do I do now?" I had some stuff with me, and I started eating it right away. Initially I looked much less suspicious than Hetty. Why? I think it was because I had a kind of a dumb blond look. Hetty looked so dazzling—a somewhat defiant face and somewhat Jewish-looking. So I kept pretending that I didn't know anything. And they swallowed it for a while. She was the chief suspect, not me. Mrs. De

Ruiter had seen Hetty with Jan. But not me. So they didn't know whether I knew Jan.

When Gisela was arrested, Hetty had already spent several frightening hours:

Not being able to say anything is terrible. All night long they questioned me in the police station. Then I was shown the photos of how that man was killed, slumped halfway over the table, bleeding. And I kept saying: "Oh God, how awful. And I was just there." But I was trembling all over. Then I thought: "Well, I'll lean my leg against the table." But that made the whole table tremble. Terrible. Awful. I kept saying that some girls from Rotterdam had been in the hostel building and that was all I knew
   And then they asked me how I knew.
   "Well, they were turned over to me at the station." "By whom?" "By a woman wearing a big hat." I thought: "What in God's name can I tell them? How long can I keep this up?" That woman [Mies van Ginkel] appeared to only have a bullet in her lung, and she was in the hospital and could tell everything.

Hetty suffered several nasty blows during the interrogation; Kerkhove was present from time to time. But neither Hetty nor Gisela said anything that could be used against anyone, not even when they were later brought face to face with each other in the prison in Den Bosch. Hetty was shown pictures of people whose last name was Van Beusekom, but she managed to control herself when she saw the face of Jan Meulenbelt in the photo lineup. The fact that Hetty and Gisela didn't talk helped to prevent a major disaster.

Ger Kempe and Piet Meerburg wanted to get Hetty and Gisela out of Vught. Via Olga Hudig they tried to get in touch with "Aunt Jo" (Jo van Koeverden), a former espionage contact of Hetty's from the time in 1941 when she and Olga had done some spying on German fortifications. Jo lived in Buren and had previously been able to talk the Germans into releasing some prisoners. Olga went to look for Aunt Jo, and after some investigation found out that Aunt Jo was a man. However, Jo van Koeverden could do nothing because the charges against Gisela and Hetty—murder and helping Jews (*Mord und Judenhilfe*)—were too serious. Olga Hudig stayed on with Aunt Jo, and they were married after the war.

Hetty Voûte and Gisela Söhnlein were not released, and together they managed to get through two years of imprisonment. Mies van Ginkel confessed having worked for the resistance as well as for the SD. After the attack, fearing for her life, she asked the Germans to protect her. This led to a form

of semi-voluntary imprisonment. As a result, Mies van Ginkel accompanied
Gisela and Hetty on their journey through several prisons and concentration
camps, even though she enjoyed all sorts of privileges that the other two
women could only dream of. The final stop for the three women was
Ravensbrück. Hetty and Gisela survived the war. Mies van Ginkel was
fatally wounded in 1945 in an air raid while on a transport to Sweden. Samuel Kerkhove, the chief of police of Boxtel, was imprisoned in May 1948.

The fiasco in Esch had serious consequences for the Utrecht Children's
Committee. Anyone who had ever set foot in the house in Esch was in danger of being recognized by Mies van Ginkel. Jan Meulenbelt and Rut Matthijsen went into hiding and were out of circulation for two months. James
van Beusekom stayed in Amsterdam. He continued to be active in the resistance but was no longer involved in children's rescue.

The SD maintained surveillance on the house where James van
Beusekom had lived in Utrecht. This led to the arrest of Maurits Niewegt,
a young Jewish man living underground with the help of the Children's
Committee, when he went there on June 28, 1943. He died in Bergen-
Belsen in May of 1945.

Jan Meulenbelt and Rut Matthijsen did not resurface until September
1943, when it was clear that Hetty and Gisela had not revealed anything. The
card system was placed in safekeeping at the archbishop's palace in Utrecht.
Jewish children who went into hiding after June 12, 1943 are not recorded
in it.

AFTER ESCH

After the operation in Esch, a number of children in the provinces of Utrecht
and Zeeland had to be moved at once. No one knew whether Hetty, who
had been responsible for keeping the card system up to date, would be able
to keep silent.

After Jan Meulenbelt dropped out, Jelle de Jong became the most
important figure in the Utrecht area. In Rut Matthijsen's absence he kept the
office going and probably set up a new contact address, but its location is
unknown. Office meetings often took place at the home of Frits Iordens's
landlady, Jitske Eding. She and her husband ran a large rooming house for
students on Voorstraat in Utrecht. Ankie Stork recalls: "It was a rooming
house for students—a barn of a place. And all sorts of young people lived
there. It was like a beehive. Everyone running in and out—very dangerous
in retrospect."

Jelle de Jong didn't continue very long as coordinator. In September 1943, he left the Utrecht group for personal reasons. An de Waard took over the coordination of the Utrecht region. Jelle de Jong joined the armed resistance and survived the war.[6]

On August 2, 1943 Frits Iordens and Anne Maclaine Pont were married in private. Since all of the other committee members were either under arrest, in hiding, or working elsewhere, only An de Waard, Geert Lubberhuizen, and probably Kempe knew about it.

Paul Terwindt and Tini van de Bilt expanded the branch in Arnhem by making connections with as many organizations as possible.[7] Terwindt wrote:

> We very methodically tried to make contact with Calvinist, Dutch Reformed, liberal Protestant, Catholic, Socialist, and Communist circles. Activists from interdenominational Christian, Catholic, and humanist groups—probably separated for many years—got to know one another. These connections brought in the addresses of prospective foster parents. The Jewish parents were not told where the helpers and the foster parents lived, and they didn't even know the city or town where their beloved children were placed. As a matter of principle, children were always placed far away from their homes; for example, those from Amsterdam went to Arnhem, and vice versa, to avoid being recognized accidentally.

Ankie Stork was one of the greatest new assets of the Utrecht Children's Committee in the summer of 1943, and she recalls:

> I have already mentioned the sale of "The Eighteen Dead"; and then my cousin Anne Maclaine Pont came and asked me to go and look for foster homes. After all, I was living in Twente, where there were lots of farmers and which was so remote, and to her it looked like an ideal area to place children. In addition she had already arranged a hiding place for the Sarluy family through my father. So there was obvious cooperation. . . . I asked my father: "Where can I ask for advice? Who would be able to help me?" Then I got many addresses near Nijverdal, and I went there and explained: "Yes, we have to put up children. We have to find places to house Jews." And I did that first in the area around Nijverdal, where I was in touch with Tijhuis and with Tiemen de Jonge among others, and with farmers in Zuna and Haarle.

Tijhuis was the principal of an elementary school in Nijverdal. Tiemen de Jonge was the local head of the National Organization to Help Those in Hiding (Landelijke Organisatie voor Hulp aan Onderduikers), known as the

LO, and he used his connections at the distribution center to obtain ration cards and whatever else was needed.[8]

Shortly before this, Ankie Stork had already been involved independently in sheltering students who had refused to sign the declaration of loyalty. For this she had made contact with Jan Vloedgraven in Lemele, a fifty-one-year-old farmer who worked as a machine operator in her father's factory, whom she had known since before the war. Through this contact, Lemele became a center for hiding children. The central person was the Reverend H. Berkhof, who in 1938 became the minister of the Reformed churches of Lemele and Archem, which together comprised a total of 790 souls. Berkhof had studied in Berlin in the thirties and had experienced Nazism up close, so there was no need for Ankie to explain much to him. He gave her a list of reliable addresses. Berkhof had already done good work in Lemele by obtaining forged permits (*Ausweise*) for those threatened with forced labor (*Arbeitseinsatz*). In his sermons he preached strongly against National Socialism. Ankie recalls:

> He was courageous and didn't mince words. Father felt that you had to support that. And then I thought: "I'll go to Minister Berkhof, he'll know lots of addresses." . . . And then I spent a whole morning with him, and he gave me a whole list with addresses. The addresses were reliable, and I think that the five most important families were on the list. . . . He said: "This is where you should go. These people will help you."

The members of the five families soon began to suggest other possibilities. As a result, many of the children who were hidden after June 12, 1943 by the Children's Committee were placed in Nijverdal or Lemele or with farmers in the surrounding area. Ankie Stork used her parents' home in Nijverdal as temporary shelter. Most of the time she picked up the children in Amsterdam, especially in the Apollolaan and Sarphatipark neighborhoods.

Anne Maclaine Pont sometimes asked Ankie to put up adults. Of all the committee members, Anne was the one who least often followed Jan Meulenbelt's guideline about limiting their efforts to children.

> I would receive a request from Anne: "Do you have a place for a married couple? We're stuck with a couple." So then I'd begin looking until I found something—also in my own circle. People about whom I figured: "Well, they have space, let's try there." My parents had two Jewish girls in their house. Jews were always coming and going there. In a small village like Nijverdal—for Nijverdal really was a small

village—you knew exactly who could be trusted and who couldn't.
. . . If I didn't know the people, I didn't use my real name.

Ankie had male and female contacts in Nijverdal, Ommen, and Lemele.
The rapidity with which Ankie was able to organize her branch reflected the
change in attitude toward the German occupiers after the strikes in April and
May of 1943

After Anne Maclaine Pont introduced her to Adri Knappert in a house
called Weversnest in Nieuwebrug, Ankie often stayed there. Anne and Frits
often did too, so that they could get together and discuss matters.

In August 1943, twenty-year-old Dora Matthijsen, a cousin of Rut,
joined the Children's Committee. At first she acted as the contact between
Jan Meulenbelt and Rut Matthijsen, who were in hiding, and the rest of the
committee. Dora reported regularly at the office so that she could keep Jan
up to date on the latest developments. From time to time she would also
escort a child somewhere, and in due course she began to function more and
more as a kind of secretary to Geert Lubberhuizen.

On September 1, 1943, Jan Meulenbelt and Rut Matthijsen returned to
Utrecht in order to resume their activities. Matthijsen says:

> It was somewhat nervous-making . . . being back in Utrecht. . . . All
> sorts of policemen on duty could recognize you. It would be easy to
> walk into a trap. But nothing like that happened, so we were able to
> just go on with our work. I simply picked up where I had left off with
> Geert. Hetty and Gisela had never been to the Bezige Bij publishing
> house, so they couldn't possibly reveal its address.

Sometimes there were strange coincidences. For example, Geertruida
(Truitje) van Lier ran into trouble because of the murder of G. J. Kerlen, the
superintendent of police of Utrecht. This attack took place on September 3,
1943, and was carried out by Gertrude (Truus) van Lier, a cousin of Geertruida (Truitje) van Lier. The cousin lived on Prins Hendriklaan in Utrecht,
the same street where Geertruida (Truitje) had established Kindjeshaven.
The confusion this stirred up for the Germans as well as for the Children's
Committee caused a good deal of trouble for the director of Kindjeshaven.
The Germans initially suspected her, but she was able to prove that she was
innocent. Her cousin was arrested on September 14 and was executed by a
firing squad two months later. When the Children's Committee found out
about the attack, several committee members took their hidden Jewish children out of Kindjeshaven and put them up elsewhere despite Truitje's protests.

## THE AMSTERDAM STUDENT GROUP

All the groups expanded their operations in the summer of 1943. The Amsterdam Student Group was no exception. New branches were started, mostly in the southern part of the country.

### AMSTERDAM, WIJDENES, AND NIJKERKERVEEN

Wouter van Zeytveld and Tineke Haak traveled regularly to Cees and Lien Kracht in Wijdenes. Wouter remembers:

> I poked around in [the northern part of] Noord-Holland. . . . There wasn't much of an organization compared to Friesland or Limburg. . . . We had Cees and Lien, who, in turn, had connections near Nieuwe Niedorp and Winkel. They knew quite a few former conscientious objectors who lived in the area. A number of children had been hidden there.

Cees and Lien were careful. They made it a rule never to do more than one illegal thing at the same time. On May 13, 1943, the day all radios had to be turned in, they were uncertain what to do. They decided to comply. That way they would be able to post a certificate on the door confirming that they had turned in their radio, and that would prevent a search that might uncover the child they were hiding.

Lien made sure that she dutifully deposited a quarter in the can for Winterhulp, a relief fund operated by the Dutch Nazi organization, when the NSB teacher came by for a contribution. This helped to erect a wall of allegiance behind which the Jewish identity of their hidden child, Bob de Groot, was concealed. The NSB teacher never suspected Cees and Lien and wasn't at all suspicious when Bobbie was registered in the school. Until the "hunger winter" of 1944–45, Bobbie went to school like all the other children. Lien explained:

> There was no school that last winter [of the war]. But then we had school at home. The teacher would come to our house. She would be at our house for a few hours in the morning, and in the afternoon she'd go somewhere else. That was every day, and the children got homework so that they completed that year anyhow.

A girl of about four had been hidden with Cees and Lien but later was transferred to the home of Piet and Annie de Vries in Andijk. Lien Kracht recalls:

FIGURE 10

*The Children's Committee at the wedding of*
*Geert Lubberhuizen and Willy van Reenen*

From the collection of Mr. Rutger Matthijsen (Oss)

The girl looked terribly Jewish. I tried to keep her on the premises, but that was almost impossible. And then she'd tell everyone she saw: "Those horrible Germans took my father and mother." So Annie brought her back to us and said: "Well, Lien, I hope you can work this out because it's simply impossible on our little street."

Later a place was found for the child in an out-of-the-way village in the polder.

Tineke Haak attended college until the summer of 1943, then devoted herself full-time to taking care of children. This entailed accompanying children, but above all it meant looking for secure refuges throughout the country. To do this she visited her friends' parents, among others:

Addresses were important. I remember that I considered many people. Like: "They should be able to take care of a child, shouldn't they?" And then I'd go there, and I'd be very surprised and upset if they said they wouldn't do it.

Tineke sometimes took the train to Friesland, but she always found traveling with children a terrifying undertaking. Her efforts found a connection in Nijkerkerveen in the Veluwe area that yielded many placements. Her parents helped in this work.

In Amsterdam, the pediatrician Fiedeldij Dop saw his practice shrink dramatically. Until September 1943 he regularly warned parents and urged them to let their children go into hiding. He received support from a good German:

> This man, a banker from Hamburg, had a conversation with the chief of police every Friday evening. . . . He was then told the details of the raids on Jews that would take place the next day. . . . This meant that early the next morning I would ride my bicycle, for I no longer had a car, past my patients and could tell them in time: "Today children will be picked up in your neighborhood. Make sure to hide." . . . It's fantastic the way these people never gave away my name. The most beautiful example of this was a boy of around sixteen who was hidden but was found and taken away. They put a pistol to his head to make him tell who had placed him there. But he never said a thing.[9]

Another person who supplied children was Lau Mazirel, an Amsterdam lawyer. Meerburg remembers:

> Many of the poor Jews lived in the area near Tugelaweg. She was there a lot, so she'd come to us with all sorts of children who had to be sheltered somewhere, but who didn't come via the child-care center. The children Lau brought in were mostly from homes where there was no money at all.

The Amsterdam group often met in Lau Mazirel's law office. Piet Meerburg recalls:

> We always needed meeting places where we could speak freely. Anyone who was around twenty years old could be picked up and sent to Germany for work. So you were never ever confident of your safety in a café, even though we all had really good forged ID's. Besides, we had to discuss things that you couldn't really talk about in public. Lau had a place; all sorts of people came there. I myself often used her place for emergency situations—for people who had to go into hiding but had to stay somewhere for a few days or a week before they could be taken to a refuge in the countryside. Well, all that was possible.

Mieke Mees joined in the spring of 1943. Piet Meerburg knew her from his vacations in Gorssel. She was a medical student and a board member of the Amsterdam Women Students Organization (AVSV). She traveled primarily to Limburg. After interviewing her in 1976, Ph. A. J. Mees wrote:

> Mieke's first task was to take nine children from Amsterdam to Geleen, and from there farther into Limburg. She succeeded with the help of another girl, but they never again escorted such a large number because the risk of being noticed was too great. This took place in 1943; the assembly point was Central Station in Amsterdam. Upon arrival in Geleen there was great anxiety because the expected contact person failed to show up. Fortunately a trustworthy girl directed them to a mineworker's family that gave the nine children and their escorts a warm welcome, offered them a meal, and took care of finding hiding places.[10]

Tineke Haak recalls that there wasn't much of a change of command in the group:

> It actually consisted of Wouter and Piet with the many women around them. . . . Wouter and Piet were the kind of people who kept the big picture in mind, the ones who organized things. And we were happy to leave it to them. . . . I think that you can't really talk about hierarchy in our group.

Wouter and Piet wanted nothing to do with the LO (National Organization to Help Those in Hiding), which was founded at the end of 1942, even though this meant that they missed out on getting the ration cards it provided. Meerburg recalls:

> We had a big conflict with the LO. The LO required names and addresses, and we refused to give them this information because we felt it was irresponsible. So we didn't get any ration cards or money from them. We could afford to do that because Utrecht supported us. But I've always been very angry about it.

In the summer of 1943 Geert Lubberhuizen asked for help in selling the illustrated poem "The Eighteen Dead." The Amsterdam group would share the profits. A supply of the poems was stored at the Haaks' house. Piet Meerburg remembers that the Amsterdam group lived completely on the proceeds from sales of "The Eighteen Dead." CS-6, the resistance group of Gideon and Jan Karel Boissevain, wanted to help with the sales. Wouter knew Gideon from high school. Piet Meerburg went to Corellistraat, the address of CS-6, to discuss the matter and was shocked when he saw that there were guns in the house. He advised Wouter as follows: "We'd better not have anything to do with these people. They're a bunch of swashbuckling cowboys."

Nevertheless, there was some cooperation with CS-6 for the sale of the poems. This led to a tragedy comparable in its consequences to the failed attack at Esch. But with a great difference: Hetty Voûte and Gisela Söhnlein returned from imprisonment, whereas the parents of Jur and Tineke Haak did not return.

On August 1, 1943, the CS-6 group was rounded up by the SD, which then installed itself in the house on Corellistraat. A few days later, Tineke Haak asked her seventeen-year-old brother Bob to take some poems to Corellistraat. In a report she wrote:

> I myself had to take a child to Friesland that day. We had never before involved Bob. Unwise and actually unnecessary. But catastrophic. At Corellistraat 6 he was arrested by Willy Lages, the head of the Sicherheitsdienst in Amsterdam. Together with another boy who had been caught in the trap, Bob was taken to the Weteringschans prison, where the Boissevain brothers [of the CS-6 group] were already being held. The same car probably continued to Lairessestraat, where they came to pick me up (Bob had told them my name when they asked who had sent him).

Tineke was not yet back from Friesland, so her parents were arrested in her place. They were taken to the municipal jail on Amstelveenseweg, but revealed nothing during their interrogation.[11] Tineke was very upset by their arrest, and when she received an indirect message that the Germans would be willing to release her parents in exchange for herself, she wanted to turn herself in. Wouter and Piet talked her out of it, arguing that one couldn't expect Germans to keep their word.[12]

Deported via the Vught prison camp, her parents ended up in German concentration camps. Her mother died at the end of 1944 in Reichenbach in Poland, and her father died early in 1945 in Sachsenhausen.[13]

After the arrest of his parents, Jur Haak decided to move back into the family home in order to help his sister, Mieke, take care of the younger children.[14]

The sisters Judith and Elly Mirjam Gross who were in hiding with the Haak family were not identified as Jewish during the August 3 raid. They were rushed to the home of a prominent family living on Oranje Nassaulaan, where they were well taken care of. Shortly afterward, the foster mother brought them to visit Jur Haak at the Haak family's home. Someone in the neighborhood recognized the children and reported them to the police. The next day there was a raid at the foster family's home on Oranje Nassaulaan. The foster mother refused to hand over the children. First, she insisted, they would have to be washed and properly dressed. It was agreed that the gentlemen would return the next day to pick up the children. Tineke Haak writes:

> Well, of course that was wonderful, and you'd think that she would have called us right away and said something like "Hurry up, guys, come and pick up the children because they're going to be taken away tomorrow morning." But no! She just handed them over! . . . When she told me, I was totally dumbfounded. And she said: "Well, you see, my husband has a position . . ."

Meanwhile, the smuggling system at the child-care center was working so well that at first Meerburg and Van Zeytveld didn't worry much about the Gross sisters when they were brought there. "We'll get them out," they figured. Alas, they came too late. Both girls were deported soon after their arrival at the child-care center. In February 1944 they were gassed in Auschwitz. The parents of Judith and Elly Mirjam Gross were later looked after by Tineke Haak. Her visits to them were very difficult. She tried not to tell them that their two little ones had been sent to Auschwitz, but eventually they found out.

The parents survived the war. After the war, the foster mother paid them a visit and told them that she was the one who had given the children to the police. Tineke Haak writes: "That's incredible, isn't it? I don't understand why they didn't kill her right then and there. They just sat and listened!"

After the raid on her parents' home, Tineke could no longer live there. She moved in with Wouter van Zeytveld and Piet Meerburg. Because they didn't have much space, Wouter van Zeytveld and Tineke Haak rented a house on Vechtstraat. This turned out to be a bad choice: the house belonged to two black marketeers who soon figured out that Wouter and Tineke were doing resistance work. They had to flee, leaving behind Tineke Haak's violin, among other things. The father of Kurt Leoni, a student, let them live in an apartment above his place of business in the Nes neighborhood.

Meerburg moved in with Hans van Loghem on Herengracht, where they stayed until the liberation. Meerburg's part (one-third) of the address administration was hidden in the meter box. The hiding place was constructed by an electrician.

Wouter van Zeytveld went through life pretending to be a student who had signed the loyalty declaration. He had a forged permit (*Ausweis*) from the Labor Bureau in Hilversum. Then he was detained in Amsterdam:

I had an *Ausweis*, but no student ID card. And that's why I was stopped at Central Station. Because I gave them the *Ausweis*, and then they wanted to see my student ID card, which I didn't have. Then they said: "Come with us." . . . I had ration cards with me, all sorts of stuff. . . . I was able to flush all of it down the toilet because all they were thinking about was a boy who was supposed to go to Germany. So that was a lucky break.

Piet Meerburg found out about Wouter's predicament; he was quite worried because he knew that Wouter was carrying incriminating material:

Then I called Krijn [van den Helm], and I said: "Damn it, Wouter has been picked up and he's in jail." Krijn came over right away. . . . And then the two of us—I would never have dared by myself—went to the university, to the registrar, and Krijn kept threatening until we got a book of one hundred blank student ID cards. And then we filled in Wouter's name and took it to the jail.

Wouter was released. He took his student ID card and immediately went to the SD headquarters on Euterpestraat in order to get a real *Ausweis*, bearing the name of a student who had signed. The document was handed to him by an enormous SS man. Wouter was able to help many others with the other ninety-nine blank ID cards.

### SNEEK

The odd threesome of Willem Mesdag, Gérard Jansen, and Mia Coulingh worked in Sneek. Jansen didn't expect much from his Catholic superiors, and Coulingh didn't expect much from her Protestant ones. Curate Jansen's superior, Pastor J. van Galkom, was a nervous man who preferred not to cooperate, and at any rate wanted as little to do with the resistance as possible. Mia Coulingh encountered the same sort of opposition in the Reformed Church. It was different for Mesdag. He was the leader of the Baptist community and the confidant of many colleagues from surrounding villages. But there were not enough Baptists to provide enough homes. That is why cooperation was necessary.

The three clerics had two advantages over other children's rescuers: because of their jobs, they had to make the rounds of community members and parishioners; getting addresses was no trouble. The faithful came to church once a week; and after services potential foster parents were taken aside. Mesdag's daughter, Nina Mesdag, remembers that one day her parents and Mia Coulingh ran out of possible refuges. But Gérard Jansen still had

FIGURE 11
*The Baptist church and parsonage, Sneek (Friesland)*
From the collection of Dr. Bert Jan Flim (Leeuwarden)

plenty of addresses. Nina's parents asked how that could be, since the Roman Catholic community was not very large.

> "Well," he said triumphantly and slightly mischievously—for he liked to make fun of himself—he said: "Well, I have a weapon you don't have. Confession." If someone came to him to confess to something and a penance had to be done, he would say: "If you do this you will be doing work agreeable to God."

The Amsterdam students took the children to Friesland across the IJsselmeer via two different routes. The first was by train to Enkhuizen, where they would catch the boat to Staveren, and then by train to Sneek. The alternative route was Amsterdam-Lemmer (the so-called Lemmerboat). From Lemmer there was a tram connection to Sneek. People very rarely went the whole distance via Zwolle by train. The crews of the ferries must have noticed that the same students kept traveling with different children. Gérard Jansen remembers: "The crew never said a word. I think that was so wonderful. . . . Those people never asked anything. Never."

It was usually Iet van Dijk who took the children to Sneek. Mia Coulingh recalls:

> Iet was a petite, blonde young woman. And I remember her arrival in Sneek. . . . She had a little baby with her who was, I believe, nine days old. And she said: "Something's not right, because the child hasn't soiled even a single diaper." So we went right to a doctor, Dr. Gerritsma. We had already asked him to do physicals before we placed the children with families. . . . And he had that baby admitted at Anthonius Hospital, a Catholic hospital. The baby was in the hospital for five weeks and turned out to have pyloric atresia, and it needed intravenous feeding. Treatment was always free. Curate Jansen had worked out with the hospital that all our Jewish children would be treated without charge as long as it was necessary. Later we placed the baby that was fed intravenously with a regular family and then made sure that a visiting nurse would come, and so on.

Nina Mesdag adds:

> Iet could look so incredibly stupid. And that saved her. I mean, she looked so stupid getting on the train—as if she didn't have all her marbles. . . . So they let her go.

Rescuing children took a lot of time. So much that Mesdag's regular work was affected. Nina Mesdag still remembers an incident when three Jewish children were sleeping in her brothers' room:

> Of course, my parents had their hands full with all this, and then my father had to attend a church council meeting for which he had been unable to do certain things. We had a chairman of the church council who was really scared for his own life. He had the nerve to accuse my father of sabotaging something that was supposed to be done. My father didn't say a thing; the man was not important, and of course my father wouldn't dream of telling him, of all people, why he was so busy. But he came back from the meeting feeling just awful, and he told my mother, and my mother was cut to the quick by it. When my father went out for something or other the next morning, my mother sent for that man—without telling my father, of course. Just like that. Could he come immediately? Well, from her tone the man understood that it was imperative. He wanted to know why, and she said: "I can't say, but you have to come right now." Well, he comes and he says: "What's it all about?" And she says: "Come upstairs!" And she opens the bedroom door and says: "*That's* sabotage! And now get out of here, I don't want to see you again." He didn't betray those children. It was

a dangerous thing to do, but my mother was hopping mad. And that's how she reacted.

The children often stayed with Mesdag for a day or so in order to become acclimatized. And sometimes they would undergo a transformation. Dark children would get a treatment with hydrogen peroxide. This was not necessary very often because the Amsterdam students usually sent blond Jewish children to Friesland, where most of the people were blond. The children's clothes were taken and divided up. One child might come with two large suitcases and another with nothing. The doctor would come to check the children's health. After a bleach treatment and a medical checkup, they were put on the back of a bike with their luggage and delivered to their hiding address with their distribution card and ration coupons for a month. The threesome in Sneek never joined the LO. Ration coupons came from Amsterdam. Many children ended up in villages around Sneek. These small villages in Friesland had a variety of religious denominations. Mia Coulingh and Mesdag placed children with Protestant families, while Gérard Jansen was responsible for placements with Catholic families.

LEEUWARDEN AND JOURE

On June 25, 1943, the resistance raided the Regional Employment Office (Gewestelijk Arbeids Bureau; GAB) in Leeuwarden. They seized all the records on those who were scheduled to go to Germany for forced labor or had already been sent there. The operation was carried out by an armed action group led by Krijn van den Helm. That is why many Frisians think of him in connection with armed resistance. But Krijn van den Helm was also involved with placing Jews in hiding until well into 1944 and with finding places for Jewish children until October 1943.

In May of 1943, Van den Helm was running out of ration cards because of the growing stream of Jews from the western part of Holland who had to go into hiding. He obtained some from the LO. The Jewish children who had been hidden by Meerburg via Van den Helm in the area surrounding Leeuwarden were taken care of by the LO. Thus Van den Helm's organization was the first branch of the Meerburg group to join the LO. Two men from Joure, Sjoerd Wiersma and Uilke Boonstra, were also important in rescuing children. Both of them were members of the "Council of Five," an umbrella organization for various Frisian districts of the LO. Piet Meerburg recalls his first conversation with Sjoerd Wiersma:

He was a man raised in a strict Calvinist tradition and he had a laundry in Joure. Every week that crazy guy went to Amsterdam with a truck that he then loaded with Jews who wanted to go into hiding. And then he just drove to Friesland and found shelters for them. . . . A very dour man. One day he had several places for children, and I went to Joure with Iet van Dijk and two or three children. . . . I wanted to know why he did all this, since I thought it was pretty dangerous, and he said: "Well, it says in the Bible: 'Love your enemies.' And the Jews are my enemies. But I have to love them. And I have to save them, because it's my Christian duty." That scared the hell out of me. So the next day I went to Krijn van den Helm as fast as I could. I said: "Jesus, Krijn, what kind of guy is he? Is it safe?" And he said: "Oh, don't pay any attention to all that. There are others around here who reason the same way. But they're the very best."

Uilke Boonstra, an architect and family man who, like Wiersma, was around thirty years old, was cut from the same cloth. Time after time, driven by his Calvinist convictions, he too risked his life and the lives of his family to help as many Jews as possible. After Krijn van den Helm's reassuring words, Meerburg decided to take his chances with these two. Since Wiersma and Boonstra also headed the LO in the southeastern corner of Friesland, Meerburg and Van Zeytveld did not have to worry about ration cards and such things. It was rarely necessary to pay for room and board. Everything was taken care of in Friesland. Meerburg recalls:

Having one more child, especially in large families, made little difference. I have one great example of a man in Friesland who really earned very little money and had seven children. He collected the buckets from privies; that was about the lowest kind of job in the world. But he absolutely refused to accept any money, and he was willing to add an extra child to his seven. . . . That's how it went in most cases.

In the case of the Leeuwarden and Joure branches, Meerburg swallowed his reservations about the LO. After all, the people who were doing the rescue work there (and therefore had to be informed of the addresses) were also the leaders of the LO. Thus there was no question of a double—and therefore doubly risky—address file. There was never more than one list. After Sneek and Leeuwarden, Joure became the third connection to Friesland for the Amsterdam Student Group.

LIMBURG

In early May of 1943, Piet Meerburg asked two students from Nijmegen to help come up with hiding addresses. He knew them from the students' resistance, and they were living underground in Venlo. That was how Meerburg was introduced to thirty-eight-year-old Hanna van de Voort in Tienray. Because of her job as midwife she was a familiar presence throughout the area. The two students, Karel Ex and Joe Russel, first asked Hanna's sister, Mien van de Voort (a member of the local resistance), if she could help them find places to hide children. Mien send them on to Hanna. But Hanna's mother was seriously ill and needed care, and this made Hanna hesitate. Nico Dohmen, a student who was in hiding with Hanna and her parents, recalls:

> I think that encouragement came in the first place from Hanna's mother. She was an exceptionally good-hearted mother. And she said: "Well, Hanna, if these little children are in danger, then we have to do something. Now you make sure to find a place for them, and I'll pray for them."

Hanna's father, Anselm van de Voort, was a retired baker who shared his wife's point of view. When they talked about "danger" they actually meant "mortal danger." According to Dohmen, the word "gassing" was mentioned during the conversation. Evidently, in May of 1943, Ex and Russel were already aware of what was happening in Poland.

In early June, Piet Meerburg and Mieke Mees visited Tienray. Meerburg introduced himself as Piet van Doorn. Hanna van de Voort and Nico Dohmen never knew his real name until after the occupation ended. It was decided that students from Amsterdam would take the children to the Venray station, where Hanna would be waiting for them. From there they would go together to Tienray, either by bus or on foot—the latter took one and a half hours. During the journey the children would have time to get acquainted with Hanna van de Voort. And the next day the students would go back to Amsterdam. For safety reasons, they had decided to concentrate on children. Nico Dohmen recalls:

> We would have run even more risks if we had expanded our area of activity. So that's why we decided to limit ourselves exclusively to children. Of course it didn't work out that way, because we helped adults too: American pilots, French prisoners-of-war. You can make all the limitations you want, but if people turn up on your doorstep, you have to do something.

This was how Hanna became an activist. Meanwhile, her mother died in December of 1943. Nico Dohmen helped his hostess as much as he could, and he recalls:

> Finding addresses was almost exclusively Hanna's work. Because she knew those people; she had their trust. If she came to them and said: "You should help this child because it's in great danger," they would reply: "Well Hanna, if you think so, we'll do it."

It took some time to find enough addresses. The inhabitants of the border villages near Tienray knew very little about the April/May strikes. And news about the deportations had not reached these remote villages. Tienray was one and a half hours by foot from Venray, the nearest railroad station. Wherever she went, Hanna had to explain what Jews were, how the Germans and their collaborators were persecuting them, and how most of them lived in Amsterdam. Then she had to explain that the Germans punished people who helped Jews, so that you had to think twice before taking a Jewish child into your home. Often the people did not believe her, and this made it very difficult to get them to cooperate. The first Jewish child to arrive in Tienray turned out to be a six-year-old handicapped boy. He stayed about two weeks in the Van de Voort household and then was taken to Kampen by Nico Dohmen's father, P. H. Dohmen. The boy was able to stay in Kampen for the remainder of the war.

From the start the Tienray center was quite independent. Meerburg and Van Zeytveld did not want to exercise close supervision. Piet Meerburg explains:

> That was their responsibility. Of course there was cooperation. Of course there were contacts. Of course we consulted when there were problems. But ultimately it was their responsibility.

All told, Hanna van de Voort and Nico Dohmen, who was in hiding himself, managed to find places for 123 Jews, the youngest of whom was fourteen days old. Nico recalls that they made a point of not keeping records because it would have been too dangerous.

The number 123 comes from a list that was drawn up in February 1945, after the liberation of Tienray. It may well have been incomplete.[15]

The busiest period was during July and August of 1943. According to Nico Dohmen, the children came straight from the child-care center in Amsterdam, which was to be closed in September. Dohmen recalls:

So many children came almost all at once. Some weeks we received five or six children per day. . . . Meerburg and Wouter van Zeytveld came several times, but it was more dangerous for them than for the girls. . . . Mieke Mees, Alice Brunner, and Ietje van Dijk made many trips back and forth, and they took many risks. Of course I must say that they really liked doing it, and they often stayed over one or two nights. There was always plenty of food in Tienray, and we always gave them food to take back with them.

Anselm van de Voort, Hanna's father, had problems accepting the sophisticated students. Nico Dohmen remembers quite well:

Ten minutes from the Van de Voort house there was a creek that you had to cross. And when Mieke got to the creek, she'd sit down and put on her stockings, and then she'd arrive properly dressed in stockings. That's why Mieke could do no wrong in the eyes of Mr. van de Voort. At least she was a respectable girl who wore stockings.

## EVACUEES FROM ROTTERDAM

It became much easier to find hiding addresses after a batch of blank evacuation documents was stolen from the Department of Children's Evacuation of the Central Evacuation Bureau on Westersingel in Rotterdam, probably by Iet van Dijk or Mieke Mees. With these documents, the children could pretend to be evacuees from Rotterdam. Mien van de Voort recalls:

. . . all the children going into hiding were provided with identity cards from the Central Bureau for the Evacuation of Children in Rotterdam. Of course they were all given new names, and their home addresses were listed as streets that had been destroyed during the 1940 bombing of Rotterdam. In this way the children became evacuees from Rotterdam. It goes without saying that they were well-coached. If necessary they could recite cover stories describing their ruined homes and the shortage of food in Rotterdam to explain why they were staying in the village.

To avoid making mistakes, the students compiled a list of 323 streets in Rotterdam that had been destroyed in the bombing.[16] This measure made things safer for prospective foster parents. Nico Dohmen relates:

The foster parents were well aware that the children were Jewish. . . . Of course we always told them that there wasn't much danger so long as they stuck to the cover story: the child was an evacuee from Rotterdam, they had proof of it, and they didn't know anything else.

Most of the children were hidden west of the Maas River between Gennep, Venray, and Venlo. Connections with the east bank of the Maas were maintained primarily by ferries situated far apart. At that time the Maas River was more of a barrier than it is today. The populace of the villages was almost one hundred percent Catholic. People were seldom exposed to different ideas. Nico Dohmen recalls:

> All the dramas we went through: children who didn't dare to say that they didn't eat pork and tried to avoid it in every possible way. . . . Most of the foster parents had no idea that Jews don't eat pork. How would they know such a thing? . . . And then, damn it, there isn't much to eat and you prepare a nice piece of meat, and they won't eat it! Then you think that they are stubborn and headstrong, and whatever else. . . . In general I must say that the foster parents could take a lot, the way they managed to accept the incomprehensible ways of their foster children. . . .
>
> I should also say that practically no one in the whole area believed the stories about the children being evacuees from Rotterdam. I'm still astonished at how incredibly all these people played along, for there is no doubt that an enormous amount of people knew what was going on.

Thanks to Nico Dohmen, we were able to find information about 101 of the 123 Jews that he and Hanna found places for. There were sixteen adults and eighty-five children: fifty-seven boys and twenty-eight girls. Dohmen recalls that they used code words in their correspondence with Meerburg and Van Zeytveld. Boys were referred to as coffee, and girls as tea. There was always one big problem: "people much preferred tea to coffee."

Apparently Meerburg, Van Zeytveld, and their comrades sent the "difficult cases" to Tienray. Dark children were the most difficult category, but as Dohmen recalled, "the people in Limburg are somewhat darker, so it was a bit easier there."

Older children were more difficult to place than younger ones. An example is Thomas (Tom) Stein, who had just turned twelve. He was born in Germany in 1931, and in 1937 he emigrated from Hamburg to Amsterdam with his parents and his brothers. At present Tom Stein lives in California.

> My father had been fortunate in that he had managed to get various kinds of protective papers. Until one day in the summer of 1943, when our pediatrician came in the middle of the night and told us to get out. I think he had been active in the underground. His name was Dr. Fiedeldij Dop.

Tom Stein relates that it was impossible at first to find a placement for him, so Nico Dohmen decided to take him along on his search:

> We would go from farm to farm, basically trying to find lodge [sic] for me. To find someone who would be willing to take me in. And the way Nico did it: he would go to a farmer and introduce me as an orphan. A child who was orphaned during the bombing of Rotterdam. And asked them whether they would be willing to take me in. He said he would be able to give them ration cards and that money would probably not be available. . . . We had been walking all day. It had been a very discouraging day and we finally got to this guy. Both Nico and I were really quite discouraged because of the many rejections. And we got to this guy and he actually . . . He said he didn't feel very comfortable about it, to take in a boy, because he had five daughters. He said he would consider it, but he wasn't sure whether his wife would want to do it. So Nico asked to talk to the wife. Let me digress for a minute. They were really illiterate farmers. This was a Roman Catholic area of Holland. They were devoutly Catholic. And basically Nico said to them that if they would take in this boy, then that would guarantee them a place in heaven. That basically was kind of like religious bribery, if you wish. So they agreed to do it on that basis. Plus the fact they saw that we were tired and discouraged. And I think they were also interested in getting someone to help them with their farm.

Tom slept in the attic with the farmhand. He stayed there for fifteen months, worked hard on the farm, and soon adjusted to the primitive conditions.

Tom's story is the second instance we know of where religion was used to pressure people. Nico Dohmen, like Curate Jansen, denies ever using such a weapon.

Nico Dohmen's job included taking children to the foster homes found by Hanna, providing ration cards for them when needed, and periodically looking in to see how they were doing. In this respect the branch in Tienray was methodologically very similar to the NV. Nico Dohmen explains the details:

> The children always went to Stationsstraat [the Van de Voort family's home] first. There they were told what to say, their names were changed, and they got an evacuation card. Then they were instructed in more detail and were told to contact us if anything went wrong. And we kept in touch with the children on a regular basis. Every two months we'd come by to see if everything was in order.

The evacuation cards gave the children more freedom of movement, so that they were able to play outside and go to school. Of course Dohmen would stop in at the school to urge the teachers to say as little as possible about the Jewish background of the new pupil. If there were two or more children in the same school, they generally knew nothing about each other. As mentioned before, it was only children of elementary school age who were able to go to school. Tom Stein, for example, was too old, so he did not go to school while in hiding.

In most cases the local priest was the head of the school's governing body. Usually his consent was obtained; usually, but not always. In such instances the children could not attend school unless the principal dared to secretly go against the wishes of his superior. Nico Dohmen recalls:

> We would go and talk with the priest. . . . But sometimes, when we knew that the priest wasn't all that brave, we'd "forget" to do so. Instead we'd go and talk directly with the principal. I don't know the exact numbers because we kept very poor records. But I do think, and this is on the low side, that there were about fifty children who went to elementary school.

Nico Dohmen remembers especially Father H. J. Vullinghs in Grubbenvorst, who was "very easy." Later it turned out that Vullinghs was one of the leaders of the Limburg branch of the Westerweel Group, a partly Jewish resistance organization. Thanks to its efforts, somewhere between 100 and 150 Jews (including numerous children) found places to hide in Limburg. He himself died in Bergen-Belsen.[17]

The organization in Tienray did not become affiliated with the LO; Nico and Hanna wanted to retain their independence. When necessary, the Amsterdam group supplied them with ration cards. But Nico and Hanna were not big customers because the Jewish children usually landed in large households with enough food. And hardly any room and board had to be paid. Nico Dohmen remembers that they received 130 guilders per month from Amsterdam. From this they paid 30 guilders to the Nabben family in Swolgen.[18] This was a poor family that eventually took in three children.

Clothing and shoes were provided by friendly shopkeepers. Nico and Hanna soon had their hands full with rescue work. Hanna also had her full-time job as midwife. Around the end of August they began getting help from Kurt Löwenstein (alias Ben), a young Jew who was in hiding. Kurt (born in 1925) and his parents had been on the way to America when they were stranded in Rotterdam on May 9, 1940. The ship was supposed to depart on

May 13 or 14. Kurt ended up in Tienray via Venlo. He was lodged with the Mooren family in Megelsum. Dohmen recalls:

> "Ben didn't look very Jewish at all. He had reddish hair but had more of a Dutch snub-nose than a typically Jewish nose. . . . And he became my closest co-worker. He always went out with me.

The Amsterdam students brought about fifty Jewish children to southern Limburg students. Early in 1943 Piet Meerburg made contact with Arie van Mansum in Maastricht. Van Mansum, a salesman, was an active member of the Calvinist Church and had already organized an underground network when some female students from Amsterdam, among them certainly Mieke Mees,[19] delivered several Jewish children to him on the train platform at Sittard. His organization had already hidden dozens of Jewish children in the region, many of them sent to him by Derk van Assen, the bailiff of direct taxes in Maastricht, who was also a Calvinist. In the summer of 1943, Derk van Assen was caught, and on September 14, 1943 he was executed by a firing squad.

> Almost every week Van Mansum received Jewish children from Meerburg at the Sittard train station. He took them to the temporary shelter of S. and J. Bosch in Hoensbroek, whom he knew through the Calvinist Youth Organization, and to Reformed families in the Treebeek region. The Bosch family and Miss A. Prins were Mansum's most important contacts in the mining region. They located new foster families. Workers with big families, in particular, turned out to be willing to take in Jewish children. And that's where they were probably safest, because they were hardly noticed amidst the other children. Thirty-three children were housed in Brunssum, Heerlen, Ubach-over-Worms, Eys-Wittem, and Vaals. Bosch provided ration cards, shoes, and clothing.[20]

Twenty-five-year-old Jan Bosch never asked for the names of the people who brought these Jewish children to him. He knew them as the "W. and T. organization," most likely an abbreviation for Wouter and Tineke. All thirty-three children survived the war.[21] On October 1, 1943 Van Mansum was arrested. His sister Margreet took over his work. Van Mansum survived the war. The activities of Jan Bosch and Arie van Mansum are discussed extensively in A. P. M. Cammaert's book.[22]

## THE NAAMLOZE VENNOOTSCHAP

By April of 1943, the NV had hidden approximately eighty Jews in the Heerlen-Kerkrade area, almost all of them children. In September the number had increased to approximately 225. Children were taken from the child-care center every day, and others were picked up at their homes. A large number of new recruits, many of whom were women, did this work.

The three founders of the Naamlooze Vennootschap (Anonymous Association), or NV, Jaap and Gerard Musch and Dick Groenewegen van Wijk, were living under cover in the mining region, and each of them had a permit (*Ausweis*) stating that he was employed in the Emma State Mine. They kept in touch with Joop and Semmy Woortman, the Kinsbergens, the people who escorted the children, and the three in Limburg through a pharmacy in Amsterdam.

Woortman was one of the 300,000 former soldiers who was supposed to go to Germany. He reported on August 3, 1943. Since he was working for the NVV labor union (Nederlands Verbond van Vakverenigingen), he was exempted at the last minute. As a result he was able to continue providing material support.

The area in Limburg around Heerlen and Kerkrade was "filled." Via Pontier, the Calvinist clergyman Hendrik Bouma was able to deliver a list of reliable parishioners, thus opening the new territory of Brunssum/Treebeek. Ration cards and financial help were provided by the LO in Heerlen. After some time new foster homes became available in this area. New territories in Geleen/Sittard and Venlo/Blerick were added later on.

A record number of children were smuggled out of the child-care center just before it closed. The Musch brothers and Dick Groenewegen van Wijk once took fourteen at the same time. Rosie Colthof, who was eleven at the time, and seven other children were pulled out of the line during their daily walk. Because so many children were taken at once—one informant remembers fifty-two in a single week—they were photographed so that their identities could be established later on. The widow of Dick Groenewegen van Wijk donated the photo album to the Dutch Institute for War Documentation (NIOD).

## THE TROUW GROUP

The unit of the Trouw Group involved in hiding children was very active under the leadership of Hester van Lennep and Gesina van der Molen. Starting in May 1943, Hester van Lennep and her friend Paulien van Waasdijk handed most of the Jewish children over to members of the Trouw Group. The children left the child-care center via the teachers college, but some-times parents would get in touch with Hester's skin care institute to say that they were willing to part with their children. One pregnant woman even contacted Hester before the delivery and asked her to find a suitable foster family. After the baby, a girl named Ruth, was born, it stayed for a week with Hester and Paulien on Keizersgracht; then Paulien took her to a foster family in Purmerend. The family wanted to keep the baby permanently. Hester and Paulien could not go along with this. Hester van Lennep recalls:

> Neither of us was married, and we had a baby in the house. An impos-sible situation. "I'll become its mother," I said. "Darn," says Paulien, 'I just discussed it with my mother, and I want to be the mother." So we sat bickering over who would take the child. Finally we tossed a coin. And she won, so she was the mother. I went to register the baby at the registry office in Amsterdam. I went to the window and didn't know how to register a child. So the man says: "Please give me your distribution card (*stamkaart*) and your ID," and I say: "Gee, I totally forgot all that." So I went back home. I walked the whole distance— it seemed like I walked forever. So I got my distribution card and my ID, and then went back to the same window. And the man said: "But ma'am, your friend didn't request extra food during her pregnancy." And I answered as follows: "Sir, she was so embarrassed." At that time you could still be embarrassed as an unmarried woman. Nowadays it's very different. . . . The man got up and came back with a huge stack of ration cards, so I got extra food retroactively! Even though my feet were killing me by now, I practically flew home.

They called the baby Marijke van Waasdijk, and she survived the war with-out having to go into hiding.

Like the other groups, the Trouw Group didn't inform the parents about their children's whereabouts. But on one occasion they broke the rule for a girl named Betty.

Hester van Lennep:

> The parents couldn't manage without the child and just had to know where she was. . . . We allowed them to take a walk with the child. Then they took her to Vondelpark, I don't remember exactly, or to the Amsterdam woods.

Sándor Baracs:

> And the father brought a snow-white fur coat for the child, so striking that everyone had to look, of course.

Hester:

And then they were arrested. . . . The father was killed.

Betty was brought to the child-care center and taken out by Mieke Mees or Iet van Dijk. She survived the war in Oudega in Friesland.

The rescue workers never revealed their private addresses. A Jewish child from Amsterdam-Oost was lodged temporarily in Amsterdam-Zuid with a Jewish couple who had a six-month-old baby. After some time, Mien Bouwman, a fellow worker of Gesina van der Molen, came to take the child to a permanent refuge. The couple, fearing, correctly, that the razzias would spread to Amsterdam-Zuid, had meanwhile decided to let their own child go into hiding. Mien Bouwman recalls:

> Then they said: "Can you give me an address so that if it starts here we can reach you for our child." And then I said no. Because I couldn't give an address. . . . And then I said: "I'm willing to come and pick up your child next week." Well, they weren't ready for that yet, and in retrospect I understand their attitude very well. But at the time I thought: "How stupid!"

Mien Bouwman took most of the Jewish children to the provinces of Groningen, Friesland, Drente, and Overijssel. In July 1943, she traveled to Groningen with a fourteen-month-old baby:

> He wasn't toilet-trained. . . . He was circumcised, so that wasn't very pleasant, of course. And back then you didn't have plastic pants and such. If a child peed, everything was soaked. Well, I wasn't too eager to change that baby. From Amersfoort until Zwolle an NSB woman [the NSB was the Dutch Nazi movement] was sitting across from me. The little boy didn't look at all Jewish. He had blond hair, so he didn't attract attention. And the woman said: "What a sweet child." And she started a whole story. Of course I had my own story ready as well: he was my sister's child, and he had to go to her family in Groningen. He came from Rotterdam. Anyway, the story had no flaws. But the strange thing was that I thought: "Either you or I will have to get off the train." Somewhere inside I was so incredibly angry! For I was thinking: "You bitch! You say he's such a sweet child. But if you had your way, you'd kill him." That's what I really thought.

Mien Bouwman recalls that the child sensed the tension and somehow controlled himself:

> Of course, you were afraid at times. . . . And sometimes that fear would be transmitted to the children. David didn't pee until I got to the farm

in Middelstum. Then I put him on a chair and he peed, and it ran across the floor like a river. That was *my* tension.

Mien Bouwman remembers taking Rivka (Riekje) to an address in Hoogeveen found via Van Aalderen, a member of the Trouw Group:

> Rivka Vleeschhouwer. . . . Yes, that's when I missed the train. I was supposed to leave her in Hoogeveen. Then I caught a later train . . . and it got dark in the train. And all the way from Amsterdam Rivka was singing Jewish songs. No matter what I did. . . . Mr. Baracs always said: "Just whisper them a story." Forget it! She kept on singing Jewish songs.

Sometimes things did not work out as planned when Mien Bouwman brought a child to what she thought would be a secure placement. For instance, she brought baby David to Middelstum in northern Groningen without preliminary consultation. She had no idea that the family was already taking care of a mentally handicapped family member:

> I didn't ask beforehand because the child had to go right then, so I simply went for it. It didn't work out. The child was very fearful, very restless. And these people couldn't handle it. So after a week there was a note for me in Groningen: "If you don't come and take this child away, we'll take it to my aunt." The aunt turned out to be the mother of a friend in the Trouw Group whom we often visited. . . . With the help of another girlfriend in Groningen, he ended up at this woman's sister, and that's where he stayed the whole war. . . . My contacts at Trouw knew that Jewish children had to get away. So then you'd say: "Guys, if you ever find out about a place where they might take in a Jewish child, keep it in mind and let me know."

Trouw maintained close ties with the LO, which delivered ration cards for most of the people who had gone into hiding with its help. When the CS-6 group with Hester van Lennep's nephews Gideon and Jan Karel Bois-sevain was rounded up on August 1, 1943, Hester and her operation were endangered because no one knew whether the young men would talk or not. Sándor Baracs begged Hester to go into hiding. After two weeks she let herself be persuaded. Hester hid out in the home of acquaintances in Amstelveen, and that very night the SD raided the skin care institute. Hester continued her resistance work in Amstelveen until the child-care center was closed.

## NOTES

1. L. de Jong, *Het Koninkrijk der Nederlanden in de Tweede Wereldoorlog* (1975), pt. VI, pp. 793–860.

2. The Oranje-Vrijbuiters (Orange Buccaneers) was an armed action group. At the end of August 1943, they were rounded up by the Sicherheitspolizei; eighteen members were condemned to death and executed by firing squad in February 1944. The group had connections with the Landelijke Organisatie voor hulp aan onderduikers (LO; National Organization for Assistance to Those in Hiding). See L. de Jong, *Het Koninkrijk der Nederlanden in de Tweede Wereldoorlog*, pt. VII, p. 739.

3. Telephone conversation with Clara Kien-Hes; see Sources.

4. Telephone conversation with Rut Matthijsen; see Sources.

5. Ibid.

6. Interview with Rut Matthijsen; see Sources.

7. Unless otherwise indicated, our information about the Arnhem branch comes from A. P. M. Cammaert, *Het verborgen front. Een geschiedenis van de illegaliteit in de provincie Limburg tijdens de Tweede Wereldoorlog* (Leeuwarden and Mechelen, 1994), pp. 663–668.

8. See, e.g., H. W. Poorterman, *Van Bezetting naar Bevrijding* (Enschede, 1978), pp. 139–142.

9. P. J. M. Dolfsma, Interview with Ph. H. Fiedeldij Dop; see Sources.

10. Ph. A. J. Mees, "Mieke Louwers-Mees en haar aandeel in de redding van Joodse kinderen in de oorlog 1940–1945," *Kroniek van de Stichting Geslacht Mees*, no. 25 (Rotterdam, July 1976).

11. Interview with Tineke Haak; see Sources.

12. Ibid.

13. Tineke Haak's written account of her experiences during the war; see Sources.

14. Ibid.

15. Unfortunately the list has been lost. The number 123 lived on in the memories of those involved.

16. Collection of N. J. P. Dohmen (Baarn).

17. A. P. M. Cammaert, *Het verborgen front*, XXVIII, pp. 421–422, 446.

18. Dohmen no longer remembers how the remaining 100 guilders was spent. For that matter, the anonymous author of the document "Tienray, verzet en bevrijding" reports that room and board came to 180 guilders per month. Source: anonymous, *Tienray, verzet en bevrijding. Het grote gezin van "Tante Hanna" en "Oom Nico,"* Collection of N. J. P. Dohmen (Baarn), p. 3.

19. Ph. A. J. Mees, "Mieke Louwers-Mees en haar aandeel in de redding van Joodse kinderen," p. 3.

20. A. P. M. Cammaert, *Het verborgen front*, p. 403.

21. Jan van Lieshout, "Jan Bosch. Vader van 33 kinderen," *Limburgs Dagblad* May 18, 1977.

22. See above, n. 7.

# FAITHFUL RESCUERS
## October 1943–May 1945

Now that all of Holland's Jews except for those in hiding had been deported, the rescuers faced the challenge of keeping the hidden children safe until liberation. No one doubted that liberation would come soon. Meanwhile, new places had to be found for any children who were having difficulties in their foster homes. Conditions were becoming more and more difficult. Most of the young men who were active in the rescue movement were no longer able to travel freely, since almost everyone in their age group could be picked up and sent to Germany for forced labor (*Arbeitseinsatz*); hundreds of thousands were already working there. There was a very severe food shortage in the western part of the Netherlands, and the local people could no longer do much for the Jewish children hidden in Friesland, Overijssel, and Limburg. The local branches of the movement had to make themselves self-sustaining.

## THE UTRECHT CHILDREN'S COMMITTEE

In October 1943, Jan Meulenbelt, An de Waard, and Manfred Lewinsohn were the only activists doing children's rescue work in Utrecht. Starting in September 1943, Rut Matthijsen was again responsible for managing the "office" as a place for meetings. By the beginning of 1944, Geert Lubberhuizen and Rut Matthijsen were deeply involved in the work of forging documents. What with this and the need to sell the illegal publications of De Bezige Bij, they no longer played a direct role in rescuing children.

Jan Meulenbelt was arrested in 1944. He was soon released, but Ger Kempe asked him to go into hiding and withdraw from other activities because he posed too great a risk for the organization. Jan went into hiding with relatives of Rut or his fiancée, where he stayed until liberation.

Frits Iordens and Anne Maclaine Pont moved into a small house adjacent to the Oude Kerk in Amsterdam. From there they continued rescuing downed Allied pilots and taking them to safety. On March 2, 1944 Frits was arrested in the Belgian town of Hasselt while guiding a group of Allied pilots. He tried to run, but was shot and died of his wounds. The news was an enormous shock for the Utrecht Group. An de Waard recalls:

> It was terrible. You were never certain about anyone. In the evening, if you said: "Well, see you soon, I hope," you meant *hoped*. . . . You were always anxious about whether your best friends would manage to stay alive.

Anne Maclaine Pont never recovered from this loss. She lived through the time until liberation as if in a fog. After the war Frits was buried on the rural estate of Eerde near Ommen that he loved. Anne died in May of 1969 after an accident.

James van Beusekom remained in Amsterdam, where he did resistance work but was no longer active in children's rescue activities. In August of 1944 he was caught while in hiding and was sent to the camp at Amersfoort. From there he was sent to the Neuengamme concentration camp and later to Hamburg. He died before the liberation.[1]

An de Waard began working with Ger Kempe in the Packard espionage group. Together with her sorority sister Titia Timmenga, she continued, all through the Hunger Winter of 1944–1945, to take care of children in Utrecht:

> Together we did the work in Utrecht, distributing supplies. Because somehow there was always something to be had. We'd suddenly receive the message: "Fifty red cabbages have arrived. Could you deliver them to various addresses?" Or the message: "There's a bread distribution, can you come to pick up the loaves?" Or: "There is a meat distribution," meaning that there had been a clandestine slaughter. In Utrecht there was a group of Jews who were engaged in this sort of thing. They just bicycled around without wearing a star. There was a Mr. Hartog. . . . I don't know whether the group had a name or not. Hartog was originally a butcher, so he could butcher illegally. And then we would be notified to come and get meat. We had a little four-wheeled cart, and we all happily walked along, and we went to all our addresses. Some of them were very far away. And since we no longer had bicycles, we had to do it all on foot.

Since Ankie Stork's network in Overijssel was well-organized, she often helped out in Utrecht after the death of Frits Iordens. There she worked for

Manfred Lewinsohn as a courier. Manfred often took the children to the Stork residence in Nijverdal. Ankie recalls: "I didn't know that his name was Lewinsohn. We called each other Manfred and Ankie. That was all there was to it."

On April 19, 1944, after a ten-year engagement, Geert Lubberhuizen and Willy van Reenen got married. Matthijsen remembers:

> We went to the reception in Velp, and to our great surprise there were two fraternity employees, as we called them, in uniform. . . . They were old fellows, so they probably weren't running too much of a risk. . . . Besides, if I remember correctly, Willy was a pharmacist's assistant and had good connections in circles where people had supplies of one hundred percent ethanol. . . . So they wangled a lot of it. She made plenty of drinks, diluted three to one with some essence in them—you could still get that: old jenever [Dutch gin]. It was delicious. And I think that we were quite under the influence for a few hours.

Geert and Willy moved to Amsterdam, and Dora Matthijsen was brought in as a liaison between Amsterdam (Geert Lubberhuizen) and Utrecht (Rut Matthijsen). Following his predecessor Lubberhuizen, Rut Matthijsen moved into Maarten Vink's attic. There he continued his forgery work.

On Monday, May 29, 1944, Ankie Stork stashed a suitcase and a handbag with ten thousand food stamps printed by Rut Matthijsen in Jitske and Henk Eding's place in Utrecht because her own room was no longer safe. When she returned at half past seven that evening to pick up her things, she was welcomed by the Dutch SD. The house had been betrayed, and several people had been trapped. After several hours she was able to get to her handbag without being noticed and flushed the food stamps down the toilet. Ankie recalls:

> . . . of course, I had to explain why I had come there so late that evening. The only thing they found in the suitcase was the *Wilhelmus* [the Dutch national anthem] printed by the publisher of the *Bezige Bij*. Of course that was a strictly forbidden item and was incriminating. But that was all they found. . . . They took me with them; after six weeks I was released. They couldn't pin anything on me, and the others didn't say anything either.

Olga Hudig visited her in prison:

> I thought: "Oh, they've caught her too." So I didn't want to say anything. . . . I didn't know how much I could trust the police. . . .

One policeman who could be trusted asked me: "Do you know this person?" I didn't want to say yes . . . But then Olga turned and waved at me behind the glass wall. Then I knew that it was all right. And I said: "Yes, I know her. She's the sister of one of my very good friends." I thought: "That's very neutral; it should be all right." Then Olga asked me if they had found anything. And I was able to make it clear that they didn't have to worry about me. That was good, and it was of course important for them to know that.

Ankie's interrogators asked about her connection with the Edings. Fortunately she was prepared for this question. She and Jitske had agreed to say that Ankie had come to the house to check on Jitske's six-year-old daughter, who was ill with pneumonia. She stuck to the story. No one asked anything about the *Wilhelmus* pamphlet. Ankie was released. Jitske Eding was taken to Vught, where she met Hetty and Gisela. Henk Eding died in a camp in Germany.

Things weren't going well for the group. That August Manfred Lewinsohn was arrested. He was taken to Vught and ended up in the cell above Hetty Voûte. Via the "pipe telephone" he informed her that Geert Lubberhuizen and Rut Matthijsen had put aside two copies of every issue of the *Bezige Bij*, one for her and one for Gisela. The news cheered Hetty enormously. Manfred also told Hetty that his arrest had nothing to do with rescuing children. Two weeks later he was taken to Westerbork because he was a Jew, and from there he was deported to Bergen-Belsen in September. At the end of the war the Nazis began evacuating the camp. Manfred Lewinsohn died on March 14, 1945 during one of those hellish evacuation transports. Meanwhile, Sara Blok-Roozenboom replaced him in watching over the small group of children in Amsterdam.

At the end of August, Ger Kempe was arrested on a train while traveling to the south. He was released and celebrated the liberation in Utrecht with Rut and Dora Matthijsen.

Truitje van Lier continued her work as long as possible. She and Jet refused to flee when danger threatened. They were unwilling to run out on the children in Kindjeshaven. Truitje thought of a way to protect them: She took in some babies fathered by German soldiers who had been transferred. In the absence of the father, they were the responsibility of the *Ortskommandant* (army commander) of Utrecht, and he placed them in Kindjeshaven. Truitje recalls:

If people came in saying: "There are Jews around here," I would say: "Yes, that does seem to be the case. It's because of those Jewish mothers, and I can't help it." But if they insisted and said: "We're going to take them away," I'd say: "Go ahead, but then they'll all have to go. And don't forget, I'll have to warn the *Ortskommandant* because he's their guardian." Well, that usually made them back down. And I always said: "They'll all have to go. If you take one of them, they'll all have to go. I'll put them all out on the street. You'll have to work it out."

Sometimes circumstances forced drastic measures. Once, for instance, Truitje and Jet were confronted with a Jew-hunter looking for a Jewish child who was staying at Kindjeshaven. Truitje remembers:

There was a police inspector named Smorenburg.[2] And he was so nice, he helped Jews. Oh, he helped them so well. He'd take all their money. And when the money was gone, he would blackmail them for a while through the children, and then would turn in the whole bunch. On one occasion this friendly guy was after two children, one of whom was with us as far as I know. The child was named Pim de Wit. . . . As long as the child was with us, we figured that Smorenburg might show up. I decided: "He's not going to get this child. He isn't getting any child!" I would station myself on the stairs, with a solid, heavy frying pan ready in a corner. And I planned to beat his brains in with that pan. How we would then have gotten him out was another matter, but I think I would have done it. . . . I was so angry and so outraged. I might really have done it. The resistance would have helped me to get him out. But it didn't happen, fortunately. He never came.

As a toddler Truitje had lived through the First World War, and, as she remembered:

Hunger is part of war. In the beginning things may be better than expected, but before it's over there will be hunger. I knew that from my earliest youth. . . . So I started stocking up whenever I had extra rations. We bought canned butter with the butter coupons. And with the bread coupons we bought a sort of hardtack that you could keep a very long time. And you could also get cans of meat when it was still reasonable. Everything that was left over went into a closet. And you couldn't see it at all. We taped a small strip of paper over it. . . . We had a nice stockpile there.

In mid-August of 1944 there was a raid on Kindjeshaven. Since the beginning of the summer Truitje had been living in Zeist with her fiancé, who was hiding there and was in poor health. Jet took over for her at Kindjeshaven and stayed there overnight. During the raid, Jet repeated the threat that if even one child was taken, she would turn all the children out into the

street, including those of the *Ortskommandant*. She pretended to know nothing about anything else. The agents, intimidated, just left.

After this, Truitje and her fiancé moved to Culemborg, and Jet continued to run Kindjeshaven. In February 1945 she could no longer keep
Kindjeshaven open. The electricity had been turned off. The non-Jewish
children were returned to the guardianship board, and she found foster families for the Jewish children. Most of them ended up with the families of people who worked at Kindjeshaven. Jet was able to give each child a generous
portion of the canned food supply. All of the Jewish children were lodged
without any problems.

## HUNGER

In the western part of the country, everyone was preoccupied with the
search for food. Interest in the *Bezige Bij* began to flag. But the forging of
documents had to go on, and it cost money. Rut Matthijsen would bicycle
to Amsterdam to get money from someone at the National Assistance Fund
(Nationaal Steunfonds).

By October 1944, it was no longer safe for Rut Matthijsen to continue
forging documents in Maarten Vink's attic. His equipment was moved to the
attic of a store on Janskerkhof with the help of the two owners, the Fels
brothers. Rut managed somehow to get through the Hunger Winter.

When Utrecht was liberated, Rut and some other members of the Utrecht Student Association tried to reopen the association's building as quickly
as possible. They took back things belonging to the association from a bar
that had been frequented by German soldiers. Rut describes:

> They had furniture and glassware that belonged to the student associ-
> ation. So we went there with the police and a cart: "Let's get the stuff
> out of there." And everything we pointed at—it was like a command.
> Nothing was really checked, but we made sure that we had some glasses
> and plates, and that we at least got our chairs back.

Before long, the students emerging from hiding were once again able to get
a glass of beer at the student association.

## BRANCHES IN THE NORTH, EAST, AND SOUTH

How did the branches of the Utrecht Group in Friesland, Overijssel, and
Arnhem fare?

In Friesland, clothing and shoes were supplied locally, often by the foster parents themselves. If needed, the LO provided new addresses. As far as is known, all the children who were placed there survived the war. This is also true for the children placed in the south of the country by the Utrecht Group (with one exception: a child in the Maastricht area was betrayed and fell into German hands).

It was hard work. Sometimes a child had to be transferred twenty times, as in the case of Lottie Broekman. On January 12, 1943, on her eighth birthday, Paul Terwindt took Lottie to a Protestant minister, W. J. Val, in a village near Arnhem. She went to school there, and everything was fine. In November German troops were billeted in the family's house. Minister Val asked for Lottie to be transferred. Either Paul Terwindt or Tini van de Bilt took Lottie to Venlo, to a father and his sons, who sometimes treated her roughly, then to a convent school, where a priest took her on his lap and groped her, then to a country estate near Maasbracht, where the aristocratic foster parents were too eager to convert her; next she was on a refrigerated barge in which she went up and down the Maas River for a week, and so on. She was uncontrollable by the time all this came to an end, but fortunately she was reunited with her mother after the liberation. Paul and Tini's regular visits had been the only constant in her life. They brought her ration cards and even letters from her mother. Terwindt protected her with his own body when British planes bombed the train that was taking them to yet another possible hiding address.

From October 1943 on, the Overijssel branch operated independently of Utrecht. Ankie Stork continued to deliver ration cards, but after the summer of 1944 this was no longer necessary. In the Weversnest in Nieuwebrug near Ommen, Adri Knappert took care of a constantly changing group of children. By February 1944, nine or more Jewish children had been noticed, and people were talking, so Adri had to move. Ankie Stork found a new accommodation, a huge summer home called De Eelerberg that belonged to F. A. Vening Meinesz, one of her professors at Utrecht who also happened to be a friend of her parents. The children were moved to the new place in a horse-drawn cart.

Adri recalls the move:

> The odd thing is that you don't worry in a case like that. You don't even think about it. We crossed the heath on foot with the children to a farmer's cart that would take us away. All the way we sat in the cart and sang songs.

In the end thirteen children were housed in De Eelerberg. Everything went well. One day Adri was warned that officers of the *Grüne Polizei* (German police) were on the way to De Eelerberg by car. She and the children hid deep in the woods until late that night. The *Polizei* just drove past.

After the children left Nieuwebrug, Ankie concentrated her efforts in Nijverdal, Hellendoorn, and Lemele. Early in 1944, she made contact with an organization headed by Leendert Overduin, a Calvinist minister in Enschede. This organization is estimated to have hidden seven hundred Jews, primarily from the surrounding region.[3] Several times Ankie took people in hiding from Overduin, and vice versa. Ankie was arrested on May 29, 1944 and was not released until mid-July. The Jewish children in Nijverdal received no help from the resistance during this time. Later, even when she herself had to go into hiding, Ankie managed nonetheless to continue taking care of her charges who were in hiding.

At De Eelerberg Adri worried about a frightened neighbor across the street who kept asking her to move elsewhere. Eventually, she took the thirteen children in her care for a six-week vacation at a summer camp called Zonneoord in Ede. From there she went out on her own, without Ankie, to look for new places. The children were distributed all over the eastern part of the country.

## THE AMSTERDAM STUDENT GROUP

After September 1943, the influx of Jewish children from Amsterdam to Friesland, Limburg, and other outlying areas decreased. After the railroad strike in September 1944, the organization split into smaller, independently operating divisions that Meerburg and Van Zeytveld in Amsterdam were barely involved with.

### AMSTERDAM

Children who ran into difficulties in one foster home in Amsterdam would be placed in another, but most of the children remained where they were. Since the Sneek (Friesland) and Tienray (Limburg) branches did not accept help from the LO, Wouter van Zeytveld had to make sure that there was money for them.

At the end of 1943, Hanns Rauter, the German chief of police in the Netherlands, came up with a plan to use starvation as a way to force the many people in hiding out of their hiding-places. To this end, he introduced the Second Distribution Card, or *Tweede Distributiestamkaart* (TD), which had to be added to the ID card. Of course people in hiding could not get one legally, and this meant that they were no longer able to obtain food. The Second Distribution Card was introduced around the middle of 1944. It was a great failure because the LO was prepared. Thanks to fraud by the civil registrars at many city halls, the number of local inhabitants rose by leaps and bounds. Wouter van Zeytveld had a contact in the municipal registry of Amsterdam who added fictitious children to the rolls who were then issued Second Distribution Cards. As a result, Wouter was not dependent on the LO or the armed action group. The resistance workers themselves needed ration cards. Krijn van den Helm made sure that the LO in Friesland reserved ration cards for the Amsterdam Group. He had begun doing this early in 1944 when the food situation in the western part of the country became acute. Meerburg saw to it that his own people did not raid the trough that was fairly well-stocked thanks to Van den Helm. Wouter van Zeytveld remembers:

> Piet was very principled about this. I thought it was great. Once there was a shortage of milk. And we had milk coupons and difficult situations because of that Second Distribution Card. I still remember vividly that he blocked all those milk coupons so that no one could get to them. . . . In the resistance there were, of course, all kinds of people who had extra cards, and they sometimes used them for themselves. . . . Piet was on top of it; he didn't want them to be misused.

On April 29, 1944 Piet Meerburg and Hansje van Loghem were married in Laren in the province of Noord-Holland. Because they did not want to be married by the city's NSB (pro-German) mayor, they went looking for a "good" civil servant. During the marriage ceremony, the mayor angrily stood outside the door and listened. Arriving late, Wouter van Zeytveld saw the mayor and immediately took off. The couple spent their honeymoon in Tienray.

At the end of 1943, Wouter van Zeytveld and Tineke Haak moved to Sarphatistraat in Amsterdam. They took in four adult Jews. In addition, Arnold van Zuilen, a half-Jewish former high school classmate of Wouter, often stayed with them. Van Zuilen worked in the resistance and sometimes gave Wouter information about Jewish children who were having difficulties with their foster families in Amsterdam.

As mentioned in Chapter 3, Virrie Cohen had to go into hiding at the end of September 1943. For a while she went underground in the maternity clinic of the Lutherse Diaconessen Hospital in Amsterdam, where she worked as a nurse. Virrie recalls:

Every week I had a day off, and I didn't know where to go. . . . So I went upstairs to my room and acted as if I were away. I had to pretend somehow. It wasn't easy. But we worked so terribly hard there that spending your day off in bed wasn't so bad.

Once, when there was a raid, Virrie simply walked out of the hospital so as not to endanger anyone if she was caught. In a roundabout way she ended up with Wouter and Tineke, and thus became the fifth person hiding out in their house. Two weeks later Alice Brunner took her to Tienray.

Soon afterwards the police raided Wouter and Tineke's house. Everyone was well hidden, and Wouter had good forged papers. But the address could no longer be considered safe. Wouter and Tineke moved into the house on Oude Kerks Square that Anne Maclaine Pont had vacated after Frits Iordens's death. They spent the summer there.

The fake papers that Piet Meerburg got from Geert Lubberhuizen were as safe as Wouter van Zeytveld's. Meerburg worked for the Dutch Railways as a supervisor in the signaling system. This was a big help to the transportation budget, because he was able to travel for free.

All rail traffic stopped after the railroad strike on September 18, 1944. The Amsterdam students no longer had a role in rescuing children because they were unable to get to the branches in other areas. Everyone saw that the end of the war was approaching, and that the main thing was to keep themselves and their few charges in and around Amsterdam alive. This turned out to be quite difficult, so much so that Wouter van Zeytveld approached the National Assistance Fund (Nationaal Steunfonds), which had been established by then, with a request for assistance. This brought in a small amount of money.

Around September 5, 1944, known as "Dolle Dinsdag" (Mad Tuesday), the day that hundreds of NSB members tried to flee to Germany, Wouter van Zeytveld and Tineke Haak decided that the upstairs apartment in the large house in Sarphatistraat was safe again and moved back there. That is where they endured the Hunger Winter. In the last month of the war they took in some people who had to leave their hiding-place in Wieringermeer because the polder was being flooded. Wouter and Tineke celebrated the liberation in Sarphatistraat and were married when the war ended.

After the cessation of rail traffic on September 18, Alice Brunner settled in Utrecht to look after her mother. Since she had to resign from the Amsterdam Student Group when she moved, she no longer received the minimal extras afforded by rescue work. From then on she had to scrounge for food to stave off starvation:

First we'd go to the immediate area, to Bunnik and later farther east, around the Veluwe. And I also went across the IJssel bridge several times. Toward Overijssel and Friesland. . . . I'd just go to a farm and ask if I could buy a pound of butter or a bag of rye. Most of the time it was possible. And sometimes I'd stay overnight; then I'd be given a plate of delicious food. . . . The best way to describe hunger is that you can't think about anything but food.

Alice never had hunger edema. But she stood on the roof of her parents' house, crying with happiness, when large bags of Swedish white flour came down from the skies at the end of April 1945.

WIJDENES

There was more food in Wijdenes than in the large cities. Meerburg and his group were unable to offer much help to Cees and Lien Kracht.

BY BOAT TO GET BREAD

In February 1945, Meerburg and Van Zeytveld helped Truus Weismuller take groups of starving children from Amsterdam to the relative abundance of Friesland. This was a completely legal undertaking even though the groups always included a few Jewish children. Each time a few hundred children would be taken by boat to get bread. Tineke Haak remembers one such trip:

> It was a very tense journey. All the children were very ill and throwing up. Almost everyone was throwing up. So there was a lot to do. And then we finally arrived in Sneek, but we hadn't arranged anything because all our contacts had been severed.

Nina Mesdag adds:

> The boat was moored at Harinxsmakade, almost behind our house. . . . Well, when the hold was opened . . . those children who were sitting there—it was really terrible. Just awful! And my mother said: "We don't have any addresses, but I don't think it matters. I'll just ring doorbells." And then she rang all the doorbells on the quay and said: "Come with me for a moment." And before you knew it, all the children had homes. There was one child left who couldn't walk anymore, and my parents took the poor thing home with them.

Looking back, Tineke knows what motivated her:

I did resistance work purely and simply because of the persecution of the Jews. Of course I was also against Nazism in general, aside from the Jews. But I'm not sure I would have been involved so intensely and so completely if there had been no persecution of the Jews.

## TIENRAY

In 1943 and 1944, Hanna van de Voort, Nico Dohmen, and Kurt ("Ben") Löwenstein developed the Tienray branch into an independent enterprise. Following the example of Piet Meerburg, they wanted nothing to do with the LO. This meant that ration cards had to come from Amsterdam. But in Tienray there was practically no need for ration cards. The only thing people might be interested in were sugar coupons. And these were extremely difficult to get. Eighty percent of the families never received ration cards. This meant that the children's material care was wholly in the hands of the foster families. Nico and Kurt were able to keep in regular touch with the families until October of 1944. Nico Dohmen recalls:

> Those people had infinitely exaggerated faith in us. They really thought that we knew everything. And of course at times you did have to act as if you knew everything. In order to be convincing.

Aside from being separated from their parents, the transitions from city to countryside and from kosher to non-kosher were big shocks for some children. Nico Dohmen has kept the following letter, written in the spring of 1944:

> Dear Daddy and Mommy,
>
> Right now I'm somewhere in Limburg at a farmer's house. I don't know exactly where I am—I just got here. Don't look at how I'm writing because I'm very nervous. I still have lots of trouble with my fanny—lots of yucky stuff is still coming out. First I was with emergency people because there was nothing for me. But I said that I could never get used to it. And I cried so much when they brought me here. The woman is nice—I don't know the man yet. Maybe I'll get another address. I can't go to school. I have to work here on the farm—peeling potatoes, sweeping up, digging up potatoes, and all sorts of nasty things. I hope to be with you soon. It's Saturday afternoon—I just ate a piece of bread with pork. I think it's terrible; I think it's so very nasty. I liked it with the emergency people—but not now. Monday this letter will be sent and someone will come to visit me. Later—after dinner—I'll write more. Bye-bye and a kiss from Annie.
>
> I wish I could be with middle-class people—it is terrible here, yuck.

The trip went OK.

How is Mrs. Vredenburg?

It's Sunday and I'm not allowed to mend my sock—I think they're terrible people. You eat bread from the table.

Still, this ten-year-old girl adjusted quickly. Nico Dohmen can't remember having any other problems with her. Nico tried to arrange for all of the children up to age twelve to attend school. The report card of a twelve-year-old boy has been saved; he had the highest grades in Catholic subjects: attending Holy Mass and Catechism.

Nico Dohmen recalls:

> Practically all the children between seven and twelve went to school there. . . . But there was one problem: all the schools were Catholic. There wasn't one non-religious school. . . . Of course that created the problem that we had to make it clear to the children that they had to pray along with everyone else, cross themselves, and not show that they weren't Catholic.

This did not always work. Ten-year-old Chaim Lindner told everyone at school that he was Jewish and asked them not to mention it to anyone else. Nico and Kurt took Chaim to another school and prepped him carefully. He promised to follow their instructions. When Leo, Chaim's older brother, heard that Chaim was at a Catholic school, he protested so fiercely that the family where he was staying warned Hanna. Nico visited Leo at the end of a hard day:

> The minute he sees me he starts screaming and screeching and kicking my shins and lashing out. The boy was completely hysterical. So the first thing I did was to whack him and say: "Are you completely out of your mind? Now sit down and howl, and then tell me what's the matter." Well, then it tumbled out: "You filthy swine! Trying to make my brother into a Roman Catholic! I'm going to report myself to the police because I'd rather get caught than have my brother become a Catholic." It was impossible to reason with him. The boy was so completely mixed up. And I was dead-tired that day. And I'd had it too. I said: "OK, Leo, go and do it. Go to the police, report yourself. And report me as well. Because I've had it!" Then we went for a stroll. I didn't do anything. . . . It was really kind of nasty, but I needed to unburden myself. I told him about the awful stuff I had to deal with. Why everything was going wrong. Well, we walked back to the house. There wasn't another peep out of him. The problems were gone for good.

FIGURE 12
*Home of the Van de Voort family*
From the collection of Mrs. W. E. M. Kötter-Van de Voort (Maastricht)

As has already been mentioned, far more boys than girls had been sent to Tienray. Hanna, Nico, and Kurt often fell back on the Nabben family, who lived in Swolgen, when they had boys who were difficult to place:

> Once we gave a girl as a bonus to a couple who already had two boys. The family's attitude was perfect, and they had nothing but boys. So we said: "Well, Mrs. Nabben, the next one coming to you will be a girl." . . . On December 5, 1943 we took Rietje Dasberg, a three-year-old girl, to them. It was the biggest favor we could do them. Finally they had a girl, in addition to their own sons and two Jewish boys in hiding. They were so thankful for her.

In December 1943, the Tienray threesome were asked to find a place for a Jewish couple with a three-year-old child who had run into difficulties in Oldenbroek (Gelderland). Nico passed the word that the three were welcome and said he would pick them up in Nijmegen. This was the only time he had ventured outside the area of the remote villages near Tienray since his arrival there. Nico recalls:

It was—on purpose—the first or second day of Christmas, because the Germans were so busy celebrating *Weihnacht* that they ignored almost everything. The plan was that at eleven in the morning I would go to the second platform under the clock in Nijmegen. A couple with a small boy and the person accompanying them would be there. As soon as I approached them, the escort would leave and I would take over. . . . I arrived a few minutes ahead of time, and I saw them from a hundred meters away. But guess who was standing next to them as escort? My own father. So we didn't follow the plan, and instead we talked.

## HUNTING JEWS

The Germans found out that a large number of Jews had found a refuge in the small border villages of Brabant and Limburg. The subject was raised at an NSB meeting in Venray, and a series of raids followed. Eleven people were caught in Oirlo. An even worse disaster was prevented by a tip from a village policeman in Meerlo:

> After the raid in Oirlo we received a flood of requests asking us to find new places for the children who were being hidden. It goes without saying that we often worked until deep in the night. It was a time of worry, turmoil, and action. Sometimes it seemed as if transferring the poor refugees would never end, especially when foster parents turned up late at night.[4]

Hanna and Nico were unaware that Lucien Nahon, an inspector for the Landstand (a Nazi agricultural organization) who was staying in a hotel in Tienray, was a spy. Nahon ferreted out the addresses of foster families in Tienray and the neighboring villages of Oirlo, Broekhuizenvorst, and Castenray, and reported them to O. Couperus, the chief of police in Venlo.[5] who then sent the following report to the Aussendienststelle der SA und SS (the SA and SS field office):

> My informant told me the following:
> Miss Hanna van de Voort who lives in Tienray is the secretary of an organization that puts up Jewish children for a fee of 100 guilders per month, per child.[6]
> Two Jewish children are living with this Van de Voort. In addition, the following children are also being put up at:
> Bartels, one girl, approximately 11 years old.
> Hendriks, one boy, approximately 12 years old
> P. Nabben, one boy, approximately 9 years old

Mrs. Gielen, 2 small children
Mooren, one child
Janssen (father of a mailman) one child
Van Geffen, one child
Kruysberg, one child.[7]

As a result, on the night of July 30, 1944, a disaster without equal in the children's rescue effort took place in Tienray. The police raided the home of Hanna van de Voort. Nico escaped via the roof and was able to warn several foster families in Tienray. However, he could not prevent the capture and deportation of seven children.[8] After the liberation, Hanna van de Voort charged Lieutenant Van Es, the policeman who carried out the raid, with the murder of:

> (1) Floortje de Pauw, 8 years old; (2) Wim de Pauw, 7 years old; (3) Louis van Wezel, 7 years old; (4) Dick van Wezel, 10 years old. After staying with me in a cell for two days, the De Pauw and Van Wezel children were sent to Westerbork and then to Auschwitz, where they were murdered, according to the latest report. Bep Aldewereld, 19 years old, was sent to Westerbork and then to Bergen-Belsen and was repatriated after liberation.
>
> Therefore I accuse Lieutenant Van Es of the murder of four underage Jewish children.

The traitor was sentenced to five years in prison. Bep Aldewereld was the only one of the children to survive. Six foster parents and Hanna van de Voort were arrested. Under interrogation Hanna admitted that she had given evacuation documents to the six others. As a result the six were released on August 2. When interrogated, they all stuck to the story that they knew nothing except that the children were evacuees from Rotterdam, and they had proof. Nico recalls:

> One of the fathers who returned from the interrogation in Eindhoven said that Hanna would be taken to Ravensbrück. . . . they kept asking about me. And she couldn't convince them that I was an evacuee from Rotterdam. That was the problem. . . . Then we succeeded in getting in touch with Mieke Mees. Mieke Mees dashed off to Eindhoven.

Mieke Mees was a beautiful woman. She visited the Eindhoven office of the SD and flirted with the commander. Mieke indicated that she would be glad to go out with him some evening, but made it clear that she was rather put out about the imprisonment of a naïve, simple woman from Tienray who had nothing to do with anything. As a result Hanna was released. Mieke did not show up for her date with the SD officer.

Another raid failed. On August 13, 1944, several SD members from The Hague went to Broekhuizenvorst to arrest the Peres family: father, mother, and two grown sons. But word of the impending raid had preceded them, and the family was transferred elsewhere. Sometimes warnings came in time to save people.

During a chance meeting in Amsterdam, Meerburg and Van Zeytveld asked the NV to help find new housing for children from Tienray whose addresses were known to the police. Many children had to sleep outdoors until new places were found. Two slightly older boys remained with their foster families but from then spent the nights away from the farmhouse. One of them, Tom Stein, remembers:

> The farmer was too scared to have me stay there. He got more and more frightened. It was very understandable. I mean his family's life was at stake. Yet at the same time I needed to eat. And so I made this arrangement that I would spend the nights in the forest and I would spend the daytime working for him, but I would stay away from the farmhouse. . . . I usually met a bunch of two or three young Dutch guys, who were trying to avoid forced labor. And so we would usually meet at a certain prearranged place. We had a kind of an underground shelter built with straw and we slept there. . . . The Germans were afraid to go into the forest because they were worried about the underground there.

## ON THE FRONT LINES

Later, as the Allied forces advanced in the south, Tom's situation became even more frightening. The front lines were located so nearby that German soldiers were quartered with many of the local families. Tom was working on the farm when the German quartermasters came into the farmyard. A German field kitchen was billeted at the farm. Now Tom was stuck there:

> We just said I was a son. And they believed it. . . . I was afraid to leave. I would have liked to hide in the forest, but I knew that if I hid in the forest, I would endanger the life of the farmer and his daughters. Because the Germans . . . would have been suspicious about why the so-called son had disappeared. So I stayed there the whole time.

Every day Tom had to peel potatoes for the regiment. He saw dead soldiers laid out, and wounded ones receiving first aid. He was scared to death that the soldiers would become suspicious. Still, there was nothing to do but stay and make sure to play his role. This situation continued until the liberation.

> I was living right on the farm together with the Germans, doing the
> farm work for at least two months, I think, trying to avoid interacting
> with the Germans. Unfortunately there was . . . one German who had
> designs on me, who made a play for me. I thought at the time that he
> suspected I was Jewish and wanted to find out whether I was circum-
> cised. It was only after the war that I realized that this guy was a homo-
> sexual who was trying to make a play for me. I managed to avoid it.
> It was very uncomfortable but I managed to avoid it.

Tom will never forget the liberation, which finally came at the end of
November.

> I remember it because it was so frightening. We were very scared,
> because we were under the impression that usually, before the libera-
> tion, the SS would come through, and naturally everyone was terrified
> by them. There was major shelling going on for, I think, more than a
> day. Very frightening. We saw the Germans retreat. . . . We were liber-
> ated by a British and, I believe, an Irish regiment. . . . I was just terribly
> excited, deliriously happy, and felt wonderful about it. . . . I was very
> proud that I was Jewish and that I had survived the war. And then,
> just at that time, I actually overheard some of the soldiers making anti-
> Semitic remarks, and that was a major blow for me. It was a terrible
> disappointment.

At the end of August 1944, an Allied bomber was shot down above Blerick. The bombardier and the pilot parachuted out, and managed to come
down near Meerloo. Kurt Löwenstein, who had seen them jump, took them
to the Van de Voort house, where they stayed for a few weeks. Then they
spent some time at an intermediate address and were taken to the convent of
Tienray.[9]

This incident shows that even the Tienray trio gradually deviated from
the original concept of devoting themselves to helping Jewish children.
Nonetheless, the children were their principal activity—at least until the
front arrived.

After September 1944, when the forces commanded by General Bernard
L. Montgomery were unable to capture the bridge across the Rhine at Arnhem, the liberated area of the Netherlands was restricted to a narrow strip of
territory from Eindhoven to Nijmegen. In early October the front was near
Venray and Overloon, where the Allied troops got bogged down in the
mud. Hanna, Nico, Kurt, and the Jewish children in their care were now
virtually on the battlefield. The Germans urged the inhabitants to leave.
Many people did just that. Some asked Nico for advice, and he told them:

Don't go away, stay here, otherwise you'll end up following the front, and you'll be miserable. Most of them took his advice. A seven-year-old girl staying with one of Hanna's neighbors was killed by a shell burst. Almost all of the 123 Jews put up by the trio were liberated in 1944. One of them was Virrie Cohen, who had been brought to Tienray by Kurt ("Ben") Löwenstein as the Allied troops approached. Virrie and Hanna, dressed in nurse's uniforms (Virrie didn't really have anything else), ventured out into the street in the daytime to help where it was needed. Nico and Kurt buried many a dead villager.

Nico Dohmen and Anselm van de Voort managed to save the "Madonna of Tienray" from destruction when the Germans planted demolition charges in the church. The Madonna was a holy statue dating from 1440, crafted shortly after the apparition of the Holy Virgin in Tienray.[10] They hid it under the floor of the Van de Voort house. On November 21, 1944 the church was blown up.[11]

During the period when the front ran through Tienray, many houses were uninhabitable because of the fighting. Many of the children had to be taken to other places. Nico and Kurt preferred, when possible, to move the whole family, and not just the Jewish foster child. That way the attachment between child and foster parents was not disturbed. Since there was no real administration, a few children were unaccounted for. However, most of the foster parents reported back to the trio right after the end of hostilities.

As far as we know, only one of the children hidden in Tienray was baptized during the occupation. Hanna, Nico, and Kurt opposed this practice. The exception was a very special case. It took place in November 1944, right before the liberation of Tienray, and the child in question was a sixteen-month-old baby named Herman. The baby was hidden in nearby Swolgen and, along with some other children, came down with diphtheria. Since there was no serum, Herman and the others seemed doomed to die. Seventy-four-year-old Anselm van de Voort, risking his life, made the two-hour walk to the convent in Horst, but they did not have any serum either. Finally, Hanna van de Voort and Virrie Cohen decided to chance going to Arcen, across the Maas River. They bicycled to Lottum. Virrie recalls:

> The Germans were in the castle of Arcen, and somehow we knew that they had serum. And Hanna wanted to get that serum for the children. So we went to the Germans [in Lottum] and we got a *Bescheinigung* [crossing permit]: a piece of paper that said we were allowed to cross the Maas, which wasn't allowed at all. I got that paper too; they didn't know that I was Jewish.

Virrie continues:

> Taking that piece of paper, we crossed the Maas in a small boat. Then
> someone shot at us. I don't know if it was the British or the Germans.
> We lay flat in the boat. When we arrived in Arcen we got the serum,
> and we grabbed whatever we could get our hands on in the way of
> candies and licorice—everything that was lying around there—which
> the Germans had stolen anyway. And then back again in that little boat.
> And then we returned with the serum, but one very young baby died
> anyway.

While Hanna and Virrie were gone, Nico and Kurt stayed in touch with
the foster family. When they learned that Herman would not live much
longer, Nico rushed to Swolgen. He recalls:

> It became very clear that Herman was near death. He was suffocating
> slowly but surely. . . . I was with them, and the foster mother said: "I
> can't bear the thought that Herman won't go to heaven because he
> isn't baptized. He is a child of mine too. Can't I please baptize him?"
> And I said: "You have taken him into your house to save him. If you
> think that Herman can only be happy if you baptize him, then you
> may do so. But only do it when he is actually dying. You shouldn't
> do it before then." Well, that's what happened. . . . Herman's mother
> came back from a concentration camp. . . . The conversation with her
> wasn't too pleasant. And finally they had him exhumed because he had
> to be buried in a Jewish cemetery. I thought it was so terrible for those
> foster parents. Because as they saw it they were only doing what they
> thought was good. . . . I sometimes get angry about it. If there is a God,
> why does he arrange things that way? Couldn't he have done it differ-
> ently?

The last two months before the liberation were a nightmare in the Van
de Voort household because so many people were staying there. In addition
to Hanna and her father Anselm van de Voort, Nico Dohmen, and Virrie
Cohen, the house sheltered, among others, two very old and dazed ladies.
They had been fired at while fleeing from the home for the aged in Vier-
lingsbeek and had been picked up from the streets and taken to the Van de
Voort house by Nico and Kurt. Unfortunately they were covered with lice.
For nights on end everyone slept together in an airless cellar.

A few days before the liberation, Nico decided that it would be safer for
him to pitch his tent elsewhere. Together with two American pilots, he left
for the convent of Tienray, where a hiding place had been arranged near the
heater. They were barely installed when some Germans came to inspect the

convent, but they did not find the Americans. Meanwhile, the convent gradually filled up with homeless people. In the infirmary, where Hanna and Virrie were working as nurses, soldiers from both sides were cared for. Mien van de Voort estimates the total number of people in the convent to have been "several hundred." Together they awaited the approach of the Allied troops.

The day before the area was liberated, Hanna, Nico, and Virrie decided that it would be safer to take the two pilots to the liberated area. In the early morning of November 20, 1944 the five of them crossed the lines to Oirlo. Hanna and Virrie, unwilling to abandon their work, returned to occupied territory. Virrie comments:

> People always ask me: "How could you go back to those Germans?" Because Tienray was still occupied by the Germans. Where was I supposed to go? On a tank, along with the Americans? What nonsense. No, I went back with Hanna. I belonged with Hanna. We were together.

Nico and the pilots went to the local American commander, a certain Major Montgomery. Nico was on the verge of a breakdown because of the endless shelling, and he reproached the major for not advancing, since there were very few German soldiers west of the Maas River. He remembers:

> I was very emotional. Then the major said something that I'll never forget: "You have to understand that for me the life of one soldier is more important than that of a thousand civilians."

Nevertheless, one cannot help wondering whether Nico's plea played a role in speeding up the Allied advance. The very next day, November 21, 1944, Tienray was liberated without any prior artillery bombardment.

Nico took the pilots to Helmond and then went to the office that the Jewish Coordination Commission (JCC) had opened in Eindhoven. They asked Nico for a list of the Jewish children that Hanna and he had placed in foster homes. Nico responded that there was no such list because they had never bothered with administrative niceties and asked why a list was needed. An argument followed:

> They said: "We want to take all these children away from there as soon as possible. Because it is still a front-line situation, and it's much too dangerous for them. We want to take them to Eindhoven." I said: "I won't do it. I won't give you just one address. . . . I will give you addresses, but only if you will take all the children away from here. Because all the children are equally in danger. We have made a special effort to help Jewish children because we regard them exactly the same

as other children. So I want to be consistent." Well, they practically called me an anti-Semite.

Hanna and Nico had no definite plans about what to do with the children after the war. However, they would have liked it if the foster parents were able to personally return the children to their parents. Until a guardianship decision was made, the children would have to stay with their "hiding" parents; this was another reason for Nico's initial reluctance to cooperate with the JCC. After several days Nico returned to Tienray. He was exhausted when liberation finally came, worn out by the combined tension of living under the Germans, of being on the front lines after the Allied invasion, and of the constant sense of responsibility for the many people he helped.

The same was certainly true for Hanna van de Voort. The strain of the rescue work and the interrogations by the SD in Eindhoven must have contributed to the heart condition she developed after the war. She died in 1956, one day after a heart operation.

A few children stayed with their foster parents after the war. Two became Catholics of their own volition. One of them, Helmut Willinger, entered upon a program to become a priest but did not complete it. One foster family was glad their child was leaving. On January 30, 1945, Nico Dohmen received the following letter:

Dear Friend Nico,

  We have taken the liberty of sending [name of the child] to Tienray. You probably expected her sooner. Well, this morning I finally threw her out of the house after first throwing a plate (unfortunately it hit the wall instead of her head), a fork, and an ashtray at her. What with her name-calling and insults, our parting was something that a well-schooled, impertinent, and brazen tramp of the worst sort could not have improved on. I was really surprised when she returned, even the most barefaced rascal wouldn't have done that with such a straight face (a hallmark of her character). . . . Not a word of thanks.

Nico and Hanna brought this unmanageable girl to Eindhoven, where Abraham de Jong of the JCC took her under his wing. The rest of the children were invited to a traditional Purim party that was organized in February 1945 in Tienray. In order to be able to send out invitations, a list was made— for the first and last time—of all the Jews who had been hidden by Hanna, Nico, and Kurt. Unfortunately, the list has since been lost. The number 123 lived on in the memories of those involved.

---

## FRIESLAND

The hundred children in Leeuwarden and the eastern part of Friesland were cared for by the LO. They consulted Piet Meerburg about their problems with a difficult girl:

> The girl was probably a bit of a nymphomaniac. She was about fourteen or fifteen. And wherever we put her up, she was bothering the foster father. And I remember quite well that I discussed with Krijn what we should do with her because we really were at our wit's end.

Krijn van den Helm considered bringing the matter before the *veemgericht*, a secret three-member tribunal, set up by the resistance, to try serious crimes against the resistance. Only two sentences were possible: death penalty or no death penalty. In the end the matter was not brought before the tribunal.

Krijn was also involved in the armed resistance. For his own safety he left Friesland, but the SD tracked him down. When he pulled a pistol, the arresting officers shot him dead.

Another leader of the resistance in Joure, Uilke Boonstra, was also killed. He was arrested on August 8, 1944, and on August 18 he was executed by a firing squad in Vught. The 130 Jewish children for whom his organization had been responsible were now cared for by the LO and were moved whenever there was trouble. All of these children survived the war.

## SNEEK

Willem Mesdag, Gérard Jansen, and Mia Coelingh remained committed to rescue work; the children were their first priority. Nina Mesdag remembers:

> I think that my parents deliberately decided: "One kind of resistance work, otherwise everything can be betrayed, and then we'll have nothing." . . . Later I did have brief contacts with adults who needed our help, but they weren't only Jews—there were also non-Jewish people in hiding. In 1944 there were rescued Polish, British, and American pilots and flight crews; we provided them with reading material because they were on farms where no one understood any English.

Gérard Jansen started on the slippery slope of being a "fixer," just like Wouter van Zeytveld in Amsterdam. He combed the surrounding area for provisions for "his" children and encountered all sorts of people of quite divergent religious convictions who helped in many different ways. He even found a barber who was willing to cut the "too Jewish-looking" curls of the hidden children. He also managed to get hold of fuel.[12] An unidentified civil servant in the city of Sneek supplied the threesome with a good many of the ration cards they needed.[13] As has already been mentioned, the supply of cards was sporadically supplemented by the Amsterdam Group until the railroad strike. Iet van Dijk brought the ration cards. Jansen divided the take proportionally among the three of them, and personally distributed his share of the cards.

Jansen once made a bad contact when looking for new addresses. A family he approached tried to blackmail him. They took the money from him and threatened to report him to the Germans. Of course he couldn't hide behind an alias with his own parishioners. It is not known how this blackmail was stopped.

The Sneek branch checked regularly on the well-being of the children. Mia Coelingh recalls that no records were kept: "No one had anything written down or had anything on them. Everything was in our heads."

Neither Jansen nor Coelingh could remember any Jewish child ever being in danger. To the best of their knowledge, there were no raids on any of the foster homes. The strict secrecy they maintained, and the generally non-Jewish appearance of "their" children, must have helped.

When asked how often she visited the hiding addresses, Mia Coelingh answered:

> At least once a month—because of the ration cards. The children needed a distribution card and had already received one upon their arrival. . . . We felt it was a good idea for the three of us to keep in touch with the families. So: how did both sides like this temporary placement? Were they worried about anything? Was there anything they wanted to talk over? For example, we had some very musical children who found a church organ in rural Friesland. . . . Then people noticed that the child was very musical. This led us to discuss music lessons, which were arranged.

Mia Coelingh recalls that they even found a way to deal with the small number of dark-haired children who were sent to Friesland:

> There were no Jews at all in Bolsward, so that's where we took the most Jewish-looking children. And we said that they were from Indonesia. . . . No one knew what a Jew looked like. So it was very simple: the "worst" of them went to Bolsward.

Of course, the foster parents themselves were aware that the children they were hiding were Jewish.

Piet Meerburg had an agreement with Jansen and Mesdag that Jewish children would not be baptized during the occupation.[14] Mia Coelingh remembers Lidy van Gelder, a young woman who was staying in the Mesdag home, who wanted to be baptized. Willem and Sjoukje Mesdag consulted with Jansen and Coelingh:

> We said no unanimously. Of course it was sad for Lidy, who had asked for it, but in the end she understood that it was better this way. In those times of unrest we didn't want to let these children make big decisions. What if the parents came back? We had to be able to return the children to them as Jewish children.

The three tried to arrange for the children to go to school, as was done in Tienray.

Nina Mesdag remembers Jaap van Meer, a four-year-old toddler from an Orthodox family. In the spring of 1943 he was taken in by the Mesdag family.

> It used to be that you would wear your Sunday clothes on Sundays. But Jaapje would say: "Oh, Sabbath?" Naturally we couldn't let him say that. And we had a children's picture book, one of those books about a farm. There were pigs in it, of course, and he'd say: "Yuck, dirty, dirty, dirty." And then we'd say other things about the pig: "What a pretty curly tail," or "Look, he walks on tiptoes." But all that eventually ended. . . . When he was really used to us, he turned out to be a very adventurous, cute little boy. He kept running off. Despite his blue eyes, he was a real Jewish boy—circumcised and all. Then— it happened several times—he'd come back with money. People gave it to him; they felt sorry for him. Well, that frightened my parents, because we had Lidy as well. So Jaapje was sent to a farm where he had lots of freedom in the village.

The cows on the farm were calving. Jaapje was fascinated and soon felt quite at home. On moving to the farm he was given an evacuation certificate. Jaapje spent his time in hiding under his own name, as an evacuee from Rotterdam. Mrs. Akkerman-Piersman still has the certificate, which even gives his address in Rotterdam. As time went by, he became so Frisian that he was no longer at all different from the other children in the neighborhood. Early in December he celebrated Sinterklaas with the Akkerman family. And then something went wrong. Someone became suspicious and checked with the Central Evacuation Bureau in Rotterdam; no one there had ever heard of a Jaap van Meer. In great haste he was moved to a farm in Drachtster-compagnie in eastern Friesland, where he stayed until liberation. Afterwards he was again taken in by the Mesdag family, and after a short time he was

reunited with his parents, his brother, and his sister. Nina Mesdag vividly
remembers that moment:

> Jaap didn't say a word! But Mrs. Van Meer said that she could see a
> look of recognition in the child's eyes. Then we all ate together, with
> tears in our eyes. And Jaapje, whom we had taught to eat with a fork,
> could hardly eat at all. Because he was so excited and nervous he
> dropped his fork. The first thing he said was in Frisian: "*Dèr dondert
> mien vörke*" [I dropped my fork]. And that was so good because it broke
> the tension.

After the disastrous battle of Arnhem and the subsequent railroad strike
in September 1944, it became much more difficult to take care of the Jewish
children in Sneek. The three kept it up for several more months, covering
many miles on bicycles with tires made of rope. There were fewer and fewer
ration cards. But there was more available in Friesland than in the western
part of the Netherlands. Gérard Jansen was the first of the trio to drop out.
At the end of October he was transferred to Enschede. By the end of
November, the situation in Sneek had become too dangerous for Mia Coelingh. She went into hiding in Enschede, and at the end of March 1945 she
went to Bussum to help her parents:

> Life was becoming too hard for them—the terrible hunger and no help.
> With great difficulty I was able to make my way over the hermetically
> sealed IJssel River crossing and arrived safely in Bussum. That's where
> I went through the last few months of hunger; it was terrible, but we
> managed. Mother was the hungriest; she gave my father more than his
> share, but he really needed it badly. My mother got hunger edema.

The Baptist community in Sneek gave what help they could to Sjoukje
Mesdag. Farmers from the surrounding area delivered milk clandestinely.
People from Mesdag's previous congregation in Zijldijk in northern
Groningen sent peas, potatoes, and wheat—enough to feed the many guests
and boarders. Sneek was liberated on April 15, 1945.

Despite their exemplary mutual cooperation, the three activists in Sneek
kept one another in the dark as much as possible about what they were
doing. Mia Coelingh never knew where Gérard Jansen obtained ration
cards. When a child was moved, she didn't know where. The Amsterdam
students never revealed that there were branches in Leeuwarden and Joure.
The less one knew, the safer it was. Both student organizations made this an
ironclad rule. It held for the Jewish children too: some "forgot" who they
were and were totally caught up in their new identity.

## The Naamloze Vennootschap
### Amsterdam

After October 1943, there was no longer much work for the Amsterdam members of the NV, including Joop Woortman, his wife Semmy, and the Kinsbergen family. Once in a while Semmy would accompany a child to Limburg or would bring photos of Jewish children to their parents. Joop took care of Jews and non-Jews who were in hiding in Amsterdam, and as a former soldier he participated in the armed resistance. Hans Kinsbergen was Joop's right-hand man. Together with his stepfather, Hans tracked Jewish children who had got into difficulties in their foster homes. In March of 1944, Hans was called up for German military service (because he was German). He wanted to go into hiding, but that meant that his half-Jewish stepfather, Samuel Kinsbergen, would also have to go into hiding. This would have been difficult because their home was the NV's most important safe house. Woortman asked Hans to report for military service so that they could go on using his stepfather's house. Hans did so. He survived the war but had a terrible time. Samuel Kinsbergen and his wife Lea were able to continue helping children until the railroad strike. Both survived the Hunger Winter and were liberated in Amsterdam.

The following case illustrates the danger of recruiting people for resistance work. Joop Woortman met a former classmate who complained bitterly about the German occupation. Joop invited him to join the resistance. Semmy Woortman recalls:

> Half an hour later he returned to buy a pack of cigarettes in the cigar store where they had been talking. And then the storekeeper said to him: "Are you Joop Woortman? Weren't you just standing and talking outside the door? Be careful, because the guy you were talking to just called the SD from here to report a Joop Woortman." So then he came home and said: "Damn, I've been betrayed under my own name." . . . That's when we went into hiding.

Semmy and her stepdaughter, Hetty, went into hiding in Apeldoorn. Joop wanted to continue his resistance work, so he went into hiding in Amsterdam. He was involved in the preparations for the raid on the jail on Weteringschans on July 14, 1944. The raid failed. Joop wasn't there because he was ill, but he was arrested at home. On September 4 he was sent to Bergen-Belsen. Semmy took care of Joop's people in hiding, insofar as she could find their addresses.

LIMBURG

The Bockma family continued to take care of the remaining children in the Heerlen area. They also took over a few Jewish children from Father Leendert Overduin, who had 700 people to hide and not enough places to house them.

During a five-month period, 145 children were placed in Limburg. Finding new homes for people transferred from someplace else was difficult, and the NV was not the only hiding organization in southern Limburg. At the end of September, the NV had 200 people hiding in a rather small area. An estimated 2,500–3,000 Jews were hidden in Limburg at that time. The NV decided that when it was necessary to move people, they would attempt to place them outside Limburg. But the organization in Limburg would still be responsible for their care. And that is how it came about that Truus Vermeer took 100 Jewish children from Limburg to the provinces of Gelderland and Overijssel.

Pastor Pontier was arrested in Heerlen. A few minutes before his arrest he had been tipped off by someone from the resistance. He could have fled but did not, because then his house would have been searched, and the police would have found the Silber family, who were living on the top floor. The Silbers came from Heerlen and would have been recognized on the street. Lies Pontier, the pastor's daughter, took a Jewish toddler, Lily de Goede, to friends. Gérard Pontier was held in solitary confinement in Scheveningen for half a year. The news of Pontier's arrest was announced to the Vermeer family in Brunssum. At that very moment a policeman arrived to warn them about a major raid that was going to take place in Brunssum and Treebeek. The families were quickly warned, and the children were bundled up and taken to a swimming pool on the heath. The twenty-five children stayed in the swimming pool buildings for at least two nights. Some of them were able to return to their foster parents. But other foster parents were so frightened that they gave up, and new placements had to be found for their children. Several children had to stay in a cellar and a pumping station for quite a while. The cellar was a limestone cave underneath the house of a family that had German relatives. The entrance was via the hinged bottom of a kitchen cupboard. Eighteen Jewish children hid underground, led by Ted Meines and Roosje de Goede, Lily's mother. After several days, Ben Fritz came to help them. Dick Groenewegen van Wijk knew him from before, and when he met Ben on the street in Amsterdam he asked him to come and help. By early December, a month after the warning about the raid, new addresses had been found for all the children.

Twenty-one children slept in two rooms in the pumping station. Because the pumping station provided water and fresh air for a mine and was of great importance for coal production, it was guarded night and day by German soldiers. The Jewish children were moved to the house of Jo Broers, an engineer, who lived with his wife and their eleven children in a large house on the premises. Jaap Musch also moved in. Maria Paulina Cals, the district nurse, took care of the children; early in December she brought them Sinterklaas presents, and a week later Chanukah lights. On December 25 and 26, the last of the younger children left. The older ones did not leave until March 2, 1944.

The NV had nine full-time members in Limburg; many more worked part-time or helped in any way possible. The NV did not approve of foster parents baptizing children. Only a very small number of children was baptized.

In Limburg there was a problem child, a slightly older Jewish girl who had dyed her hair red and dated German soldiers. Her caretaker, Cor Grootendorst, brought up the problem at a staff meeting, and it was decided that the girl had to be liquidated. There was some difficulty in finding someone willing to carry out the decision. Cor Grootendorst recalls:

> Everyone looked at me because I knew the young woman and knew where she was. No one else knew where she was. I said: "I won't do it. I can't." . . . Then Ben, putting a brave face on it and wanting to do the right thing, said: "I'll do it." The two of us walked out together. and I still remember that we were very quiet. We were thinking and thinking, and that train kept getting closer. "How in the world are we going to do it?" I would hold her and he would strangle her. . . . Then we arrived at the house and she had flown the coop. Ben and I were so incredibly happy. You can't imagine what a relief it was. I can't really imagine that we would have gone through with it.

The girl disappeared and was never heard from again.

The Limburg NV got money from "Father Beatus" (his real name was G. L. J. van Beckhoven), who gave them a sizable sum of money every month. Dick Groenewegen van Wijk did not know that Beatus was the head of a large relief organization in Heerlen with a membership of Protestants, Catholics, and Social Democrats. In February 1944 Beatus had to go into hiding. This meant that Dick once again had to travel throughout the country for donations.

In April 1944 the LO asked for an accounting of the ration cards. The list compiled by the NV is still extant. There were forty-eight children in Brunssum, forty-four in Heerlen, thirty-three in Geleen, seventeen in Venlo, forty-five in the Betuwe area south of Utrecht, forty-four in Hengelo; a total of 231 children.

On May 9, 1944, Dick Groenewegen van Wijk and Gerard Musch were arrested. Dick was picked up one evening during a police identity check, and his alias, "Richard Hofman, worker at the Hendrik mine," was not on a list of mineworkers checked by the Landwacht, the pro-German police corps. He was punished for being in hiding and was sent to a prison camp near Burscheid in Germany. Gerard Musch was detained while carrying false identity cards. The punishment for transporting fake ID cards was a one-way trip to Germany. Imprisoned for a while in Amsterdam and in Scheveningen, he was eventually sent to Oranienburg, where he was liberated by the Russians on April 22, 1945.

On May 17, 1944, Gerard Pontier returned from prison. The next day he visited Salomon Silber at his new hideout to wish him a happy birthday. Silber wrote in his diary:

> I was really surprised when I saw him standing in front of me. I could hardly recognize him. He must have lost at least twenty kilos. We embraced warmly. . . . I asked him in which prison he had been. "The worst prison in the country, Scheveningen. They tortured and tormented me to tell them who I had helped. I answered: 'The duty of a clergyman is to help everyone, friend and even foe, if he asks for help, and I am forbidden to name names.'"[15]

A month later, June 17, 1944, Beatus (Gerard van Beckhoven) was arrested. On September 6 he was sent to Sachsenhausen. Gerard Musch was on the same train. In February 1945 Beatus was transferred to Bergen-Belsen. There he and Joop Woortman died of typhus in March of 1945.

On July 7, Dick Groenewegen van Wijk knocked at the door of the Vermeer family in Brunssum. He had escaped from Burscheid and had been walking for four days without food.

The NV territories in Limburg, except for Venlo and the surrounding area, were liberated between September 17 and 20, 1944.

Shortly after the liberation of the mining region in Limburg, a certain Mr. Frank, a Jewish soldier, visited the Vermeer family. The Jewish Coordination Commission had delegated him to check on the Jewish children. He asked for and was given a list with addresses; after this the care of about 110 Jews was transferred to the Jewish community. That was the end of the NV's rescue work in the southern part of the Netherlands.

## BETUWE

Forty-five children were hidden in the Betuwe and adjacent areas. Truus Vermeer had taken them there, but for various reasons things did not work out. The organization decided to transfer the children to Twente. Truus Vermeer was again the one who took them to their new addresses.

## TWENTE

At the end of 1943, two new territories were opened up in Twente and Salland (areas in the province of Overijssel). Because of the impending raid in Brunssum in November, about forty-five children in Limburg needed new accommodations. Fortunately, thanks to the efforts of Piet Vermeer, there were several foster parents and places in school ready for them in Hengelo. Vermeer's fiancée, Hieke Meines, was a nurse in Hengelo, and she was able to obtain the assistance of some of her former patients.

## NIJVERDAL

The members of the NV were haunted by the raid in Brunssum that had been called off. They began to feel the need for a permanently available safe house where people could flee.

Piet Vermeer found a vacation house in Nijverdal with the help of Berend Jan Flim, a Calvinist baker. In mid-January Jaap Musch and Truus Vermeer moved into the house in Nijverdal. They were soon followed by five Jewish girls who had experienced many horrors and therefore needed extra attention. Jaap Musch took care of them. Herman Flim, who worked in his father's bakery, visited customers to ask if they might be able to house a Jewish child. So many were willing that it was possible to transfer a considerable number of Jewish children from Limburg. On August 17, 1944, ten-year-old Ed van Thijn, who had been hidden in the mining region of south Limburg for over a year, was placed in a new home by Herman Flim. After living for brief periods at eight different addresses, Ed was arrested in December 1944 and sent to Westerbork. Because the transports from Westerbork had ceased, he was liberated there in April 1945.

Dick Groenewegen van Wijk and Gerard Musch lived in the vacation house, and from time to time were joined by Piet Vermeer. The three discussed the postwar prospects of the children entrusted to them. They felt that many of the deported parents would not survive. Jaap Musch came up with an idealistic plan to establish a community in which the older orphans would take care of the younger ones. Nothing came of the plan, but it shows Jaap

Musch's single-mindedness. Lea Winnik, who earlier, together with her sister, had escaped from the child-care center in Amsterdam, wound up living with Jaap Musch from March, 1944 onwards. She got to know him very well and remembers his irritation when the other NV members indicated that they would sometimes like to take it easy.

Jaap could not understand their attitude, she said. "He gave up everything. He gave up his whole life to this purpose."

The five girls boarding in the vacation house led a carefree existence, interrupted only by a teacher from Nijverdal, who came from time to time to give them lessons. One of the five was eventually moved to another address. Jaap stayed behind with the other four.

But a disaster struck the NV too. On September 8, 1944, the vacation house was accidentally discovered by K. L. Diepgrond, the Dutch commander of the Erika prison camp near Ommen. He and his men saw four girls running into the woods. When they asked Jaap's name, his response made them suspicious: "Jaap Musch; no, Jaap Vogel" (*musch* = sparrow, *vogel* = bird). His papers indicated that he was a miner from Limburg. Jaap Musch had always told the other NV members that he would keep silent rather than lie. Angered by his refusal to speak, his interrogators, after one and a half days, gave the order to execute him. He was shot at Erika. After the war he was reburied with military honors in the cemetery of Ommen. The four girls were taken to other addresses. The author has spoken with three of them; they think the world of Jaap.

On March 22, 1945 the central part of Nijverdal was destroyed by British bombers, and Flim's bakery received a direct hit. The Flim family and the Jewish children hidden with them survived the bombing in a shelter. On April 8 they were liberated while staying with a farmer in the area.

Herman Flim was once accidentally involved in another kind of resistance: helping Hans Kinsbergen, a German deserter. Kinsbergen had gone through a series of horrors after he had taken Joop Woortman's advice in March of 1944 and reported to the Wehrmacht, sacrificing himself to help the resistance. In October, while in Poland with his unit, Hans volunteered for special training in Holland, in a village seven kilometers from Nijverdal. Once in Holland, he deserted and was able to make contact with Flim. We agree with Hans that urging him to join the German army must be seen as one of the biggest mistakes in the history of the NV.

## THE TROUW GROUP

After 1943, the Trouw Group no longer engaged in children's rescue work. One hundred children were provided with ration cards by local LO or Trouw workers. Sándor Baracs began writing for the organization's newspaper. After the execution of Gideon and Jan Karel Boissevain on October 1, 1943, Hester van Lennep took over the care of the people hidden by the CS-6 group.

On January 20, 1945 Sándor Baracs and Hester van Lennep were married. They wanted the officiating official to be one who had been appointed before the war by Queen Wilhelmina (and not by the German occupation authorities). They found what they were looking for in Tienhoven in the province of Utrecht. Mayor Van den Hoorn told his fellow villagers that the wedding guests were members of the land consolidation commission and their wives. After a tour of the fields, the wedding was celebrated under a portrait of Queen Wilhelmina that was taken down from the attic for the occasion. All of the Trouw Group's regular workers survived the war, and only one of the seventy-five children known to the author was caught.

The Trouw Group also gave some thought to what would happen to the children after the war. Sándor Baracs was against a community like the one suggested by Jaap Musch. Five rescue activists with legal training—Gesina van der Molen, Ger Kempe, An de Waard, Lau Mazirel, and Piet Meerburg—drafted a proposal for a law. Curiously, only one article in the proposal dealt with the orphans:

> In cases where it can be assumed with reasonable certainty that there is no longer any chance of the parents returning, the commission will help to ease the formal absorption of the children into the foster families; for example, by name changes.[16]

They were so completely in agreement about turning the orphans over to their foster families that they devoted only one sentence to the subject. It never occurred to them that the Jewish community would claim the Jewish orphans after the war. They had complete confidence in the foster families they themselves had found for the children. Having the courage to take in a child during the occupation, they felt, automatically attested to nobility of character. Very often they knew nothing about the problems in some of the foster families. The members of the NV knew a little about such matters because of their bi-weekly visits. In his plan Jaap Musch said not a word about leaving children with their foster families. He knew how much could go wrong. The NV was not represented on the commission; Jaap Musch was regarded as a dreamer.

The proposed law deals in great detail with the difficulties that might arise if children were reunited with parents returning either from concentration camps or from being in hiding. It was expected that the returning parents would be destitute, physically weak, and emotionally unstable.[17] According to the commission. it would be better in many cases not to reunite parents and children immediately. Reality turned out to be different.

The archives of the Bureau of War Foster Children (OPK) contain files on 259 Jewish children who were reunited with either one or both parents after the war.[18] The reunions were effected quickly and without any problems.[19] The OPK, headed by Sándor Baracs, did everything it could to help. Baracs and his people spared neither time nor effort in trying to establish the identity of babies whose true names were unknown. Most of the time the babies turned out to be orphans. In a very small number of cases the parents returned. In such instances parent and child were almost always reunited within less than a year.

Custody of Jewish children who were now orphans presented difficult problems. Encouraged by the Dutch government, the Jewish community arranged to place the majority of Jewish orphans with Jewish foster families or in a Jewish children's home. There was no question of an automatic transfer of guardianship to the hiding parents.

A number of children were not reported and thus did not come under the jurisdiction of the OPK bureau. One man who was taken into hiding as a baby did not discover until a few years ago that he was not who he thought he was. Despite intensive investigations, he is still not sure of his real name and date of birth. No one can tell him whether or not he has any living relatives. His foster mother refused to give him any information.

## SUMMARY
### THE UTRECHT CHILDREN'S COMMITTEE

At least 339 children and 46 adults were hidden by the Utrecht Children's Committee; a total of almost 400 people. From the summer of 1943 until the Hunger Winter of 1945, financial support was provided by Bezige Bij, the illegal publishing operation. Geert Lubberhuizen estimated that the total amount earned from publications must have reached 800,000 guilders.[20]

After the railroad strike of September 18, 1944, every branch had to arrange for its own supplies. None of the founders of the Utrecht Children's

Committee was able to resume children's rescue work until the end of the war.

## THE AMSTERDAM STUDENT GROUP

The Amsterdam Student Group saved the lives of an estimated 350 Jews: 10 in Wijdenes, 10 in Nijkerkerveen, 60 to 80 in Sneek, 100 in Leeuwarden, 30 in Joure, 50 to 60 in southern Limburg, 123 in Tienray.[21] Money was no problem until the Hunger Winter. The group shared the proceeds from Geert Lubberhuizen's publications. In addition, the National Assistance Fund (Nationaal Steunfonds) helped out. All the rescuers who started at the very beginning continued as long as possible, that is, until the railroad strike.

## THE NAAMLOZE VENNOOTSCHAP

The routine of the NV differed in important ways from that of the student organizations. For example, the NV members themselves retained responsibility for the children. Until well into 1944, the NV continued to find new places for Jewish children who were having difficulties in their foster homes.

Two of the 252 persons (including 20 adults) hidden by the NV were caught; one of them escaped deportation because of the railroad strike, but the other was gassed. One child died of natural causes. The NV's bi-weekly visits to the Jewish children occasionally turned up signs of abuse in the foster families. The student groups, with fewer activists, were able to provide more Jewish children with hiding places. The NV members only rarely deviated from the idea of restricting their efforts to rescuing children. In contrast to the other groups, whose membership steadily decreased, very few people dropped out of the NV, which grew explosively after the child-care center was closed in September 1943.

## THE TROUW GROUP

The Trouw Group was active from May through September of 1943. This period coincides with the peak period of smuggling children from the child-care center. The Trouw organization was a "pick-up" organization that managed to find accommodations for 100 children.

## NOTES

1. *Utrechtsche Studenten Almanak* 1946 (Utrecht, 1946), p. 123. The exact date of James van Beusekom's death is uncertain. Shortly after the war, Clara Hes met his parents. They told her that on May 3, 1945, James was aboard one of the three prison ships in Lübecker Bocht that were accidentally torpedoed by British fighter-bombers. This incident caused the death of almost 7,000 prisoners, James van Beusekom among them.

2. He was the brother of the "good" police officer mentioned in Chapter 4.

3. For a short history of this resistance group, see Coen Hilbrink, *De illegalen. Illegaliteit in Twente & het aangrenzende Salland 1940–1945* (The Hague, 1989), pp. 109–114.

4. Mien van de Voort, Plakboek Tienray; see Sources.

5. A. P. M. Cammaert, *Het verborgen front*, pp. 407–409.

6. The police chief implies in his report that money (the large amount paid for room and board) was the reason for helping Jewish children; that was absolutely not true.

7. Mien van de Voort, Plakboek Tienray; see Sources.

8. Ibid. Also see Jan van Lieshout, "Het verraad van Tienray," *Limburgs Dagblad*, May 5, 1974.

9. Mien van de Voort, *Plakboek Tienray*; see "Sources: Bibliography and Other Documentation."

10. Because of this, Tienray had been a place of pilgrimage for more than 500 years; of course, this was good for the income of Anselm van de Voort, who was a baker.

11. Interview with Nico Dohmen, October 3, 1989, Collection of the author (Groningen). Also see Mien van de Voort, *Plakboek Tienray*; see Sources.

12. Interviews with Mia Coelingh and Nina Treffers-Mesdag; see Sources.

13. Nina Treffers-Mesdag reports that her father received money from Mrs. Sminia, a tax officer. Source: N. Treffers-Mesdag, letter to the author; see Sources.

14. Elma Verhey, "Kind, jij hoeft geen Poerim te vieren. De Here Jezus is ook voor jou opgestaan," *Vrij Nederland*, October 8, 1990, p. 34.

15. Salomon Silber, Unpublished diary from the war period; see Sources.

16. Comments in the final version of the OPK proposal; see Sources.

17. Comments in the early version of the OPK proposal; see Sources.

18. This is only a small part of the Jewish children involved. There are no files in the OPK archives about the other children (approximately 1,500) whose parents returned.

19. In many cases the reunions of Jewish children and their parents were very difficult. See Bloeme Evers-Emden and Bert-Jan Flim, *Ondergedoken geweest – een afgesloten verleden?* (Kampen, 1995), pp. 106–115.

20. Richter Roegholt, *De Geschiedenis van de Bezige Bij 1942–1972* (Amsterdam, 1972), p. 71.

21. This adds up to 383–413, but these figures include the children that the Amsterdam Student Group took over from the Utrecht Children's Committee. Thus the author's estimate of 350.

# THE CHILDREN

6

The children's rescuers are the subject of this book. But we want to try and answer some questions about the children even though the data are limited. We hoped to find out the following about the children:

- Their dates of birth and where they lived before going into hiding.
- Their parents' income and occupation.
- Whether their parents lived in a rich or a poor area.
- When they went into hiding.
- How religious their parents were (it was impossible to find this out).
- The number of places where each child was hidden (a certain percentage of the children stayed in more than one place).
- The distribution of placements by province.

There were also some questions about the foster parents:

- How did they treat the children?
- Did they receive money for board and lodging?
- How many of them were childless?
- What was their religion?
- What was their income?

Finally, we wanted to know how many Jewish children were captured while in hiding during the occupation.

## RESEARCH METHODS AND DATA

Eleven hundred Jews were hidden by the four organizations that are the subject of this book. We were unable to track down 265 of them, so the research in this book is based only on the 835 Jews about whom we have information. These names were collected from various sources, including the surviving lists compiled by the Utrecht Children's Committee (UCC), the NV, the Tienray branch of the Amsterdam Student Group (ASG), and the Trouw Group, 263 OPK files, 17 interviews; 75 questionnaires,[1] and a number of other sources ranging from newspaper clippings to extensive reports.

The figures in the lists kept by the four hiding organizations are shown in Table 1. The addition of the figures in Table 2 gives a grand total of 739 children and 96 adults.

TABLE 1

| Hetty Voûte's card index (part of the UCC children) | 243 children, 41 adults |
| --- | --- |
| NV list | 214 children, 28 adults |
| Tienray list (part of the ASG children) | 85 children, 16 adults |
| Trouw list | 64 children |

TABLE 2

| UCC | 50 children, 5 adults |
| --- | --- |
| NV | 12 children |
| ASG | 60 children, 5 adults |
| Trouw Group | 11 children, 1 adult |

THE DATABASE

The database for the study consists of 835 Jews (739 children and 96 adults). The children's database includes 739 children. Many of the 265 hidden Jews that we could not track down were probably cared for by the ASG. The total number of Jews it hid is estimated to be 350.

We know very little even about those we could track down. For example, we were not able to identify the provinces in which eighty-nine of the children were hidden. We do not know the names of twenty-one of the children. We do not know how many placements were made for eighty-nine of the children. And so on.

All told, there are 345 girls, 381 boys, 58 women, 38 men, and 16 persons of undetermined gender in the database (see Table 3).

TABLE 3

| Group | Girls | Boys | Women | Men | Unknown | Total |
|-------|-------|------|-------|-----|---------|-------|
| UCC | 135 | 146 | 25 | 19 | 14 | 339 |
| ASG | 55 | 90 | 12 | 9 | 0 | 166 |
| NV | 118 | 107 | 20 | 7 | 2 | 254 |
| Trouw | 37 | 38 | 1 | 0 | 0 | 76 |

The over-representation of boys in the Amsterdam group can be attributed entirely to the Tienray rescuers (see Chapter 4). The majority of the adults were women. They were mostly the mothers of children who had also been hidden, especially in the case of those helped by the NV.

AGES OF CHILDREN IN 1943

The ages of the children who were saved, as of 1943, are shown in Table 4. Note that more than 42 percent of them were younger than six, and 78 percent were younger than twelve.

TABLE 4

| | |
|---|---|
| 0–2 years old | 20.4% |
| 3–5 years old | 22.0% |
| 6–8 years old | 20.8% |
| 9–11 years old | 14.8% |
| 12–14 years old | 13.2% |
| 15 years old or older | 8.8% |
| Total: | 100.0% |

LAST ADDRESS BEFORE GOING INTO HIDING

Table 5 shows the provinces where 441 children lived before going into hiding. (Noord-Holland is the province where Amsterdam is located, and the city of Utrecht is the capital of the province of the same name.)

TABLE 5

| | | |
|---|---|---|
| Groningen | 2 | 0.4% |
| Friesland | 2 | 0.4% |
| Drenthe | 0 | 0.0% |
| Overijssel | 8 | 1.8% |
| Gelderland | 9 | 2.0% |
| Utrecht | 26 | 5.9% |
| Noord-Holland | 361 | 81.9% |
| Zuid-Holland | 23 | 5.2% |
| Zeeland | 0 | 0.0% |
| Noord-Brabant | 6 | 1.4% |
| Limburg | 4 | 0.9% |

The four groups concentrated on rescuing Jewish children from Amsterdam. No group made a special effort to rescue children from any other locality. Eleven children from Utrecht were hidden by the UCC, ten were hidden by the NV, four were hidden by the ASG, and one by the Trouw Group.

PARENTS' INCOME AND OCCUPATION

Parental incomes and occupations, shown in Table 6, were of interest in our research because many people assume that the "Jewish proletariat" had practically no opportunity to go into hiding.

TABLE 6

| Income | UCC | ASG | NV | Trouw Group | Total |
|---|---|---|---|---|---|
| High | 14.1% | 7.9% | 13.1% | 12.1% | 12.1% |
| Middle | 54.1% | 49.2% | 41.5% | 42.4% | 46.6% |
| Low | 31.8% | 42.9% | 45.4% | 45.5% | 41.2% |

We asked about the parents' occupations and incomes in our previous research on a cross-section of 310 hidden Dutch children.[2] Eighteen of the children did not know their parents' occupations. The answers of the other 292 are roughly approximated by the three occupational categories in Table 7.

TABLE 7

| High | 111 | 38.0% |
|---|---|---|
| Middle | 144 | 49.3% |
| Low | 37 | 12.7% |

On average, the parents of the children hidden by the rescuers were apparently lower on the social scale than those from the cross-section of 310. Wouter van Zeytveld and Joop Woortman enjoyed the confidence of a great many Jews who were not rich. If parents did not have enough money to "buy" a hiding address, they could ask the children's rescuers.

The student rescuers obtained children through Dr. Fiedeldij Dop, who must have had patients in the middle- and higher-income groups. This explains the relative over-representation of the middle class among the children rescued by the ASG. The NV and the Trouw Group are over-represented in the lower-income group. The Trouw members obtained three-quarters of their children from the child-care center. The Kinsbergen family and Joop Woortman of the NV group were especially concerned about helping the very poorest.

RENTAL VALUES OF HOUSES IN JEWISH AREAS

We know the home addresses of 303 children in Amsterdam. Three-quarters of the Jews in Amsterdam lived in rental housing.[3] The average rental value of housing per district gives a rough indication of the income level of the inhabitants. This information about the Jewish populace of Amsterdam is provided in Table 8. The last legal addresses of the Jewish children in the data are given in Table 9.

TABLE 8

| High rent<br>Apollolaan district, Museum and<br>Concertgebouw district | 10.8% |
|---|---|
| Higher than average rent<br>Noorder and Zuider Amstellaan, Stadion<br>area, Amstelkade and surrounding area,<br>Lekstraat and surrounding area, Plantage<br>district and Sarphatistraat, Transvaal area | 41.8% |
| Average rent<br>Weesperstraat and surrounding area,<br>Nieuwe Pijp, Weesperzijde and<br>surrounding area | 17.5% |
| Lower than average rent<br>Oosterpark district | 8.8% |
| Low rent<br>Old Jewish district, Oude Pijp | 13.6% |
| Elsewhere in the city | 7.6% |

TABLE 9

| High rent<br>Apollolaan district, Museum and<br>Concertgebouw district | 3.0% |
|---|---|
| Higher than average rent<br>Noorder and Zuider Amstellaan, Stadion<br>area, Amstelkade and surrounding area,<br>Lekstraat and surrounding area, Plantage<br>district and Sarphatistraat, Transvaal area | 46.5% |

| | |
|---|---|
| **Average rent**<br>Weesperstraat and surrounding area,<br>Nieuwe Pijp, Weesperzijde and<br>surrounding area | 20.8% |
| **Lower than average rent**<br>Oosterpark district | 8.9% |
| **Low rent**<br>Old Jewish district, Oude Pijp | 9.2% |
| **Elsewhere** in the city | 11.6% |

The children from non-Jewish districts are over-represented at 11.6 per-cent, The first razzias took place in districts where there was a large Jewish population, such as the Weesperstraat and the surrounding area. Districts with few Jewish residents were the last to be raided, which explains why the children from these districts are over-represented at 11.6 percent.

The middle rent group is best represented, followed by the lower rent groups. We can therefore conclude, with some caution, that children from the middle class had the first opportunity to go into hiding with the help of the four rescue groups. As regards the children's rescuers, we have not found any support for the notion that the Jewish proletariat had little or no chance to go into hiding.

RELIGION

The respondents to the questionnaire reported that their parents were not very religious or not at all religious.

GOING INTO HIDING

Almost everyone in the files of the Bureau for War Foster Children (OPK files) was an orphan. A number of children had already been in hiding before they were brought to the child care center and then came under the care of one of the four groups. The UCC and the ASG found places for 32.2 percent of the children before May 1, 1943. Twenty-seven of the thirty-four chil-dren (79.4%) rescued by the Trouw Group were placed during the period from May through September 1943. The initial amateurism of the rescuers and the lack of cooperation in the countryside explain why Jewish children with long-term *gesperrden* (special permits postponing deportation) were most likely to be successfully placed by the student groups.

The statistics indicate that children with long-term *gesperrden* who lived in Amsterdam, were less than six years old, and came from middle-income families had the best chance of being placed.

HIDING PLACES

We know that 650 children lived with 1,355 foster families; 261 of the families are unknown. Table 10 shows the breakdown of the 1,355 known foster homes by province and rescue organization.

There were more than 107 children in Friesland; Iet van Dijk was able to find places for 230 children, but there are no further data. Other sources indicate that each child stayed in three or four places on average. This means that an estimated 3,300–4,400 hiding addresses were needed for the approximately 1,100 Jews in hiding.

TABLE 10

| Placed in province by: | Trouw | NV | ASG | UCC |
|---|---|---|---|---|
| Friesland | 22 | 5 | 46 | 34 |
| Groningen | 6 | – | 1 | 3 |
| Drenthe | 6 | – | 1 | – |
| Overijssel | 3 | 77 | 6 | 6 |
| Gelderland | 6 | 22 | 3 | 33 |
| Utrecht | 2 | 9 | 3 | 124 |
| Noord-Holland | 24 | 12 | 22 | 27 |
| Zuid-Holland | 17 | 19 | 7 | 21 |
| Zeeland | 2 | 7 | – | 9 |
| Noord-Brabant | 2 | 6 | 5 | 12 |
| Limburg | 8 | 278 | 113 | 35 |
| Total known | 98 | 435 | 207 | 354 |
| Unknown | 27 | 62 | 62 | 110 |
| TOTAL | 125 | 497 | 269 | 464 |

PROFILE OF FOSTER PARENTS

We studied the 650 longest-lasting placements. One-third of them were in large cities or in provincial centers.[4] The other two-thirds were in the countryside.

TREATMENT OF THE CHILDREN

There is information about the treatment of war foster children by their host families in 263 files of the Bureau of War Foster Children (OPK). As shown in Table 11, the files mention psychological cruelty (e.g., threats to hand the child over to the Germans), an indifferent attitude and/or a lack of affection, hospitality, and security, neglect in favor of their own children, exploitation of the child as a worker, physical neglect, sexual abuse, religious pressure, and anti-Semitism. No conclusions can be draw from these data because the group is too small.

TABLE 11

| Well treated | 105 | 39.9% |
|---|---|---|
| Physical abuse | 2 | 0.8% |
| Psychological abuse | 2 | 0.8% |
| Neglect in favor of own children | 0 | 0.0% |
| Exploitation as worker | 1 | 0.4% |
| Neglect | 3 | 1.1% |
| Sexual abuse | 0 | 0.0% |
| Religious pressure | 29 | 11.0% |
| Anti-Semitism | 3[a] | 1.1% |
| No data | 124 | 47.1% |

[a] The three cases of anti-Semitism were coupled with religious pressure in two instances and with abuse in one, so that the numbers add up to 266 (instead of 263), and the percentages to 101.1 (instead of 100).

ROOM AND BOARD

In a number of cases the rescuers paid a monthly stipend (sometimes through the LO) to provide for the care of the foster children. On average this came to 42 guilders from the UCC, 31 guilders from the ASG, and 28 guilders from the NV. The stipends went mostly to families of modest means. In very rare instances Nico Dohmen and Hanna van de Voort provided money for room and board. Herman Flim gave money more often. The UCC gave subsidies to twenty-two families.

CHILDLESS FOSTER PARENTS

Before the war, approximately 10 percent of Dutch couples were childless. Such couples were especially willing to take care of a Jewish child temporarily. Two very small databases show that 30 percent of the foster parents were childless.

RELIGION OF PRINCIPAL HOST FAMILIES

What was the religious background of the families that took in Jewish children? The breakdown, based on a database of 194 children, is shown in Table 12. Calvinists comprise the largest single group. This is because Calvinist activists from the NV and the Trouw Group often recruited co-religionists to shelter Jewish children. These two rescue groups lodged 69.1 percent of their charges with Calvinists. Twenty-six of the sixty Catholic foster families were found by the ASG, and twenty-one by the three workers in Tienray. The under-representation of Baptists (parishioners of Willem and Sjoukje Mesdag) is misleading. In most cases Mesdag, Jansen, and Coelingh only knew the children's "hiding" names. This made it very difficult to identify children who were hidden in Friesland and, therefore, the families that sheltered them.

TABLE 12

| | | |
|---|---|---|
| Calvinist | 68 | 35.0% |
| Roman Catholic | 60 | 30.1% |
| Dutch Reformed | 29 | 14.9% |
| Not religious | 15 | 7.7% |
| Liberal Reformed | 8 | 4.1% |
| Protestant | 5 | 2.6% |
| Dutch Arminian | 2 | 1.0% |
| Free Evangelical | 2 | 1.0% |
| Baptist | 2 | 1.0% |
| Christian Reformed | 2 | 1.0% |
| Old Catholic | 1 | 0.5% |

INCOME OF HOST FAMILIES

The income of a total of 208 foster families is shown in Table 13.

TABLE 13

| High | 18 | 8.6% |
|---|---|---|
| Middle | 129 | 62.0% |
| Low | 61 | 29.3% |

NUMBER OF CHILDREN CAPTURED

At least forty-seven Jewish children (from the children's database) were caught during their time in hiding. This is 6.4 percent of the total. Twenty-one of these forty-seven children survived the war. The UCC managed to save three children under its care who were captured. Seven other children were hidden again by other groups via the child-care center. Eleven children survived deportation. The remaining twenty-six (3.5%) were murdered. If we look at this percentage in light of the total of 974 children, then we have to conclude that approximately 940 Jewish children escaped death thanks to the efforts of the rescuers.

NOTES

1. We interviewed one former hidden child, Roosje Colthof, in 1984. Eight years later she filled out a questionnaire. Thus there is one overlap between the questionnaires and the interviews; this brings the total number of respondents to ninety-one.

2. This sampling cannot be considered representative, nor can the data from our children's database.

3. In 1976 S. Wijnberg estimated the total number of Jews in Amsterdam to have been 79,410. The difference of 46 with J. Th. M. Houwink ten Cate, *Alfons Zündler*, is too small to worry about.

4. This pertains to the number of hidden children in the following cities and provincial centers: Almelo: 2; Amersfoort: 4; Amstelveen: 2; Amsterdam: 9; Arnhem: 4; Breda: 1; Bussum: 1; Delft: 1; Den Bosch: 3; Den Haag: 8; Deventer: 5; Eindhoven: 1; Enschede: 4; Geleen: 15; Groningen: 2; Haarlem: 1; Heerenveen: 1; Heerlen: 26; Hengelo: 12; Hilversum: 6; Hoogeveen: 2; Kampen: 2; Kerkrade: 6; Leeuwarden: 6; Leiden: 2; Middelburg: 4; Rotterdam: 5; Scheveningen: 1; Sneek: 13; Utrecht: 48; Venlo: 10; Wageningen: 1.

# SUMMARY

7

The student groups organized quickly after the deportations of Jews began. They were able to fall back on umbrella organizations like the Utrecht Student Association, the Amsterdam Student Association, the Utrecht Women Students Organization, and the Amsterdam Women Students Organization. The students were able to put children up throughout the country without much difficulty because they themselves came from outside the university cities. Their families and friends, understanding that their help was needed, opened their homes and their wallets. The 10,000 guilders collected by the four bishops lasted until the end of 1942.

Early on, the students received support from the pediatrician Fiedeldij Dop. This trusted person helped Jewish parents take the step of handing their child over to a student, thereby making it possible for approximately seventy Jewish children and several adults to go into hiding by the end of August 1942. By the end of April 1943, the number had reached 250. After a rapid start, student efforts to hide Jewish children began to slow down. This happened because a number of activists resumed their studies after the summer vacation, and the supply of available placement addresses (family and friends of fellow students) was exhausted. As a result, the Utrecht students had to try and find hiding addresses in unknown territory, which was much more difficult.

The success of Fiedeldij Dop meant that the Amsterdam students could deliver more children than the Utrecht group could place. That is why Piet Meerburg went to Friesland in an attempt to find people (ministers, pastors, etc.) who could help him find host families, but he encountered skepticism and disbelief. The extent of the deportations and the rapidity with which they were being carried out were not known in the countryside. It was not until January 1943, when Meerburg happened to run into his cousin Mia

Coelingh, that the Amsterdam Student Group was able to establish its first branch in Friesland.

In January 1943, the NV had very few channels to the outside at its disposal. The members of the NV had their roots in Amsterdam. During the first one and a half months, Gerard Musch and Dick Groenewegen van Wijk tried unsuccessfully to find homes in the province of Groningen. When they heard that Jaap Musch was successful in Heerlen, they joined him. Contact with Joop Woortman (the Fiedeldij Dop of the NV) was established, at the earliest, around the beginning of October 1942, two and one-half months after the start of the deportations. As long as the NV members could find addresses in Heerlen, there was no need to look elsewhere. About eighty Jewish children were lodged in that area during the period from September 1942 to April 1943. The foster families received very little financial support. During this early period the bishop of Roermond was quite out of reach because this was primarily a Calvinist activity. Very few people contributed anything.

Hester van Lennep used the "snowball" method. She counted on her friends and acquaintances, and they, in turn, on their own friends and acquaintances. The cooperation of the Boissevain family who were members of the CS-6 resistance group was very important for her. She was also helped by her clients. Slowly but surely, it became known in Jewish districts that there was a woman living on Keizersgracht in Amsterdam who could help Jewish children go into hiding. Hester worked on demand, and starting at Christmas 1942 she was aided by Sándor Baracs. Later on they joined the Trouw Group. Through April 1943 they were able to help twenty children go into hiding.

By April 30, 1943, the three groups of children's rescuers had found refuges for 350 Jews; this was roughly a third of the total of 1,100. By that time more than 56 percent of Dutch Jewry had already been gassed.

The Jewish rescuers looked for a channel by which they could smuggle Jewish children out of the child-care center and the Hollandsche Schouwburg. This called for extreme caution because the rescuers were under direct German surveillance. In January 1943 Süskind finally found a person he could trust in Joop Woortman, who came recommended by his old friend Hans Kinsbergen. From that moment on it was possible to let children disappear in very small numbers. The method of smuggling from the child-care center was perfected after its director, Henriette Pimentel, approached Johan van Hulst, the head of the Protestant Teachers College. Larger numbers of Jewish children could escape via the college. At the same time, Felix Halverstad and Walter Süskind became ever more creative in tampering with the card files of the German administration. Starting in the summer of 1943, pickup points were established in the neighborhood of the child-care center. Children from the center who were to be rescued were taken to these points while on their daily walks. These improved methods led to greater effectiveness in the period from May to September: one out of ten children could be taken to safety. At the end of September the Germans closed the child-care center. Until November 9, the annex in the building next-door (no. 29) functioned as a detention center for Jewish children who were caught. Several children were rescued even from the annex. A total of about 600 children were rescued from the child-care center, and approximately 385 were hidden by the rescuers.

## HOW WERE THE RESCUE GROUPS ORGANIZED?

In a nutshell, the answer is: effectively, but in very different ways. The most important difference was the way in which the members viewed their task. The NV members continued to feel responsible for the children after they found placements for them. They made home visits to see whether all was well, and when they noticed problems the child was transferred. This called for a large number of care-givers.

The two student groups and the Trouw Group transferred the responsibility for the children to the foster parents—with the exception of the Amsterdam student branches in Sneek (Friesland) and Tienray (Limburg), which did check on the children, just like the NV. Often children were entrusted to other organizations, such as the LO in Friesland and Limburg. We have called the children's rescue branch of the Trouw Group a "pickup" organization because of its methods. When picking up ended because of a lack of children, the Trouw Group ended its involvement in children's rescue work. The greater emphasis on the pickup aspect of the work was the reason that these groups had fewer workers than the NV even though they could rescue more children.

With fewer workers, it was necessary to have a less-structured organization. Any hierarchy was out of the question in the student groups. Given the abundance of strong personalities, a bureaucratic structure would probably not have been accepted. Everyone did what they thought needed to be done. Coordination came about as a result of informal discussions. The Trouw Group had no clear hierarchy.

The NV, on the other hand, had a well-defined power structure. Policies were formulated by the three leaders: Jaap and Gerard Musch, and Dick Groenewegen van Wijk. In Amsterdam Joop Woortman ran the show.

Initially all the groups tried to finance their work in the same way: they traveled all over, in cities and throughout the countryside, in search of ration cards and money. The Utrecht Children's Committee was the most successful in this respect. It did not link up with any other organization and owed its continued existence to the sale of *The Eighteen Dead*, the first product of Geert Lubberhuizen's publishing activities, and of other pamphlets. This also brought in enough income for the Amsterdam Student Group.

For the NV and for Hester van Lennep, their income relied on occasional gifts until the summer of 1943. This must have been why they joined with other organizations when the opportunity presented itself. In August 1943, the NV linked up with the LO, although it remained in charge of the children's care. The Trouw Group's organization that Gesina van der Molen brought with her was a godsend for Hester van Lennep and Sándor Baracs.

Meerburg and Van Zeytveld handed children over to the LO only if the accompanying registration requirement could be circumvented. This worked in the case of the Leeuwarden, Joure, and South Limburg branches because the children's rescuers were also part of the LO leadership. The activists in Tienray and Sneek remained independent.

After the strikes in April/May 1943, a great many people had to go into hiding, and as a result there was more readiness to take in people in need of a refuge, including Jews. Around the same time, the children's rescuers had their organizations in order, and Jewish parents were recognizing that it was better to give up their children. These three circumstances brought about the increase in the number of Jewish children picked up and hidden between May and September 1943. During these five months, more than 54 percent of the children were brought to safety.

The Utrecht Children's Committee experienced a serious setback during that crucial summer of 1943: the failed raid in Esch. In consequence the Utrecht Group was unable to profit from the opportunity to rescue children from the child-care center. After June 12, the group's activities had to be suspended for the most part. In September 1943 it managed to resume its activities. The small number of children added in the intervening period (most likely thanks to Anne Maclaine Pont) came primarily under the care of Ankie Stork.

Thanks to the efforts of the Kinsbergen family in Amsterdam, Jewish children could still be saved from deportation after September 1943. It should also be noted that the NV, which percentage-wise did not have much success at the outset, was able to take on "new" children longer than the other groups.

The NV also experienced setbacks, however. Early in November 1943, in addition to the arrest of Pontier, there was the canceled razzia in Treebeek/Brunssum that resulted in the decision to disperse the children over a larger area. The NV now made transferring children its official policy, and as a result its branches in the Betuwe and Twente areas came into existence. Early in 1944 Jaap Musch moved into the country cottage in Nijverdal. Because of a fatal coincidence he fell into the hands of the Germans and their Dutch collaborators in camp Erika; this cost him his life.

## HOW DID THE FOUR GROUPS DIFFER?

Several differences have already been mentioned. But the difference in religion has not yet been discussed. The NV and the Trouw Group were both Calvinist. Since the Trouw Group used the distribution channel of its underground newspaper to obtain addresses, it found housing for most of its children in the Protestant northern part of the country. There is nothing surprising about this.

However, the NV found its first safe haven amidst a sea of Catholics in South Limburg. The reason for this has already been mentioned: Jaap Musch came in contact with Gérard Pontier, and one thing led to another. The NV members met with only mixed success in their effort to win acceptance in Catholic circles. Starting in June 1943 they increased their territory northward with the help of Calvinist clergy. It seems very likely that old religious barriers contributed to the NV's difficult start. The increase in the number of Jewish children picked up coincided with the NV's joining the LO, which in Limburg was run primarily by the Catholic clergy. From then on Catholic foster families could also be recruited.

Most of the students were not very religious and willingly took help from anyone who offered it. Frits Iordens was not put off by the very strict Reformed beliefs of Paul Terwindt; Wouter van Zeytveld, a leftist, made contact with deeply religious people in Breukelen; Truitje van Lier received Jewish children who had stayed with Calvinist as well as Communist families. Piet Meerburg did have to swallow a few times after his first conversation with Sjoerd Wiersma, but he nevertheless threw in his lot with him. The branch in Sneek was a model of religious tolerance thanks to the cooperation of a Baptist minister, a Catholic curate, and a female Liberal Reformed assistant minister.

In Chapter 5, we discussed the question of how faithful the groups were to the objectives set forth in 1942. We can conclude that up to and including the closing of the child-care center, the majority were faithful to the goal of rescuing children. After the child-care center was closed, many devoted themselves to other forms of resistance. Most of the NV members, who from the beginning had emphasized the care of children, continued this work until liberation.

## THE CHILDREN

We wish to remind our readers, perhaps unnecessarily, that the data available are not sufficient for solid conclusions. The results of the research point to an average of three or four residences per hidden child. This comes to 3,300 to 4,400 hiding addresses, located primarily in the provinces of Limburg and Friesland, and found by around a hundred full-time or part-time children's rescuers.[1]

These numbers mean very little until you try to imagine the amount of work all this entailed. Time and time again, the rescue activists approached untold thousands of possible foster parents (often introduced by the local minister) and very cautiously asked them if they would be willing to risk their own safety and that of their children by taking in a Jewish child. The number of times the answer was no cannot even be estimated, but it must certainly have been far more than 3,300 to 4,400. The numbers begin to take on meaning if you then add the efforts the rescuers made to ensure the supply of children (just consider the personnel in the child-care center) and to obtain ration cards, clothing, shoes, and funds for room and board. Only then do you become aware of what an extremely difficult task this aspect of the resistance actually was.

And the clock kept ticking. Every Tuesday a train left Westerbork with death as its destination. The children's rescuers managed to arrange refuges for the small remnant of 600 Jews who had been spared so far because they possessed special documents (*Sperre*) that gave them a temporary stay of deportation.

The four rescue groups helped to hide a total of 1,100 children and adults: roughly 400 by the Utrecht Children's Committee; roughly 350 by the Amsterdam Student Group; about 250 by the NV; and about 100 by the Trouw Group.

Profile of the hidden children: *gesperd* (deportation postponed by a permit) for a long time, lived in Amsterdam before going into hiding, younger than six, and (less certain) from a family of average income.

Profile of the foster parents at the principal hiding address: solicited by the children's rescuers, good to their foster children, villagers, Calvinist or Catholic, and (less certain) moderately religious and living on an average income.

There was no misconduct of any kind by the foster parents in about four-fifths of the cases known to us. Only 2 to 4 percent of the Jewish children concerned were maltreated, even though the children's rescuers usually exercised little or no control after placing them. The host parents had more power over their charges than in a normal parent-child relationship. Most of the foster families did their best to alleviate the sadness the children felt because of being separated from their parents. All praise to them.

The number of childless couples among the foster parents was three times as high as the national average. Room and board was provided in at least 20 percent of the cases.

HOW MANY CHILDREN WERE KILLED DESPITE ALL THESE EFFORTS?

Only 3.5 percent of the Jewish children were caught and subsequently killed. Thus the four rescue groups were very effective.

CONCLUSION

The wartime rescuers saw hiding children as work, or a vocation, in the highest sense of the word, and they tried to carry it out it as well as possible. Looking back, are they satisfied with the way they did their work? They see now that every mistake had fatal consequences. As a result, recollected delays and mistakes take on more importance. Today several of the rescuers feel keenly that every delay, every mistake, cost the lives of Jewish children. "Did I do my work well enough?" is a question that continues to haunt some of them.

NOTES

1. Since it is impossible to know exactly how many people were involved—just think of the great number of unknowns who occasionally helped in some way—we decided not to try and give an exact number of children's rescuers.

# SOURCES

This book recounts the history of four Dutch resistance groups that, together with a fifth, Jewish group, helped to hide Jewish children during the years 1942–1945. It is based on and summarizes the well-documented scholarly research incorporated in the dissertation of Dr. Bert Jan Flim.

Dr. Flim began his research in the second half of the 1980s and received his Ph.D. from the University of Groningen in September 1995. The late Professor M. G. Buist was his thesis adviser, and Deborah Dwork, now a professor at Clark University in Worcester, Massachusetts, followed the research closely.

In his thesis Flim summarizes the results of his research, which was obtained from among others:

- 79 published sources
- 104 written sources
- 69 interviews and other oral material
- 48 telephone interviews

In the absence of material from the period, the interviews are extremely important. He also utilized the postwar files on the children compiled by the OPK (Bureau for War Foster Children). These were supplemented with the results of a survey that obtained valuable material about 310 other Jewish children.

The methodology used—a combination of archival research, interviews, and surveys—guarantees that the thesis and the abridged adaptation by the historian Jozien Driessen has produced a historically accurate account. The translation of this work by Dr. Jeannette K. Ringold is therefore based on facts and real events.

This unique collection of data was incorporated and used by Dr. B. J. Flim in his dissertation "Omdat hun hart sprak: (Geschiedenis van de georganiseerde hulp aan joodse kinderen in Nederland 1942–1945)" [They listened to their hearts: History of the organized help for Jewish children in the Netherlands during the years 1942–1945]. In 1996 the dissertation was published by Kok in Kampen (the Netherlands), and in this form it is available for consultation and reference. Dr. Flim subsequently transferred his collection of data to the Nederlands Instituut voor Oorlogsdocumentatie (Dutch Institute for War Documentation) in Amsterdam.

# GLOSSARY

*Arbeitseinsatz*

> Call-up of Dutch men to work in German war industries or agriculture.

*Aryan declaration*

> Declaration of Aryan origin: document certifying that one had no Jewish ancestors. Government employees were required to sign it, and almost all of them did so.

*Ausweis*

> Document issued by a German official certifying that the holder had certain privileges, such as being exempt from the *Arbeitseinsatz*.

*Bevolkingsregister*

> Dutch population registry.

*Bezige Bij*

> "Busy Bee." Illegal publishing house established by Geert Lubberhuizen; its profits financed the Utrecht Children's Committee and the Amsterdam Student Group, as well as many hidden actors and writers from 1943 on. On the occasion of its sixtieth anniversary, the Bezige Bij asked Mr. Hans Renders to write a book about how this publishing firm came into existence. The book, entitled *Dangerous Printed Matter*, was published in 2004.

An important source of information for this glossary was: Bob Moore, *Victims and Survivors: The Nazi Persecution of the Jews in the Netherlands, 1940–1945* (London: Arnold, 1997), "Glossary and Abbreviations," pp. 307–314.

*Chanukah*

> Literally "dedication." Festival of lights; a midwinter Jewish holiday during which candles are lighted for eight successive days and children receive presents.

*Concentration camp*

> Camp where "undesirable persons" could be detained indefinitely, often without preceding judicial process. Such camps had existed in Germany since 1933. During the war, there were four such camps in the Netherlands, located in Amersfoort, Ommen, Schoorl, and Vught.

*"De Achttien Dooden"*

> "The Eighteen Dead." Poem by Jan Campert about eighteen men who were executed by the Germans on March 13, 1941. Published in 1943 as the first product of Bezige Bij.

*Dispuut*

> Fraternity or sorority.

*Distributiestamkaart*

> Proof of identity needed to obtain a ration card.

*Endlösung*

> "Final Solution." Nazi term for the extermination of European Jewry.

*Expositur*

> Department of the Jewish Council that used bureaucratic procedures and red tape to delay deportation of Jews who had been called up.

*February strike*

> Wave of strikes that began in Amsterdam in February 1941 in reaction to a Nazi pogrom against the Jews, the first such incident in the history of the Netherlands. The strikes also expressed general resentment of the increasingly oppressive German occupation and the WA's attempt to "conquer the street."

*Gemeentepolitie*

> Dutch municipal police, originally under the control of local mayors and the Ministry of the Interior but transferred to the jurisdiction of the Ministry of Justice by the Germans.

*Gereformeerde kerk*

> Dutch Orthodox Calvinist Church.

*Gestapo*

> *Geheime Staatspolizei.* German secret police, later known as the SD.

*Grebbelinie*

> Dutch defense line in 1940, about 40 km west of Arnhem, blocking the road to Utrecht.

*Grüne Polizei*

> "Green police." German *Ordnungspolizei* (Order Police) operating in the Netherlands; they wore green uniforms.

*Hervormde Kerk*

> Dutch Reformed Church, the former Protestant state church.

*Hollandsche Schouwburg*

> Small theater in Amsterdam near the zoo (Artis), used by the Germans as a collection point for Jews captured during razzias; the Germans called it *Joodsche Schouwburg.* In our text we have used its original name.

*Hongerwinter*

> "Hunger Winter." The winter of 1944–45, so called because the Germans prevented foodstuffs and fuel from reaching the towns and cities of the western and northwestern Netherlands, causing great privation.

*Joodsche Invalide*

> The largest Jewish hospital in Amsterdam.

*Joodsche Raad*

> "Jewish Council." Organization forced upon the Jewish community by the Germans. It was charged with communicating repressive measures to the Jewish community, making sure that they were implemented, and assisting the German administration. The Expositur was one of its departments.

*Joodsche Schouwburg*

> *See* Hollandsche Schouwburg.

*Judenhilfe*

> "Helping Jews." A serious crime under the German occupation administration. Violators were arrested and sent to concentration camps.

*Kinderwerkers*

> "Children's Rescuers." Activists who from 1942 to 1945 tried to save Jewish children from deportation by finding non-Jewish host

families for them somewhere in the Netherlands and then providing them with distribution cards and/or food, clothing, shoes, and
money for board.

*Knokploeg*

"Fighting Gang." A small mobile resistance group that broke into
distribution offices, town halls, and registry offices, liberated polit-
ical prisoners, and liquidated traitors. *See also* LKP.

*Kultuurkamer*

German-dominated organization of "cultural workers" (artists,
writers, etc.); membership was obligatory for those who wished to
live by their trade.

*Landstand*

Professional organization established by the Germans; all peasants
and fishermen were required to join.

*Landwacht*

"Alternative" police organization whose personnel were recruited
from the NSB; its object was to combat the resistance.

*Lippmann-Rosenthal*

Jewish-owned bank taken over by the Germans to administer the
collection of the assets of Jews prior to their deportation. Its employees often worked alongside those of the Zentralstelle.

*LKP*

*Landelijke Knokploegen* "National League of Action Groups."
Formed in 1943 with the primary goal of breaking into rationing
offices and population registries in order to obtain ration books and
identity cards for the LO.

*LO*

*Landelijke Organisatie voor Hulp aan Onderduikers* "National Organization for Assistance to Those in Hiding." One of the largest resistance organizations. Founded at the end of 1942, it had 15,000
members and was sheltering 200,000–300,000 people by the summer of 1944.

*Militair Gezag*

The provisional government that took over after the German capitulation in 1945.

*Mussert, Anton*

Founder and leader of the NSB. Very obedient to Hitler. Even
founded a Dutch SS. Executed in 1945 as a traitor to his country.

*Nationaal Steunfonds*

> "National Assistance Fund." Established to fund resistance and underground activities.

*NSB*

> *Nationaal-Socialistische Beweging* The Dutch National-Socialist movement, the largest Nazi party in the country, founded in 1931.

*NSDAP*

> *Nationalsozialistische Deutsche Arbeiterpartei.* The German Nazi party.

*Onderduikers*

> Those who "dive under." Term describing people who went into hiding, although it encompassed a wide range of activities and circumstances.

*OPK*

> *Oorlogspleegkinderen* "Commission for War Foster Children." Organized by the Dutch government in 1945.

*Oranjehotel*

> "Orange Hotel." Ironic name for the prison in Scheveningen.

*Persoonsbewijs (PB)*

> Identity card, made compulsory by the Germans for all Dutch civilians over fourteen. It included a photo, a signature, and a fingerprint.

*Razzia*

> "Raid." In Amsterdam and other large Dutch cities, raids were carried out to round up Jews and, later, forced labor.

*SA*

> *Sturm Abteilung.* Combat division of the NSDAP.

*Schalkhaarpolitie*

> Police recruited from the NSB and trained in a special school in Schalkhaar near Deventer (Overijssel).

*SD*

> *Sicherheitsdienst.* Security and intelligence service of the SS, closely linked to the Gestapo and German police organizations

*Sinterklaas*

> The Dutch equivalent of Santa Claus: a day on which all children receive presents. It is celebrated on December 5, the birthday of the medieval Bishop Nicolas of Myre (in present-day Turkey), who is

said to have given presents to the children in his diocese. Young
Dutch children believe that he is still alive, still gives presents, and
lives with his helpers in Spain.

*Sipo*

Sicherheitspolizei "Security Police." German police force made up
of elements of the Gestapo and the criminal police.

*Sperren*

To postpone deportation until further notice.

*Spertijd*

Curfew. Time during which ordinary citizens were forbidden to
be outside their houses. Introduced on November 1, 1940 for the
entire country between midnight and 4:00 a.m. As a punishment,
curfew sometimes started at 8:00 p.m.

*Spoorwegstaking*

Railroad strike. The third and last great strike during the occupation took place in September 1944. It began on the express orders
of the government-in-exile in London at what seemed to be a pro-
pitious moment during the battle of Arnhem.

*SS*

Schutzstaffel "Protective Detachment." Originally a kind of body-
guard for Hitler; later developed into an organization of the most
fanatical Nazis.

*WA*

Weerafdeling. Combat section of the NSB.

*Waffen-SS*

Militarized units of the SS.

*Westerweel Group*

Resistance group with Jewish members.

*Winterhulp*

German-style welfare organization of the NSB. Those who refused
to contribute could expect difficulties.

*Zentralstelle für jüdische Auswanderung*

"Bureau for Jewish Emigration." German agency in Amsterdam,
jointly run by the SIPO and the SD, that supervised the deportation of Jews from the Netherlands; Ferdinand Aus der Fünten was
in charge even though Willy Lages was its head.

# CHRONOLOGY

## 1940

May

10–15　German army attacks the Netherlands. Queen Wilhelmina and nine cabinet ministers leave for London and form a government in exile. Dutch forces surrender after the bombing of Rotterdam. Start of German occupation.

18　Hitler sets up a civilian administration led by Dr. A. Seyss-Inquart as Reichskommissar. The Secretaries-General of the Dutch ministries continue functioning under him.

June–September

Various foods, shoes, textiles, etc., are rationed. First clandestine bulletins are circulated.

July

28　Queen Wilhelmina inaugurates Radio Orange in London.

August

17　All Jewish newspapers are closed down. On April 11, 1941, one official Jewish paper is allowed to publish.

28　The College of Secretaries-General is instructed not to appoint any Jews to the civil service.

An important source of information for this chronology is: Bob Moore, *Victims and Survivors: The Nazi Persecution of the Jews in the Netherlands, 1940–1945* (London: Arnold, 1997), "Chronology of the Persecution of the Jews in the Netherlands," pp. 261–267.

September

11     Dutch SS is founded by Anton Mussert, the leader of the NSB (National Socialist Movement).

October

5     Government employees have to sign a so-called Aryan Attestation, declaring that they are not Jewish.

27     Dutch Reformed Church protests Aryan Attestation.

November

21     Government employees who are Jewish are removed from their posts on German orders. Protests at Universities of Leiden and Delft. After strike by students, both institutions are closed by the Germans. The other universities do not strike. Delft is allowed to reopen after several months.

## 1941

January

10     All Jews have to register. Everyone over the age of fourteen is issued an identity card; Jews have a large *J* stamped on it.

February

11     WA incites clashes in Jewish area of Amsterdam. A WA member is killed.

13     Germans establish a Jewish Council for Amsterdam.

22–23     In reprisal for clashes, approximately 400 young Jews are imprisoned and sent to Buchenwald and Mauthausen. This causes great public indignation.

25–26     General strike in Amsterdam as a protest. Waffen-SS takes severe measures to suppress "February strike."

March

31     Creation of Zentralstelle für Jüdische Auswanderung (Bureau for Jewish Emigration).

April

11     First issue of *Joodsche Weekblad* ("Jewish Weekly"), which announces all measures against Jews.

June

4    Freedom of movement restricted for Jews.

22   German invasion of Russia. Many Dutch communists are imprisoned.

September

15   Signs "Forbidden for Jews" appear in parks and other public places.

October

20   All Jews to be dismissed from their jobs no later than January 31.

November

7    Jews are forbidden to travel or move without a permit.

December

7–11  After Japanese attack on Pearl Harbor, Allies are at war with Japan. Germany and Italy declare war on United States. New hope in the Netherlands.

## 1942

January

10   Unemployed Jews (see October 20, 1941) sent to work camps. By February 1, 7,000 Jews are working in thirty-seven Dutch work camps.

17   Jews from the countryside are to be concentrated in Amsterdam.

20   Wannsee Conference in Berlin formulates practical measures for extermination of European Jewry.

May

3    As of this date, all Jews older than six are required to wear a yellow Star of David on their clothing.

21   Jews forced to hand over all assets and possessions valued at more than 250 guilders to Lippmann-Rosenthal bank in Amsterdam.

June

26   German administration notifies the Jewish Council that deportations will start.

July

1    Supervision of Westerbork transit camp taken over by SS.

4    First 1,000 call-up notices to report to the Zentralstelle für Jüdische Auswanderung sent out.

15   First trainload of Jews from Amsterdam to Westerbork. From there deportations to Auschwitz follow. Spontaneous actions by students in Utrecht and Amsterdam to hide Jewish children and find foster homes for them.

End of August

The Amsterdam and Utrecht students care for 70–80 Jewish children hidden in several places in the Netherlands, but mostly in the city of Utrecht.

September

2    Police in Amsterdam ordered to pick up Jews at their homes, take some of them to the Hollandsche Schouwburg, and hold them there for transport to Westerbork.

October

The NV group takes its first Jewish children to South Limburg.

5 (ca.)  Day-care center opposite the Hollandsche Schouwburg is transformed into round-the-clock child-care center for children of Jews imprisoned in the Schouwburg.

December

12   Several members of the Utrecht Children's Committee set fire to student administration of the University of Utrecht in order to sabotage impending *Arbeitseinsatz*.

End of 1942

National Organization for Assistance to Those in Hiding (LO) established.

## 1943

January

16   First Jews taken to Vught concentration camp.

February

2       German army surrenders near Stalingrad, a hopeful turning point of the war in Europe.

5–6     Attempted assassination of Dutch SS General Seyffardt by members of CS-6 resistance group. In reprisal, 602 university students are arrested and sent to Vught.

March

15     Universities reopen only for students who sign the declaration of loyalty to the German occupiers. Those who refuse will be called up for work in Germany. Only 16 percent of the students sign; many go into hiding.

April 29–May 5

The German decision to deport the entire former Dutch Army to POW camps in Germany arouses great fury throughout the country. Many Dutch doors that were closed to hiders are now opened. The rescue organizations profit immensely from the new situation.

End of May to end of September

To make the country *Judenrein*, numerous raids on Jews in Amsterdam.

Trouw Group and NV increase their efforts to smuggle children from the child care-center to safe hiding places.

September

29     The child-care center in Amsterdam is closed by the German authorities.

## 1944

June

6      D-day: Allied forces land in Normandy.

September

5      *Dolle Dinsdag* ("Mad Tuesday"). The rapid Allied advance in northern France and Belgium led people in the western part of the Netherlands to think that liberation was imminent. The populace began to celebrate (prematurely as it turned out), and in early September members of the NSB, other collaborators,

and many German soldiers began to flee in a panic that peaked on September 5.

5–6    Most of the male prisoners at Vught are sent to Sachsenhausen in freight trains, the women to Ravensbrück.

17–25   Operation Market Garden: Allied airborne landings around Nijmegen and Arnhem. Dutch government in London orders general railroad strike. Many railroad personnel go into hiding. Battle of Arnhem lost by Allies; German forces hold their positions north of the Rhine River.

Winter 1944–1945

Germans stop the transport of food to densely populated provinces in the western part of the Netherlands, causing increased starvation. Underground organizations have great difficulty getting food to those in hiding.

## 1945

May

6    Official capitulation of all German troops in the Netherlands.

# A RESCUER'S WHO'S WHO

*Baracs, Sándor* (b. 1900)

Baracs, a Hungarian Jew, emigrated to the Netherlands and was natu-
ralized in 1934. He became active in the resistance in 1940. A good friend
of the Boissevain family, he married Hester van Lennep, Mrs. Boissevain's sister, and together with her joined the Trouw Group (1943).
After the war he was head of the Bureau for War Foster Children (OPK).

*Bastiaanse, Cor*

In July 1942, Cor, then a young woman living in Utrecht, decided on
her own to hide Jewish children from Amsterdam and asked Ad
Groenendijk for help. This was the impulse for the creation of the Utrecht Children's Committee.

*Beusekom, James van*

James van Beusekom was a medical student in Utrecht. In 1942 he
joined the Utrecht Children's Committee, and around the beginning of
1943 he became a full-time worker. He fled after the raid at Esch on June
11, 1943, but was caught. He was imprisoned because he had gone into
hiding, not because of his resistance work, and died in a camp.

*Bockma family*

The Bockmas were a Calvinist family in Heerlen, Limburg. They were
recruited for the NV in October 1942 by Jaap Musch. The father and
three daughters arranged a good number of foster placements. In addition, they temporarily, or sometimes permanently, hid Jews in their
home.

*Boissevain family*

In 1940 the two Boissevain sons, Gideon and Jan Karel, founded the CS-6 armed resistance group. They and the other members were arrested in 1943. Both sons were executed by firing squad. Their mother introduced her sister, Hester van Lennep, to Sándor Baracs and Gesina van der Molen of the Trouw Group.

*Bouwman, Wilhelmina, "Mien" (b. 1920)*

Invited to participate by Gesina van der Molen, Mien escorted children to the northern provinces and to Limburg. She was known as "Mien of Trouw" because she was the fiancée of Wim Speelman, the head of the distribution apparatus of the (illegal) *Trouw* newspaper.

*Brunner, Alice (b. 1919)*

Alice, a student of English at the University of Amsterdam, dropped out in 1943 and moved to Utrecht, where she was recruited by Hetty Voûte for the Utrecht Children's Committee. From the summer of 1943 until September 1944 she worked for the Amsterdam Student Group, transporting Jewish children to Friesland and northern Limburg. Later she went into hiding in Utrecht.

*Coelingh, M.W.J., "Mia" (b. 1911)*

Mia Coelingh, an assistant Reformed minister in Sneek, was recruited by her cousin Piet Meerburg for the Amsterdam Student Group. She worked in close cooperation with Willem Mesdag, a Baptist minister, and Gérard Jansen, a Roman Catholic curate. The three of them formed the Sneek branch of the Amsterdam Student Group; each of them found hiding addresses among their own parishioners.

*Cohen, Virgenie, "Virrie" (b. 1916)*

Virrie, the eldest daughter of David Cohen, one of the two chairmen of the Jewish Council, was a registered nurse and child-care worker. From February 1943, she and her sister Mirjam were on the staff of the child-care center. Virrie assisted director Pimentel and helped children to escape. After the center was closed in September 1943, she fled to Tienray with the help of the Amsterdam Student Group. There she helped Hanna van de Voort with her resistance work until the liberation of northern Limburg in November 1944. Her sister Mirjam was deported to Theresienstadt. Both of them survived the war.

*Delft, Rebecca van* (b. 1924)

Gerard Musch recruited Rebecca, a student of Dutch, to help transport children for the NV. Around Christmas of 1942, her work was taken over by Annemarie van Verschuer. Rebecca recruited another friend, Jooske de Neve, to help the NV, and she continued her work until the summer of 1943.

*Dijk, I.J. van, "Iet"*

Iet was a medical student in Amsterdam. Beginning in 1943 she escorted a great number of children to Friesland and Limburg for the Amsterdam Student Group.

*Dohmen, N.J.P., "Nico"* (b. 1921)

Nico, a student from Nijmegen, refused to sign the declaration of loyalty and went into hiding in the home of Hanna van de Voort in Tienray. After Piet Meerburg recruited Hanna for the Amsterdam Student Group, Nico helped her find refuges for Jewish children and take care of them while they were in hiding.

*Eding, Henk and Jitske*

The Edings ran a large student residence in Utrecht that served as drop-in center for the Utrecht Children's Committee. They were arrested during a raid in May 1944. Henk died in a camp in Germany. Jitske was sent to the prison camp in Vught, where she met Hetty Voûte and Gisela Söhnlein. The three women survived the war.

*Fiedeldij Dop, Philip H.* (b. 1911)

Fiedeldij Dop, a pediatrician in South-Amsterdam, had many Jewish patients. He persuaded hesitant parents to let their children go into hiding. Starting in the summer of 1942, Piet Meerburg of the Amsterdam Student Group supplied him with addresses where the children could be hidden.

*Flim family*

Jan Flim, a baker in Nijverdal, provided a summer cottage where Piet Vermeer of the NV was able to hide people. From March 1944, Jan's son, Herman (b. 1922), found new host families among the bakery's customers.

*Fritz, B., "Ben"* (b. 1922)

At the suggestion of his friend Dick Groenewegen van Wijk, Ben helped the NV branch in Brunssum (South Limburg).

*Groenendijk, Ad*

Ad knew Jan Meulenbelt at the university and asked his mother to hide some Jewish children from Amsterdam. This contact led to the creation of the Utrecht Children's Committee.

*Groenewegen van Wijk, "Dick"* (b. 1921)

Together with his friends, the brothers Jaap and Gerard Musch, Dick founded the NV in July 1942. The goal was to help Jewish children, for whom they found host families thanks to contacts with clergymen. Arrested in May of 1944, Dick managed to escape and fled back to the Vermeer family in Limburg.

*Haak family*

After refusing to sign the declaration of loyalty, Jur Haak (b. 1919), the family's eldest child, dropped out of the university, where he was a mathematics student, and became a teacher in Amsterdam. At Jan Meulenbelt's request, he arranged for Jewish children to be taken from Amsterdam to Utrecht. Jur involved his sister Tineke, her friend Wouter van Zeytveld, and another friend, Piet Meerburg, in this work, and that was how the Amsterdam Student Group came into being. The Haak parents were arrested during a house search in August 1943. The Germans were actually looking for Tineke, who was not home at the time. The parents were deported and died in German camps. Jur and Tineke survived the war.

*Halverstad, Felix*

Felix was director Süskind's first assistant in the Schouwburg. He doctored the records so that children could "disappear" administratively. He went into hiding in September 1943 and survived the war.

*Helm, Krijn van den* (b. 1912)

Krijn was a tax official in Leeuwarden when he met Piet Meerburg in 1942. He found addresses and transportation for the Amsterdam Student Group. Active in the armed resistance, he was killed during his arrest in August 1944.

*Hudig sisters, Olga and To*

Olga, the elder of the two, was a biology student in Utrecht and a friend of Hetty Voûte. Both sisters were prominent members of the Women's Student Association in Utrecht. In the fall of 1942 Jan Meulenbelt brought them into the Utrecht Children's Committee. The younger sister, To, had begun her medical studies in 1941 and was committed to taking care of children who were already in hiding. Both sisters had to go into hiding after the raid at the Edings' house in May 1944, but they continued their work during the last year of the war.

*Hulst, Johan van* (b. 1911)

Johan van Hulst was the principal of the Protestant Teachers College in Amsterdam, situated just next-door to the child-care center. Together with the director of the center, Henriette Pimentel, he arranged for children to escape via the college; this was done in cooperation with the NV and the Trouw Group. After the child-care center was closed in September of 1943, Van Hulst continued to take care of people in hiding.

*Iordens, F.H., "Frits"* (b. 1919)

Originally from Arnhem, Frits was a law student in Utrecht and a prominent member of the Utrecht Student Association for men (USC). In August 1942, Jan Meulenbelt recruited him and his girlfriend, Anne Maclaine Pont, for the Utrecht Children's Committee. Iordens was involved in several "special actions" and helped to kidnap several children from the child-care center. After their marriage, Frits and Anne organized an escape route for downed pilots. While escorting some pilots to safety he was shot and killed at a train check by the SD in March 1944.

*Jansen, G.M.A., "Gérard"* (b. 1925)

Jansen was a curate in Sneek. From 1943 to 1944, he and the Protestant ministers Coelingh and Mesdag worked together for the local branch of the Amsterdam Student Group.

*Kattenburg, Sieny* (b. 1924)

Sieny worked in the child-care center and was very active in smuggling children out. She and Harry Cohen, who worked in the Expositur, married in June of 1943 and went into hiding when the center was closed. They survived the war.

*Kempe, Dr. G. Th., "Ger"* (b. 1911)

As the senior assistant at the Criminological Institute in Utrecht, Kempe was Jan Meulenbelt's supervisor. Together with Meulenbelt, he organized the Utrecht Children's Committee in July 1942. Kempe served as its adviser and through his supervisor, Professor Willem Pompe, obtained financial aid from the Catholic Church. He later became involved with an espionage group.

*Kinsbergen family*

Samuel Kinsbergen was half-Jewish and an acquaintance of the Musch brothers. He was married to Lea Schmidt, who was German. In this way he became the stepfather of Lea's son, Heinz Schmidt, alias Hans Kinsbergen (b. 1925). Father and son were active in the NV with Joop Woortman, and the Kinsbergen home became a safe house for the organization. In order to avoid arousing suspicion so that it could continue in this capacity, Hans (who was a German citizen) sacrificed himself by reporting for duty when called up to serve in the Wehrmacht. He later managed to desert, and he as well as his parents survived the war.

*Knappert, Adri* (b. 1904)

Knappert was the director of a summer camp near Ommen. Toward the end of the summer of 1942 she worked with the Utrecht Children's Committee, housing many children for Anne Maclaine Pont and also for Ankie Stork. Later she had to go into hiding, but she and the children survived.

*Kracht–Van Dok, Cees and Lien* (married couple)

Cees and Lien became involved with the Amsterdam Student Group through Van Emde-Boas, an Amsterdam psychiatrist, and Wouter van Zeytveld. They established a large network from Wijdenes in West Friesland (the northern part of the province of Noord-Holland).

*Lennep, H.J.O. van, "Hester"* (b. 1916)

Hester was the younger sister of Mrs. Boissevain. Together with her friend Paulien van Waasdijk, she operated a skin care institute in Amsterdam where, starting in October 1942, she hid the children of her Jewish clients. Through the Boissevain family, she met her future husband, Sándor Baracs, and was introduced to the Trouw Group. She and Baracs had to go into hiding, but they continued to rescue children until the child-care center was closed in September 1943.

*Lewinsohn, Manfred* (b. 1912)

Lewinsohn, a German Jew, was introduced to the Utrecht Children's Committee by Frits Iordens. He was very actively involved in rescuing children and often worked with Ankie Stork, but he also engaged in other resistance activities. In August 1944 he was captured and, via Vught, was sent to Bergen-Belsen, where he died in March 1945.

*Lier, Geertruida van, "Truitje"* (b. 1914)

In 1940 Truitje founded a day-care center called Kindjeshaven in Utrecht. After a visit from Jan Meulenbelt in the fall of 1942, the Utrecht Children's Committee used it as a temporary refuge. In the summer of 1944 Truitje went into hiding. Her colleague Jet Berdenis van Berlekom continued the work in Kindjeshaven until February 1945.

*Loghem, Hansje van*

Hansje, a history student, had many contacts in the Amsterdam Women Students Association (AVSV) and was a member of the EOOS sorority. She was Piet Meerburg's girlfriend, and in the summer of 1942 she recruited Gisela Söhnlein to work for the Amsterdam Student Group. She and her roommate, Iet van Dijk, were actively involved in taking children to Friesland. In April 1944 she married Piet Meerburg; together they survived the war in Amsterdam.

*Löwenstein, Kurt, "Ben"* (b. 1925)

Ben Löwenstein, a German Jew, worked with the Tienray branch of the Amsterdam Student Group. He was engaged in rescuing children, together with Hanna van de Voort and Nico Dohmen, and also helped them save two downed pilots. He was liberated in Tienray at the end of 1944.

*Lubberhuizen, Geertjan, "Geert"* (b. 1916)

Geert, an older chemistry student, was recruited by Frits Iordens for the Utrecht Children's Committee in the fall of 1942. After the crisis about the declaration of loyalty, he began forging documents and was helped by Rut Matthijsen. In addition he founded the Bezige Bij underground publishing house, beginning with the illustrated broadsheet *De Achttien Dooden* ("The Eighteen Dead"). The income from the publishing house was used to finance the Utrecht Children's Committee, the Amsterdam Student Group, writers and actors. After his marriage to Willy van

Reenen, who was also active in rescuing children, Geert moved most of his publishing activities to Amsterdam.

*Maclaine Pont, Anne* (b. 1916)

Anne studied art history in Utrecht and was the girlfriend of Frits Iordens, with whom she worked for the Utrecht Children's Committee from mid-1942. She recruited An de Waard, a former classmate, and Ankie Stork, a cousin, for child rescue work. In August 1943 she married Frits Iordens, and they set up an escape route for downed pilots. She never got over Frits's death in March 1944.

*Matthijsen, Rutger, "Rut"* (b. 1921)

Rut Matthijsen was a chemistry student who joined the Utrecht Children's Committee in 1942. He assisted Geert Lubberhuizen in forging documents; eventually this became his full-time occupation.

*Matthijsen, Th. A., "Dora"* (b.1923)

Dora was a cousin of Rut Matthijsen and a medical student in Amsterdam. From August 1943 she worked with the Utrecht Children's Committee and often was a courier between Amsterdam and Utrecht.

*Mazirel, L.C., "Lau"*

Lau Mazirel, a lawyer in Amsterdam, was thirty when the war began. She joined the resistance and worked with Meerburg of the Amsterdam Student Group and Woortman of the NV. Her office became a drop-off place and temporary refuge.

*Meerburg, Piet* (b. 1919)

Piet Meerburg had a B.A. in law and was recruited by Jur Haak for the Amsterdam Student Group as a full-time worker in July 1942. He was engaged to Hansje van Loghem, whom he married in 1944. A visit to his cousin Mia Coelingh led to the creation (in 1943) of the Amsterdam Student Group's very active branch in Sneek. In 1943 his contact with Hanna van de Voort in Tienray led to the creation of another very active branch in North Limburg.

*Mees, Maria, "Mieke"* (b. 1917)

Mieke, a medical student in Amsterdam, was recruited by Piet Meerburg for the Amsterdam Student Group. She escorted many children to Limburg, as did Iet van Dijk.

*Mesdag, Willem* (b. 1896)

Mesdag was one of the three ministers who worked together in the Sneek branch of the Amsterdam Student Group. He was arrested during a raid in April 1945 but was released before the liberation of Sneek.

*Meulenbelt, Jan* (b. 1920)

Meulenbelt was a student of social geography and Ger Kempe's assistant at the Criminological Institute in Utrecht. In the summer of 1942, he and Kempe founded the Utrecht Children's Committee. Meulenbelt's contacts in Amsterdam led to the formation of the Amsterdam Student Group. He intervened during critical situations like the elimination of a traitor in Esch in June 1943. In 1944 he was caught but was released after four months in a camp. After this, on Kempe's advice, he abstained from further resistance activities.

*Molen, Gesina van der, "Gé"* (b. 1892)

A very principled Dutch Calvinist, Gesina van der Molen received her doctorate in law in 1937 as the first woman to attend the Free University in Amsterdam. She joined the resistance in May of 1940, just after the Dutch capitulation, and was a prominent member of the Trouw resistance organization from 1943. In this capacity she was able to give support to the activities of Hester van Lennep and Sándor Baracs, the smuggling of children out of the child-care center, and other resistance work involving children. After the war, Gesina was a member of the Commission for War Foster Children (OPK).

*Musch, brothers Jaap* (b. 1913) *and Gerard* (b. 1921)

Jaap was a chemical analyst and Gerard worked in an office, both in Amsterdam. Encouraged by their Dutch Reformed minister, Reverend Sikkel, they found a hiding address for a Dutch Reformed family who had originally been Jewish. After this, together with their friend Dick Groenewegen van Wijk, they organized the NV to help Jewish children. The children were brought to them by Joop Woortman and the Kinsbergen family. Their contact with Gérard Pontier, a Dutch Reformed minister in Heerlen, led to the development of a very active NV branch in South-Limburg. In September 1944 Jaap was caught, refused to talk, and was tortured and executed by a firing squad two days later. Gérard had already been captured in May of that year during a razzia on a train; he was sent to Sachsenhausen, where he was liberated by the Russian army in April 1945.

*Neve, Jooske de* (b. 1924)

Jooske was a language student in Utrecht from 1942. At the request of Rebecca van Delft, she began escorting children from Amsterdam to South Limburg for the NV. She continued until August 1943.

*Pimentel, Henriette Henriquez* (b. 1876)

Miss Henriette, as she was called, was the director of the child-care center in Amsterdam. She collaborated with the staff of the Schouwburg and, from May 1943, with Johan van Hulst, the principal of the adjacent Protestant Teachers College. This made it easier to smuggle children out of the center. In July 1943 Pimentel was deported to Westerbork and from there to Auschwitz, where she was gassed.

*Pontier, Gérard* (b.1888)

Pontier, a Dutch Reformed clergyman in Heerlen, began working with the NV around the end of 1942, recruited by Reverend Sikkel, a colleague in Amsterdam. Thanks to Pontier's help, the NV was able to establish what became its largest branch in Heerlen. In November 1943 he was caught by the Gestapo and tortured in the prison at Scheveningen. He was released in May 1944 and survived the war.

*Söhnlein, Gisela* (b. 1921)

Gisela was a law student in Utrecht and in 1942 was invited to join the Amsterdam Student Group by Hansje van Loghem. Gisela served as a courier between the Amsterdam Student Group and the Utrecht Children's Committee, and became increasingly active in 1943. She and Hetty Voûte were caught in the raid at Esch. They revealed nothing under interrogation and, via Vught, were sent to Ravensbrück, where they survived.

*Stork, Ankie* (b. 1921)

Ankie Stork was a student of social geography in Utrecht. Her cousin Anne Maclaine Pont persuaded her to work for the Utrecht Children's Committee. Ankie then built up the Overijssel branch of the organization from her parents' home in Nijverdal, working with Manfred Lewinsohn. In May 1944 she was caught during a raid on the Eding family's house, but was released. She barely escaped injury during the bombardment of Nijverdal in March 1945.

*Süskind, Walter* (b. 1906)

Walter emigrated from Germany to Holland in 1938 and once there helped other Jewish refugees. Because he was Jewish he lost his job at Unilever in February 1942, but was appointed director of the Hollandsche Schouwburg. In this capacity he facilitated the escapes of many Jewish children. In September 1944, he and his family were deported. They all died in concentration camps.

*Terwindt, Paul W., "Uncle Piet"*

Uncle Piet was an orthodox Dutch Calvinist and a friend of Frits Iordens, with whom he worked in the Utrecht Children's Committee starting in 1942. He organized the Utrecht Children's Committee branch in Arnhem and led it starting in October 1942. He found new hiding addresses in Noord-Brabant, Gelderland, and Limburg.

*Vermeer family*

The Vermeers were a large Dutch Calvinist family that was active in the resistance in Brunssum (South Limburg) and was recruited for the NV by Jaap Musch. Their home became an important hiding address and safe house. The father and many of the twelve children were active members of the NV. In addition, Piet, one of the sons, set up a new NV branch in Venlo and found hiding addresses in Overijssel.

*Verschuer, Baroness Annemarie van*

In December 1942 as a nineteen-year-old student, the baroness took over the job of transporting children for the NV from Rebecca van Delft. She remained active in rescue work until the child-care center was closed.

*Voort, Hanna van de* (b. 1904)

Hanna van de Voort was an unmarried midwife in Tienray (Noord-Limburg). Piet Meerburg recruited her to work for the Amsterdam Student Group. Together with Nico Dohmen, a student from Nijmegen who was hiding in her house, Hanna organized a sizable branch of the Amsterdam Student Group. In July 1944 Hanna was caught during a razzia in Tienray, but Mieke Mees managed to talk the police into letting her go. She was liberated in Tienray in November 1944.

*Voûte, Hetty* (b. 1918)

Hetty, a biology student in Utrecht, joined the resistance in 1940, soon after the capitulation. In the summer of 1942 she joined the Utrecht

Children's Committee on the invitation of Jan Meulenbelt. She and Gisela Söhnlein were caught in the raid at Esch, but neither one gave anything away under interrogation. They were sent from Vught to Ravensbrück but survived the war.

### Waard, Anna de, "An" (b. 1916)

Anna de Waard was a law student in Utrecht when, early in 1943, Anne Maclaine Pont recruited her for the Utrecht Children's Committee. An did children's rescue work and raised money. After a year she had to stop traveling because of health reasons, but she continued taking care of children until the end of the war. She also helped draft the law concerning war foster children.

### Waasdijk, Paulien van (b. 1905)

Paulien was Hester van Lennep's partner in the institute for skin care in Amsterdam. Even before they joined the Trouw Group they were active in helping Jewish clients. The institute was a favorite safe house and temporary refuge through July 1943.

### Woortman, J. T., "Joop" (b. 1905)

Joop and his wife, L. M. (Semmy) Woortman-Glasoog, lived in Amsterdam, where they joined the resistance early on. Through the Kinsbergen family they came into contact with Gerard Musch and the NV. Woortman soon became the leader of its Amsterdam branch. Through the Kinsbergens, he also made contact with Walter Süskind and the childcare center and led several escape operations. In addition to these activities, he participated in the armed resistance. In July 1944 he was caught by the SD and sent to the camp at Amersfoort and then to Bergen-Belsen, where he died.

### Zeytveld, Wouter van (b. 1923)

Wouter was engaged to Tineke Haak and worked for the Amsterdam Student Group from the summer of 1942. He began as a courier between Amsterdam and Utrecht. Later he escorted numerous children to Friesland and Limburg. He was the prime mover in setting up a branch of the Amsterdam Student Group in Wijdenes (Noord-Holland). From the end of 1943 he helped people who were hiding in Amsterdam. There he survived the Hunger Winter (1944–45) and married Tineke after the liberation (May 1945).

# A WORD OF APPRECIATION

We have received valuable advice and support from several people, in particular from Mr. H.C.S. Warendorf (Amsterdam, the Netherlands); Dr. A.J. Boerman, M.D. (Stockholm, Sweden); Mrs. A.C.E.C. Verschuren (Breda, the Netherlands); Mr. G.A. Rendsburg, Paul and Berthe Hendrix Memorial Professor of Jewish Studies, Cornell University (Ithaca, N.Y.); and Mr. D.I. Owen, The Bernard and Jane Schapiro Professor of Ancient Near Eastern and Judaic Studies, Cornell University (Ithaca, N.Y.).

We also thank the many generous donors who have supported our idealistic goal with large and small contributions. This adaptation and translation would not have been possible without these donations. Some of the generous sponsors were the Nettie van Zwanenberg Foundation, the Carel Nengermanfonds Foundation, the Het Parool Foundation, and Mr. H. Sanders (Oss, the Netherlands).

One of the major private sponsors of this publication wishes his contribution to serve as a lasting memorial to the following close relatives who were deported from the Netherlands and murdered by the Nazi regime for no other reason than that they were Jewish.

| | | |
|---|---|---|
| Esther Engeltje Arons | murdered July 9, 1943 aged eight | Sobibor, Poland |
| Mary Wennek | murdered May 31, 1943 aged twenty | Sobibor, Poland |
| Rachel Wennek-Klijnkramer | murdered September 5, 1943, aged twenty-seven | Auschwitz, Poland |

| | | |
|---|---|---|
| Rachel Kattenburg | murdered October 1944 aged thirty | Birkenau, Poland |
| Mathilda Wennek-Kattenburg | murdered April 1944 aged thirty-two | Bergen-Belsen, Germany |
| Levie Wennek | murdered August 1944 aged forty | between Kutno, Poland, and Dachau, Germany |
| Leendert Wennek | murdered March 31, 1944, aged forty-two | Auschwitz, Poland |
| Engeltje Kattenburg-Hijman | murdered July 16, 1943 aged fifty-five | Auschwitz, Poland |
| Henri Kattenburg | murdered July 16, 1943 aged sixty-two | Auschwitz, Poland |
| Marianne Wennek-Schenkkan | murdered May 21, 1943 aged sixty-two | Sobibor, Poland |
| Samuel Wennek | murdered May 21, 1943 aged sixty-three | Sobibor, Poland |